Rethinking Trafficking in Women

Rethinking Re-thinking in Women

Rethinking Trafficking in Women
Politics out of Security

Claudia Aradau

Department of Politics and International Studies,
The Open University, UK

First published 2008 by
PALGRAVE MACMILLAN
Houndmills, Basingstoke, Hampshire RG21 6XS and
175 Fifth Avenue, New York, N.Y. 10010
Companies and representatives throughout the world

PALGRAVE MACMILLAN is the global academic imprint of the Palgrave Macmillan division of St. Martin's Press, LLC and of Palgrave Macmillan Ltd. Macmillan® is a registered trademark in the United States, United Kingdom and other countries. Palgrave is a registered trademark in the European Union and other countries.

ISBN-13: 978–0–230–57331–4   hardback
ISBN-10: 0–230–57331–2   hardback

This book is printed on paper suitable for recycling and made from fully managed and sustained forest sources. Logging, pulping and manufacturing processes are expected to conform to the environmental regulations of the country of origin.

A catalogue record for this book is available from the British Library.

Library of Congress Cataloging-in-Publication Data

Aradau, Claudia, 1976–
  Rethinking trafficking in women: politics out of security / Claudia
    Aradau.
    p. cm.
  Includes bibliographical references and index.
  ISBN 0–230–57331–2 (alk. paper)
  1. Human trafficking—European Union countries. 2. Women—Violence
  against—European Union countries. 3. Prostitution—European
  Union countries. I. Title.

HQ281.A73 2007
364.15—dc22   2007050106

10   9   8   7   6   5   4   3   2   1
17   16   15   14   13   12   11   10   09   08

Printed and bound in Great Britain by
CPI Antony Rowe, Chippenham and Eastbourne

Contents

Acknowledgements

I have incurred many intellectual debts over the years I worked on this manuscript. My thanks first of all to Jef Huysmans and Raia Prokhovnik, who have been wonderful readers of this manuscript, patiently following it through its development and offering many suggestions for improvement. They have been treasured friends and critics. My gratitude extends to several people who have engaged in conversations with me over the ideas present here: Didier Bigo, Michael Dillon, Vivienne Jabri, Andrew Neal, Raia Prokhovnik, Julian Reid, Michael Saward, Rens van Munster and Rob Walker. Ongoing conversations with Tobias Blanke and Ozren Pupovac have been very helpful for thinking about the concept of politics.

I am also grateful to two European projects, Challenge and COST Action A24, 'The Evolving Social Construction of Threats', for the plentiful occasions they have offered me to sound these ideas to very different audiences. The *c.a.s.e. collective* and its unusual presence in the world of academic research deserves special mention here, as being part of a collective has made me more sensitive to different understandings of politics and security.

I am deeply appreciative of the financial help offered by an extraordinary institution: The Open University and the Department of Politics and International Studies, where I have developed these ideas over the years.

My mother has tirelessly collected newspaper clippings about human trafficking and has often joined me in my search through thick trial files which threatened to fall apart with every turn of the page.

I also owe special thanks to Dan Perjovschi for his generous permission to use his drawing 'Immigration' (2006) for the cover of this book. I hope the book engages, in its own way, with the contestation of dividing lines and boundaries.

Introduction: On the Contradictions of Trafficking in Women

In September 2005, one more story of trafficking was reported in the UK media[1] – another raid, one more massage parlour and a police rescue operation. Yet, this story of rescuing victims of trafficking did not stop where most stories of trafficking told in the media end. While 19 women were reported as having been saved from the premises of the Birmingham massage parlour, a few hours later 13 were released, as they were either legal residents or European Union (EU) citizens. Apparently they had told the police they were working voluntarily in the sex industry. The remaining six, coming mostly from Eastern Europe, were sent to a detention centre to await deportation by immigration on the grounds of being illegally in the UK. A few days later, the six women had their expulsion deferred, as activists intensely lobbied the government to change its policy on trafficking towards a victim-centred approach. However, the women did not make allegations of trafficking, thus, creating even more disarray.

This appears to be just another one of the familiar stories of trafficking that have recently gripped public opinion. However, this story has spurred confusion about what trafficking in women is and has exposed some of the contradictions that undergird the description of the phenomenon. When similar stories have surfaced in the media, police, human rights activists, journalists, lawyers and immigration officials have offered different rationales and interpretations of what happened and, particularly, attempted to tell a consistent story about what human trafficking is. Human trafficking is mostly rendered as a form of illegal migration, organized crime and prostitution, with the important proviso that the women involved are seen as victims of human rights abuses.[2] They are to a certain extent dis-identified from stories of illegal migration, organized crime and prostitution, in as much as it has been the 'use of force, fraud or coercion' (UN, 2000) that has turned them into unwilling and exploited illegal migrants or prostitutes. Yet, despite the attempts to confer an image of consistency to stories of trafficking, these narratives are riddled with contradictions. Although acknowledged as victims of human rights abuses, trafficked women are to be eventually returned to their countries of origin, often despite their manifest wishes. They are to be rescued, even when they refuse to identify themselves as victims.

Renamed as victims of trafficking, women are tentatively dis-identified from categories of illegal migrants and prostitutes. However, this dis-identification is unstable, as processes of illegal migration, sex work and organized crime intersect and overlap. Victims of trafficking cannot be dangerous as they are differentiated from illegal migrants and criminals. Therefore, they cannot undertake actions that would be deemed dangerous or risky by Western states; that is, they cannot migrate but only return to their countries of origin. As definitions of trafficking do not fail to mention, migration, prostitution and irregular work have been external forceful impositions upon these victims. Victims of trafficking are eventually *voluntarily* returned home, after having testified against their traffickers and having undergone more or less extended periods of *rehabilitation*. Instead of deportation, voluntary return. Instead of detention centres, rehabilitation shelters. Instead of illegal migrants, victims.

Although deployed upon supposedly different categories of subjects, the measures employed appear as hardly different. In the shift from illegal migration to an emphasis on the human rights of victims of trafficking – a shift that has been made possible by the mobilization of NGOs in the anti-trafficking struggle – what appears to change is rather the form of incarceration or the mode of normalization. The logic of their removal from the space of the political community they attempted to enter irregularly remains the same. The contradiction of claiming the difference between victims of trafficking and other categories of migrants, only to treat them in similar ways, does not appear as a contradiction.

The contradictions that human trafficking reveals are either read as unaccountable inconsistencies or are taken to be frictionless elements in the narrative of human trafficking. They are not apparent as contradictions. Victims are awaiting expulsion when they do not accept the identification of a victim of trafficking and avow working as prostitutes. When they do accept to be identified as victims, they are still to be returned, once they have testified against their traffickers. This difference passes unnoticed. The fact that some women can walk away freely, while others waver between the categories of illegal immigrants and victims of trafficking, is taken to be part of the process of victim identification. The reality of women having recourse to other strategies such as making asylum claims to defer their 'voluntary' return is not part of the public debate on trafficking.[3] Something in the story of trafficking obfuscates these contradictions and silences. By placing human trafficking within the social and political context from which it is derived – that of illegal migration, organized crime, prostitution and human rights abuses – this book will unravel the overarching security construction that holds together these apparently contradictory elements.

The contradictions that subtend the description of trafficking and the measures taken to tackle it emerge from the very location of the phenomenon of trafficking, at the intersection of illegal migration, organized crime and prostitution. Although presented as a new phenomenon, the reality of trafficking exists by being derived from the reality of other social phenomena. These phenomena have already been problematized as specific security issues. The EU Hague Programme on strengthening freedom, security and justice makes clear the links between the social phenomena of which human trafficking is only one aspect:

> The citizens of Europe rightly expect the European Union, while guaranteeing respect for fundamental freedoms and rights, to take a more effective, joint approach to cross-border problems such as illegal migration, trafficking in and smuggling of human beings, terrorism and organized crime, as well as the prevention thereof.
> (Council of the European Union, 2004)

The problematization of human trafficking refers to how human trafficking becomes an object of regulation, what elements constitute it and what 'ordered procedures for the production, regulation, distribution, circulation and operation of statements' about human trafficking are given as truthful (Foucault, 1980: 133). By being derived from social phenomena that are problematized in terms of security, human trafficking is subjected to the same ordered procedures of production, regulation and circulation of statements. These ordered procedures do not only make visible human trafficking as an object of knowledge, they also obscure contradictory statements in the regulation of the 'truth' about human trafficking.[4] Although trafficking is not defined as a security issue the same way that terrorism is, it is part of a 'domain of insecurity' (Huysmans, 2006), already delineated by illegal migration, organized crime and prostitution.

The first contradiction obscured by security concerns is embodied by the trafficked women themselves: they are both migrants to be deported and bearers of human rights to be protected. Uttering the sentence 'I have been trafficked' can remove women, at least temporarily, from one category to another. In the wake of the above-mentioned Birmingham raid, two prominent NGOs in the anti-trafficking struggle, Anti-Slavery and Amnesty International, started a campaign for the UK to sign up to the European Convention against Trafficking in Human Beings (Amnesty International and Anti-Slavery International, 2005), as the convention grants a 30-day reflection period to suspected victims of trafficking (Council of Europe, 2005). The reflection delay is the time span within which trafficked women, with the professional help of psychologists and NGOs, can achieve the self-identification of 'victim of trafficking' and eventually name their traffickers and testify against them.

Yet, the UK government has been wary of the provisions of the European Convention, and a consultation paper on trafficking has raised concerns that the automatic granting of reflection periods and residence permits to victims might act as a 'pull' factor for illegal migrants (Home Office, 2006). The UK is not, however, singular in such attempts, and most EU countries, even Convention signatories, try to tackle the fuzzy boundary between human trafficking and illegal migration. The distinction between victims of trafficking and illegal migrants appears as an unstable one, and the suspicion of illegal migration will continue to hover over stories of exploitation and abuse.

Moreover, some of the women identified by the police as suspected victims of trafficking in the wake of the Birmingham raid have refused to utter the sentence 'I am a victim of trafficking'. BBC Radio 4 broadcast an interview with one of the women 'freed' from the Birmingham brothel. An illegal migrant, she was waiting in a detention centre, to be deported back home – somewhere in Eastern Europe. Her decision not to admit to having been trafficked and to present herself as a free choice prostitute appeared even more contradictory when she admitted that 'nobody is happy there [in the brothel]' (BBC Radio 4, 2005). The interviewer noted it as an 'inconsistency' in the story. Can supposedly free subjects 'choose' not to be happy and refuse to be returned home, the 'natural' place of belonging? These contradictions need to be analysed against the background of the security governance of migration and illegal mobilities as a 'global system of apartheid' (Sharma, 2005).

The debate between human rights activists and the Home Office on the deportation of the six women exposes another contradiction that the stories of trafficking gloss over, namely that of 'legality'. Trafficking is solely related to those who are illegally resident. The remaining women appear as free-choice workers in the sex industry. They do not have to justify their work or the extent of their free choice, as long as they work in regulated brothels. Trafficking becomes a problem most prominently in relation to illegality. Illegal migrants are under suspicion of having been trafficked; legal residents are 'uninteresting' for the state in this situation.

Simultaneously, the reality of trafficking attempts to introduce a split, a shortcut in the logic of how states govern illegal migration. Victims of trafficking, human rights activists have argued, are vulnerable and insecure and should not be further victimized by the state (Pearson, 2002). Hence, victims of trafficking are allowed to stay until they decide whether they testify against their traffickers, or longer, depending on the European country involved in the case. While the UK, for example, has strict conditionality on granting temporary permission to stay to victims of trafficking, Italy has been singled out as a model for granting residence permits to victims of trafficking, independent of their willingness to testify. Nevertheless, the so-called 'social path' that allows victims of trafficking in Italy to train for a job and reintegrate has been shown to entail constraints upon victims to testify in court against their traffickers (Anti-Slavery International, 2002: 144). The European Commission itself has made the granting of short-term resident permits to suspected victims of trafficking dependent upon their usefulness for the judicial process and the conviction of traffickers (European Commission, 2002a). The fate of victims of trafficking is, therefore, to be decided depending on their role in the prevention of the phenomenon of trafficking. Stories of suffering and exploitation are integrated within a narrative of prevention, without any apparent friction between the techniques of policing and the subjectivity of victims of trafficking.

The Home Office measures concerning illegal migrants remain perfectly acceptable, as long as victims of trafficking are clearly differentiated from the category of illegal migrants and receive a more humane treatment. Yet, these categories are too intermingled to be clearly differentiated. Are women illegal migrants? Are they genuine victims or willing prostitutes? Have they been involved in organized crime networks? The imperative of adequately and indubitably identifying 'genuine' victims of trafficking is derived from the ambivalent relationship that human trafficking has to other social problems. Victims of trafficking are and are not illegal migrants. They are and are not prostitutes. They could be involved in organized crime networks.

The classification as victims simultaneously closes down and opens up specific possibilities of action. Women can act as victims of trafficking, press charges against traffickers, put the legal system to good use and be reintegrated into society. What is closed down in the shift of subjectivity from the category of illegal migrants to that of victims of trafficking (or vice versa) is the realization that the two categories are artificially delimited. It is in the process of irregular migration (whether understood as illegal crossing of frontiers or as a lapse into a situation of illegality from a temporary situation of legal residence) that women can be abused and exploited. The category of trafficked women is not the negation of illegal migrants who make rational choices and appear as dangerous to Western states, but emerges through the very practices of security that states deploy towards migrants.

Contradictions appear as non-contradictory through the structuring that practices of security entail upon the phenomenon of human trafficking. *Rethinking Trafficking in Women* will show that well-meaning projects that attempt to disrupt distinctions between trafficking and illegal migration, prostitution and organized crime are reincorporated within the problematization of security. Challenging the distinctions between human trafficking and other problematizations such as illegal migration does not disrupt the problematization of security. To understand how existing alternative political discourses and strategies are reappropriated and taken up by the problematization of security, it will question what 'security' does, what its effects are and how practices and discourses of insecurity can buttress or undermine the institutional and discursive construction of trafficking.

This book will argue that the overarching problematization of security allows for a symbiosis between the contradictions that undergird trafficking in women and lay the ground for their smooth functioning. Security holds together the stories of trafficking and the institutional practices that 'order' these stories.[5] The security literature has so far analysed discourses – security being a specific rhetorical structure of survival, immediacy and urgency (Buzan, Waever and Wilde, 1998) – or has focused on discursive and non-discursive practices that govern danger and contingency (Bigo, 2006; Campbell, 1992). Here, security is understood in its larger function of ordering the social. The imaginary promise of a desirable state in the future is subtended by practices in the present that represent problems, in order to intervene and manage them, act upon subjects and attempt to conduct their actions in view of the projected future.

The first part of the book explores the logic of security and the way in which human trafficking is problematized as a security issue. The second part focuses on questioning and disrupting practices of security and their effects. However, unmaking security practices becomes a relevant problem only once the a priori question of what security does has been answered. Why should we be 'against security'? The (in)security of trafficked women and their vulnerability appear to create a context in which women can be different from illegal migrants or prostitutes. They can become part of a new category, supposedly enjoying increased security.

Having unravelled the effects of security understood as a governmental practice that orders populations and constitutes forms of subjectivity through specific problematizations, the book proposes an affirmative form of politics that can emerge 'out of security'. Politics out of security stems from the conditions of possibility of security and disrupts them, reconfiguring the way power functions in a specific situation. Can human trafficking be taken 'out of security'? This book discusses different modes of thinking how 'politics out of security' can come to be and proposes a form of politics that is inspired by a hybrid reading of Alain Badiou's and Étienne Balibar's conceptualization of a politics of universality, equality and freedom.

The focus on the ordering that security does and the effects of this ordering has led me to employ a 'methodology of the surface' (Veyne, 1997). Effects are apparent on the surface; they are not hermeneutically hidden, nor are they simply an offshoot of structural causes. When asked to explain Foucault's method, Gilles Deleuze used a metaphor from Paul Valéry: 'le plus profond, c'est la peau [the most profound is the skin]' (Deleuze, 1990, translation mine).[6] This dermatological metaphor does not oppose surface to depth, but indicates that everything is on the surface, at the level of appearances.[7] Therefore, this book brings to light things that have always been there, are reported, inscribed in documents and yet rarefied, made invisible through the very encounter with power. The 'archive', as the 'system of formation and transformation of statements' (Foucault, 2002: 127) contains both that which can be said and that which can be rarefied or made invisible. In the encounter with power relations, the 'truth' of trafficking is there, and it only becomes obliterated through the exercise of power. This 'truth' does not wait to be discovered through personal encounters that would be somehow placed beyond power relations, but is already there. These 'appearances' might be invisible exactly because they are located so much on the surface.

The intersection of human trafficking and security

The first chapter looks at how human trafficking has been problematized by academics and practitioners alike. I use 'problematization' to understand the various representations of trafficking: trafficking as a problem of migration, of organized crime, prostitution or human rights abuse. Specific problematizations of trafficking enable certain interventions while limiting other representations and interventions. If the connections between trafficking and illegal migration, prostitution and crime have been the subject of numerous debates, the human rights approach has been embraced as an alternative strategy focused on victims of trafficking, rather than on repressive practices to manage illegal migration, prostitution and crime. A human rights approach is seen to provide both a more politically effective and more ethical representation of trafficking. This chapter will argue that human rights approaches take up a rhetoric of danger and representations of threat that actually render them incapable of providing an alternative strategy of security.

Given this non-attention to the problem of security, the second chapter engages in a 'problematization of the problematization' of security. It looks at how security has been problematized and what questions have been asked about what security is. It argues that the problematique of security needs to be shifted to 'how' questions, questions of effects and how security works. The limitation or the expansion of the realm of security is a historical and empirical question. How security works can be unravelled by looking at the practices of ordering the social, by preventing the recurrence of the phenomenon of trafficking. Security practices have constitutive effects in terms of subjectivity and political effects in terms of the constitution and reproduction of political communities. The subjects of these practices become 'abjects', excluded, dangerous or risky others. The constitutive effects that practices of security entail and their structuring of the social fabric in exclusionary terms raises the question of how to unmake these effects of security. Can security be thought differently, reconceptualized so as to entail other forms of subjectivity? Can a form of 'politics out of security' be thought and what would such a politics entail?

For much of critical security studies, security discourses and practices also appear as undesirable interventions upon the social. Some authors understand security in terms of urgency and exceptional practices that go beyond democratic practices (Behnke, 1999; Huysmans, 1998a; Waever, 1995). Others see security practices as unjustly converging upon the figure of the enemy, more specifically the migrant (Bigo, 2002). Still others criticize the imaginary of certainty and identity that security built into the modern political subject (Bauman, 2001; Campbell and Dillon, 1993). My critical engagement with practices of security and the endeavour to think a form of 'politics out of security' stem from an understanding of the necessary constitution and representation of a space of abjection inhabited by non-subjects or not-yet-subjects. The effects of security or what security does leads to a concern with how to suspend its logic of exclusion and tear down the closures it instantiates.

Unmaking security: a political task

Chapter 3 opens up the question of how to unmake the effects of security, by discussing three different strategies proposed in security studies and International Relations (IR): desecuritization, emancipation and ethics. While desecuritization focuses on unspeaking security and its replacement by alternative discourses, emancipation and ethics attempt to reformulate the relation of one to the other. Emancipation endorses security as a relation that can be formulated towards the 'abject' rather than simply the 'subjects' who are to be made secure, while ethics deconstruct the very relationality between subject and abject by introducing unconditional principles in politics.[8]

These theoretical attempts are formulated in relation to a specific understanding of how security works: security as discourse, security as a promise and security as the problematique of self/other. What these approaches lack is an account of the practices of security. Chapter 4 brings an account of practice and power relations to bear upon these strategies of unmaking security. Alternative discourses will be shown to be mobilized for governmental purposes. The expansion of security only shifts the spaces of abjection towards other categories of people. Various attempts at reconstituting the relation to trafficked women as dangerous illegal migrants into a relation to victims as objects of pity are reappropriated and reformulated within security practices. Rather than objects of pity, women continue to be risky bodies, abject carriers of an unmaterialized threat. Medicalized and psychologized, 'victims of trafficking' are also depoliticized; their resistance to the constitutive effects of security is rendered meaningless, read only as a pathological reaction rather than a political statement. Is there a way out of this impasse?

As the problematization of human trafficking requires the specification and identification of categories of subjects and abjects, politics that unmakes security needs to sever its connection to particularity.

Drawing inspiration from Badiou's conceptualization of a politics of excess, Chapter 5 will argue that this can be done through political events that are universal and through subjects who are divorced from the represented particularity of a situation. Political events are disconnected from the particular ways in which a situation is represented, and its subjects counted by being linked with excessive subject in the margins of the situation. These subjects mobilize universal names that address everybody in a situation and enact equality as the principle radically heterogeneous to security. Equality suspends the divisions among subjects that security practices create and unravels the particular representations of subjectivity that are needed for security to function. Security practices can be deployed only if differences between subjects and abjects, divisions and exclusions have been formulated.

This conceptualization of politics will entail a shift from the representation of trafficked women or victims of trafficking as the 'abjects' of security to the presentation of illegal migrant sex workers as excessive subjects. As victims of trafficking are caught in the representations mobilized for the purposes of prevention, new names and identifications that are not particularized in ways which divide the situation between categories of subjects need to be invented to reconfigure their situation. As illegal migrants, these women continually fall out of the representation of trafficking. They are not victims of trafficking, as the latter need to be continually dis-identified by a double negating move that separates them from both illegal migrants and sex workers. Victims of trafficking are either unwilling, forced prostitutes or unwilling, forced migrants. Illegal migrant sex workers are not workers either, as the status of 'work' is linked with clear conditions of residence and citizenship. Moreover, they are not workers because prostitution is often not considered to be work. In a nutshell, illegal migrant sex workers simply *are not*.

The politics out of security endorsed here starts from the standpoint of those who are not represented as belonging to the situation, the illegal migrant sex workers, and disrupts the logic of security on the basis of a claim to equality and universality. The profoundly inegalitarian claim of security, which separates those who are dangerous or risky from those who are not, is challenged by the enactment of equality that addresses everybody. Politics out of security takes place through the collective mobilization of workers addressed under the universal and egalitarian predicate of work. It thus breaks away both from the idea of individual resistance and bureaucratic struggles over definitions and interventions.

Yet, as Chapter 6 will show, a politics of equality cannot be restricted to the forms of collective subjectification and organization of (legal and illegal) sex. Equality and universality also exist as already inscribed in institutions – be it as a result of previous struggles against oppression or as historical contingencies. Challenging inscriptions in institutional locations can sustain or even precede events that create the political subject of the (sex) worker.

Chapter 7 will supplement the principles of politics by questioning their relation to the concept most invoked against security, liberty. Trafficking in women has been remarkable through the absence of any claims to freedom. What are the limits of liberty that make it an impossible counterpart to security in this situation, despite a long tradition of political theory that has counterposed them? Combining insights from the debates on liberty with Balibar's conceptualization of equaliberty, this chapter will formulate a 'politics out of security' as a politics of inseparable universality, equality and liberty. Freedom cannot exist without equality, as inegalitarian claims to liberty only re-enact the logic of security.

1
Problematizing Trafficking in Women: In the Absence of Security

'Some 2.5 million people throughout the world are at any given time recruited, entrapped, transported and exploited – a process called human trafficking', repeated a press release by the United Nations Office on Drugs and Crime (UNODC, 2007). As a political problem of such urgency and magnitude, human trafficking has been a recent addition to the European and international political agenda. Although concerns with human trafficking have also surfaced earlier – as academic research, especially feminist literature, has drawn attention to practices of sex tourism and trafficking in different regions of the world (Enloe, 1989; Moon, 1997; Pettman, 1996) – in Europe the issue of trafficking has been quasi-invisible until the 1990s. After the 1949 United Nations (UN) Protocol prohibiting human trade, trafficking disappeared from the political agenda. More recently, the visibility of human trafficking has been raised as a problem of numbers. Millions of people were reported to be enslaved, forcefully moved across borders and exploited. Yet, numbers were felt to be misleading, insufficient and incapable of speaking the truth about trafficking. 'How do you count something that is all underground?' asks Kristiina Kangaspunta, Chief of UNODC's Anti-Human Trafficking Unit. 'We can't go to official statistics because nobody knows about these crimes' (quoted in UNODC, 2007). Rather than numbers, what counts is the way human trafficking is seen as linked with other phenomena of concern. The phenomenon of trafficking was fuzzy and slippery and needed to be pinned down by being carefully derived from other social problems to which it was contiguous or similar.

How, therefore, is the political 'truth' of human trafficking to be rendered? If counting people who are trafficked is an insufficient strategy, human trafficking is made visible in relation to the larger spectrum of urgent social and political problems. In the midst of a context defined by the 'war on terror', where the security of the EU and its member states has acquired a new urgency (Council of the European Union, 2004), human trafficking is never far from the overarching concern with terrorism. The EU Hague Programme on the area of freedom, security and justice spells out the need for a more effective approach to 'cross-border problems such as illegal migration, trafficking in and smuggling of human beings, terrorism and organized crime, as well as the prevention thereof' (Council of the European Union, 2004: 3). The UK also made human trafficking one of its major concerns alongside terrorism for the 2005 Presidency of the European Council (UK Government, 2005).

The visibility of the phenomenon, its novelty and its protean nature, verging between concerns with immigration, organized crime, prostitution and human rights abuses, have contributed to a literature boom across disciplines. The descriptive terms include human trafficking, human trade, trafficking in human beings, trafficking in persons, trafficking in women, alien smuggling, trafficking of aliens, illegal immigrant smuggling, trade of human beings, human commodity trafficking, and the list could continue. To accommodate the protean nature of trafficking, the literature has called for a comprehensive analysis from various vantage points. The perspectives on trafficking have therefore been diverse: moral, criminal, migration, human rights, public order, labour or gender (Kelly and Regan, 2000: 4). The 'holistic' or integrated approach that the Organisation for Security and Cooperation in Europe (OSCE) has promoted since the late nineties could be described as an attempted felicitous addition of these perspectives (OSCE, 1999). Much of the research done on human trafficking has either privileged one of the perspectives Kelly and Regan enumerate or has used a method of perspective addition.

Whether done under the auspices of the EU or other international organizations such as the International Organization for Migration (IOM), by non-governmental organizations (NGOs) or independently by academics, research has 'vectored' human trafficking in the direction of migration, organized crime, prostitution or human rights. Ian Hacking has coined the term 'vector' in an analysis of how 'mad travellers' have been historically constructed (Hacking, 1998). The word is used both in mechanics and epidemiology, and Hacking uses it as a metaphor for force acting in a certain direction. In the context of human trafficking, 'vector' is also important in its epidemiological sense of 'transmitter' (Hornby, 2000). Some of the elements of migration, organized crime and prostitution are 'transmitted' to human trafficking. Human trafficking has been integrated in various taxonomies, and much of the research has focused on drawing boundaries and pointing out differences between urgent social and political problems. Human trafficking has been in turn divided into, contrasted with and assimilated to migration, organized crime, prostitution and human rights abuses in what I call a literature of vectoral transformation. This chapter will ask, in what sense has human trafficking been vectored, and what transformations have been the result of vectoring?

Most of the literature on trafficking is underpinned by the assumption that human trafficking is a phenomenon whose truth is to be discovered, that a definition can be uncovered which captures and expresses its 'real nature'. While mobilizing various theories in this search for the nature of trafficking, the literature on human trafficking also tries to grasp the 'real nature' of trafficked women. What kind of migrants, what kind of criminals or exactly what type of prostitutes are they? What category of human rights bearers could they be? The 'true' representation of victims of trafficking is derived from existing knowledge, through a refinement of existing categories. Although the category of victims of trafficking is undergoing an explicit process of social construction, the same process is not acknowledged in relation to the other categories that it evokes and rests upon. There is no recognition that these are also socially constructed categories and that debates about who is trafficked, what type of migrant, prostitute, etc. they are, are not just technical, but deeply political. These debates in which academics and practitioners alike engage accept as their starting point the taken-for-granted truths about what it means to be a migrant, a prostitute or a delinquent.

Paraphrazing Laclau and Mouffe (2001: xi), one could say that this literature partakes of the illusion of a non-discursively mediated access to things. Although I consider trafficking to be a discursive construction, it is neither an object of infinite representations nor solely a linguistic object. Language plays an important role in labelling people and creating categories of subjects; yet, this role is only made possible under certain conditions. In Hacking's formulation, discourse is to be analysed not in terms of what it says but in terms of the conditions under which those sentences will have a definite truth value (2002: 79). Among the material conditions of discourses, Foucault lists institutions, economic and social processes, systems of norms, techniques, types of classification and characterization (2002: 49). Various representations of trafficking have been made thinkable by being embedded in specific institutional configurations and in economic, social and political processes.

This constellation of language and the material conditions for the 'truth' of a discourse have been rendered by Foucault as 'problematizations'. Paul Rabinow has put in a nutshell Foucault's understanding of problematizations:

> [A] problematization ... does not mean representation of a preexistent object nor the creation through discourse of an object that did not exist. It is the ensemble of discursive and nondiscursive practices that make something enter into the play of true and false and constitute it as an object of knowledge ...
>
> (Rabinow, 2003: 18)

Through problematization, the literature on human trafficking attempts to present the truth about human trafficking and solve the uncertainty of what trafficking is. As discourses allow certain things to be said, thought and done and impede other things from being said, thought and done (Hunt and Wickham, 1994: 8), the problematization of human trafficking enables particular tools and measures to be deployed while impeding other understandings and projects. The problematization of trafficking allows the enactment of particular politics while excluding or reappropriating the prospects of different political actions.

Problematization thus makes possible the governmentality of trafficking. Something can be done about trafficking only if we know what trafficking is. The problematization of trafficking, through the various representations of the phenomenon, creates an object of knowledge that can be subsequently governed. For the purposes of this chapter, problematization is also used as a methodological tool that selects a mixture of texts from various institutional sources which share a common concern with what trafficking is. In the heterogeneous literatures that discuss the phenomenon, human trafficking appears primarily embedded in a discursive structure of migration, organized crime and prostitution. The problematization of trafficking as human rights abuses is also possible only in relation to these (modified) terms. Migration, organized crime and prostitution are taken as the starting points in the analysis of trafficking. Problematization is therefore intrinsically related to vectoral transformation. By means of problematizing trafficking in these terms – this chapter argues – the trafficking literature vectors its object in the directions already traced by knowledge accumulated in the fields of migration, organized crime or prostitution.

These representations are not natural constituents of trafficking, but are already framed in a discourse of security. Concerns with human trafficking are inseparable from the establishment of an area of security, freedom and justice, and various EU documents, most recently the Hague Programme, have not failed to point out the connections (Council of the European Union, 2004). Despite the conspicuous presence of security as an assumption in the EU documents dealing with trafficking in persons, security is mostly absent from the frameworks envisaged in the research on human trafficking. Its fleeting appearance in an OSCE document in 1999 has not led to any substantial engagement with the relation between security and human trafficking (OSCE, 1999). Human rights activists and other state and non-state practitioners in the field of trafficking have eschewed the question of security. Books or journal articles on trafficking often do not even mention 'security' as a concern. When security is mentioned or a rhetoric of threat and danger is at play, their role is still not explored.

I contend that it is important to consider this absence of security from the problematization of human trafficking or rather from the question of its un-interrogated presence. As invisible presence, security does unacknowledged work that this book will explore and bring to light. Security assumptions are present in relation to the problem of trafficking, yet absent from most of the literature on trafficking. I am interested not in why there is an absence of security considerations, but in how this absence influences and limits what can be said and done about human trafficking. Security itself becomes one of the factors of vectoral transformation, despite its absence from the visible problematizations of trafficking. Migration, organized crime and prostitution are already vectored in a discourse of threat and danger, and the representation of trafficking as a subcategory reproduces practices of security. The problematization of trafficking is already shaped by previous strategies concerning migration, organized crime and prostitution.

The work of the 'absence' is most interesting where an alternative discourse on trafficking is set in place. As the representation of trafficking as human rights abuses attempts to impose an alternative discourse to that of migration, organized crime and prostitution and challenge the interventions that these linkages entail, the approach is seen to be invariably failing. While challenging the way migration or prostitution is dealt with and the effects that these interventions have upon victims of trafficking and other categories of people, this form of critical engagement does not tackle the problematization of security that shapes the very representation of these issues. The vectoring effects that security inscribes upon trafficking and the limitations it entails for a politics that attempts to challenge the dominant ways in which human trafficking is represented will be explored later on, particularly in Chapters 3 and 4. For the purposes of this chapter, however, I shall glean intimations of the problem from the proponents of the approach themselves. The human rights approach enters a field in which there are already 'legitimate' representations of what trafficking is. Despite its opposition to the visible representations of illegal migration or prostitution, the humanitarian approach fails to conceptualize its relation to the problematization of security.

Governmentality and the problematization of human trafficking

The problematization of human trafficking is part of a concern with governing and ordering society. 'Governmentality', the term coined by Foucault to express this concern with the ordering, administration and regulation of society, is not a new term in International Relations (IR). It has been used to understand different practices of security (Bigo, 1996; Dillon, 1995b; Huysmans, 1998a), of regionalization (Walters and Larner, 2002), migration regimes (Huysmans, 2004a; Lippert, 1999), global liberal governance (Dillon, 2004; Dillon and Reid, 2001) or terrorism (Aradau and van Munster, 2007). IR scholars have been able to draw on a vast literature which has undertaken sociological analyses of governmental practices, from unemployment to the government of pregnancy, and which has employed and refined the categories and conceptual tools devised by Foucault. According to him,

> [t]his word [government] must be allowed the very broad meaning which it had in the sixteenth century. 'Government' did not refer only to political structures or the management of states; rather it designates the way in which the conduct of individuals or states might be directed: the government of children, of souls, of communities, of families, of the sick. It did not cover only the legitimately constituted forms of political or economic subjection, but also modes of action, more or less considered, which were designed to act upon the possibilities of action of other people. To govern, in this sense, is to structure the possible field of action of others.
>
> (Foucault, 1982: 221)

If government is concerned with shaping and directing the actions or the conduct of others, 'governmentality' refers to the political rationality or 'mentality' that has made this concern its own. To shape the field of action of others, it is important first to understand the problem that confronts them. It is in this sense that one can speak of the problematization of trafficking as part of a larger governmental concern. Problematizations appear in definite institutional and social locales, at a specific time and place and reflect upon a task that is at hand. They imply contestation between various actors and competing speculative interpretations about what the task at hand is.

In this sense, problematization can be thought of as a truthful and legitimate form of representation and the interventions associated with it. Representations form the object they depict and purport to tell the 'truth' about what is represented. They create a 'managed space in which some statements and depictions come to have greater value than others' (Campbell, 1992: 6). While representation has become a cherished term in cultural studies to refer to mediatic and all sorts of spaces where personal experiences and other narratives can enter, problematizations function around the element of 'knowledge'.[1] Problematizations create a managed space where knowledge plays an important role for the representation of trafficking. They are, therefore, more than simple semiotic systems of representation. Problematizations both foster and rely upon forms of knowledge and expertise. The problematization of trafficking relies upon knowledge and expertise in various fields (migration, gender, organized crime, etc.), while simultaneously fostering a new field of knowledge, human trafficking.

Problematization is close to Hacking's specific understanding of representation. Hacking has discussed representation in the context of natural sciences, thus making knowledge one of the elements of representation. By representation, he means theories rather than specific everyday instances of representation. In an almost circular definition, representations are *complicated speculations which attempt to represent our world* (Hacking, 1983: 133). Problematizations involve speculation and theory; they depend upon expert knowledge. The problematization of human trafficking involves theoretical representations which attempt to ground the truth about trafficking in knowledge. Problematizing trafficking in terms of migration, organized crime or prostitution activates a theoretical apparatus and expertise already present in the academic fields which have tackled these issues.

Knowledgeable discourses represent, and in this sense constitute, human trafficking as an object of knowledge. They confer particular identities and agencies on different actors (the trafficked victim, the migrant, NGOs, police, etc.) and make identifiable problems to be solved (the prevention of trafficking, of illegal migration) (cf. Dean and Hindess, 1998: 9).

The problematization of human trafficking creates a language and a regime of intelligibility (Rose, 1999), which make trafficking amenable to intervention. A governmental approach makes explicit the emergence of human trafficking from various sources of knowledge and its dependence upon particular forms of knowledge and expertise.

As Rose and Miller have put it, '[g]overning a sphere requires that it can be represented, depicted in a way that both grasps its truth and re-presents it in a form in which it can enter the sphere of conscious political calculation' (Miller and Rose, 1992: 182). Governing trafficking requires first the conceptualization of the situation and the set of relations at work, as governing is only possible under a certain description. The problematization of human trafficking involves competing attempts to depict the domain of trafficking in a way that grasps its real nature and represents it as a field for governmental intervention. Governmentality involves the representation of objects from reality as problematic, thereby attempting to reorder reality in terms of solvable problems. The goal of much of the literature on trafficking is to understand the 'real' nature of trafficking, thus being able to propose adequate solutions for dealing with this problem. The 'real' nature of trafficking entails the creation of a regime of truth about an object of knowledge.

The knowledge of the problem of trafficking is, however, not restricted to the knowledge of an object. It also needs to provide adequate knowledge about the subjects of governmental interventions: traffickers and trafficked people, migrants or sex workers, as well as all other categories which potential trafficked persons can encounter (clients, police, etc.). Knowledge about the people who are part of the phenomenon and their relations is seen as instrumental for better overall knowledge about trafficking, as well as for devising better ways of shaping their conduct.

Human trafficking is formulated as a problem for the authorities who need to devise methods to intervene to govern the phenomenon. Trafficking will be approached differently depending on whether it is considered a problem of illegal migration, of prostitution or organized crime. Different interventions will be developed, and trafficked women will be dealt with differently, depending on whether they are considered illegal migrants, prostitutes, victims of trickery or of ignorance, or the abused bearers of human rights. Representation is simultaneously a form of intervention, both by conferring specific identities to categories of people and by limiting and steering what can be done about these people. Interventions are inseparable from representations of the problem to be governed.

The specificity of governmentality, according to Hacking, lies in this complex interweaving of procedures for representing and intervening (1983). The complexity of the relation between representation and intervention makes impossible the distinction between knowledge that would provide insights into a phenomenon and practice-oriented knowledge that is conceptualized in relation to a goal of intervention. Inasmuch as the literature on human trafficking engages in a contestation of what trafficking is and attempts to stabilize the 'truth' about its meaning, it is governmental, a combination of representation and intervention. The concept of government in relation to the trafficking literature erases the difference between academic and policy-making literature, as in this case all authors are concerned with strategically influencing actions or the 'conduct of conduct' (Foucault, 1991). Nevertheless, I do not want to imply that the literature considered here is unaware of the political game it plays or that it brings it to a common denominator of deliberate ignorance of the political stakes. Some of the texts explicitly acknowledge their attempt to enter the political arena and change things. Most of the literature, whether academic or practice oriented, is written with the purpose of intervention in the existing regimes to govern human trafficking.

My incursion into the trafficking literature will be 'steered' by two questions. The first question is: how is human trafficking formulated as a problem? I shall look at how trafficking is represented as an object to be known, analysed and evaluated. In representing human trafficking, this literature claims to depict and tell the truth about what is represented. Trafficking needs to be conceptualized in a particular way, and it is by means of this representation that who and what is trafficked are shaped in a manageable form. As problematization is inseparable from intervention, the follow-up question is: how do these representations also intervene? The literature on trafficking is explicitly interventionist and could bear the motto of 'a plea for action' (von Struensee, 2000). However, this plea is addressed to somebody else, mainly the various authorities, and much of the literature does not perceive itself as intervening by means of the representations it puts forth. The literature on human trafficking needs to reflect on the 'governmental' work it does and on the 'governmental' space upon which it inscribes human trafficking, a space already structured and categorized in security terms. By inserting human trafficking in a space already shaped by discourses and institutional practices, the literature on trafficking is already subjected to the closure that this very space has already enacted.

Human trafficking as a problem of migration

> The European Council is determined to tackle at its source illegal immigration, especially by combating those who engage in trafficking in human beings and economic exploitation of migrants'.
>
> (European Council, 1999)

Human trafficking and migration are seen here as inseparable realities. Van Impe has defined human trafficking as an 'epiphenomenon within the continuum of the migration cycle' (Van Impe, 2000: 115). According to him, trafficking in women 'has to be seen in the larger context of illegal migration flows and analyzed against the backdrop of worldwide economic and political change' (Van Impe, 2000: 123). For many other authors too, trafficking is a subcategory of migration or rather illegal migration.

Similarly, for the IOM, one of the most important organizations involved in governing human trafficking, trafficking constitutes the antithesis of 'humane and orderly migration' that the organization upholds (for example, Anderson and O'Connell Davidson, 2003). The commitment to advancing the understanding of migration has driven the IOM research in relation to trafficking. Very early on, the IOM was involved in providing a definition for trafficking. In its initial definitions, it did not differentiate trafficking from smuggling, which involved the crossing of borders with the help of an intermediary. Trafficking was defined as occurring when 'a migrant is illicitly engaged (recruited, kidnapped, sold, etc.) and/or moved, either within national or across international borders; [or when] intermediaries (traffickers) during any part of this process obtain economic or other profit by means of deception, coercion and/or other forms of exploitation under conditions that violate the fundamental human rights of migrants' (IOM, 1999). The addition of trafficking 'within national borders' to cross-border forms of trafficking has not become politically relevant; the IOM projects on counter-trafficking or smuggling have been subsumed under the fight of illegal migration. Trafficking, just like other forms of migration, is part of an overall concern with reducing illegal migration. Even if the recent Council of Europe Convention against Trafficking in Human Beings does not specify where transportation, recruitment and exploitation is taking place, a whole section dedicated to 'border measures' places human trafficking in the context of international migration (Council of Europe, 2005).

Almost all definitions of trafficking include the element of 'movement across borders'. Even when authors note the existence of intra-border trafficking, it is considered a rather sporadic form of trafficking, which has not challenged the dominant understanding of trafficking as an international problem of managing migration (Jordan, 2002). However, subsuming human trafficking under illegal migration has been challenged by the accession of Central and Eastern European Countries (CEECs) to the EU. In the UK, the problem of trafficking appears to extend beyond connections with illegal migration, as Lithuania, one of the new EU member states, is the main country of origin for victims of trafficking. Trafficking functions within forms of labour exploitation and discrimination that remain unuttered and unexplored.

Although some scholars believe that the conceptual and definitional uncertainties concerning the issue of trafficking in human beings challenge rather than strengthen the traditional migration theories by blurring the boundaries between legality and illegality and between forced and voluntary movements (Apap, Cullen and Medved, 2002: 23), these processes of subcategorization require just a refinement of migration theories to accommodate the novel variant of trafficking. Most of the literature is rather optimistic about integrating trafficking in categories of migration and focuses on the refinement or further specification of categories.

When illegal migration is considered, Salt and Stein, for example, prefer to describe trafficked migrants as irregular or undocumented rather than illegal, because at various stages they might drift in and out of a legal status (Salt and Stein, 1997). Victims of trafficking do not always enter illegally the territory of another country as they might have obtained tourist visas, temporary work permits or legal status through marriage. Or they might enter illegally and obtain legal status at a later stage. Koser has noted that the term 'illegal', when applied to migration, has been used to cover a variety of situations normally concerning conditions of entry, residence and employment (Koser, 1998: 186). Other authors have also noted that the very notion of illegal migration covers a wide spectrum on which every sovereign state decides (Apap et al., 2002). The task of the literature is to note and monitor these various usages and integrate them within existing theories.

This task is more difficult when it comes to forms of forced or voluntary movements. Is trafficking forced or voluntary migration? The methods of recruitment can occasionally involve kidnapping, yet research has pointed out that women often wilfully undertake migratory projects.

The difference between forced and voluntary migration becomes even more complicated when one considers structural causes. Do women who choose to migrate in order to escape poverty make a voluntary choice? Moreover, if women start their journey by choice, elements of force and coercion can appear at other stages in the process of trafficking. As Koser has pointed out in the case of illegal migration, coercion covers conditions of entry, residence and employment. Even if women are not forced to leave their country of origin, they are often forced to do sex work instead of the jobs that had been advertised. The solution has been to loosen the meaning of force to cover various forms of coercion, from physical coercion to the use of deceit.[2]

Within the migration framework, the understanding of human trafficking is driven by a process of categorization. Categories of illegal, irregular, undocumented or simply deceived migrants overlap and are refined to adequately express the 'reality' of trafficking. The debate concerning the conceptual distinction between smuggling and trafficking is based on such attempts at categorization. Apap et al. (2002: 18) suggest that trafficking and smuggling should be seen as part of a continuum. Smuggling is clearly concerned with the manner in which a person enters the country and with the involvement of a 'facilitator' of illegal entry. Trafficking is supplemented by a concern with the migrants' working conditions and treatment after they enter the country (Apap et al., 2000). Unlike Apap et al., Salt is in favour of clearly differentiating trafficking from smuggling by emphasizing the exploitative element of trafficking (Salt, 2000).

Exploitation can represent an awkward intruder in the debate on the distinction between trafficking and smuggling. Migrant labourers, and especially illegal migrant labourers, frequently find themselves forced into exploitative working conditions. In this sense, they are just like the victims of trafficking. Yet, migrant labourers have not necessarily been tricked or deceived during the migration process. Trafficking, on the contrary, is taken to refer to the transportation of people within countries or across international borders using force, trickery or the abuse of power.

The conceptual distinction between smuggling and trafficking leads Wijers and van Doornick to conclude that while smuggling constitutes an offence against the state, in the case of trafficking, human rights violations give rise to certain obligations on the part of the state under international human rights law to protect victims (2002: 7). In such an approach, any movement across borders which is not sanctioned by the receiving state is problematic. Exploitation could subvert the clear distinctions that definitions of illegal or irregular migration reproduce between state-sanctioned cross-border movement and other forms of movement. Hence, considerations of labour exploitation are to be limited to the framework of trafficking, once movement and other forms of deceit have been made explicit.

Some scholars have challenged the understanding of trafficking as a specific form of migration which combines different forms of constraint and have put forward the idea that trafficking is an unintended consequence of restrictive migration policies and of the efforts to curb illegal entry and illegal employment of migrants. Koser has pointed out that the activities of smugglers and traffickers have flourished in the context of tightening political restrictions (Koser, 1998). Given that legal channels of migration are more and more reduced or restricted to specific categories such as highly skilled migrants, other types of migrants have recourse to mediating parties. Rutvica Andrijasevic has also remarked that EU visa regimes and restrictive immigration regulation work in favour of the third-party organizers of trafficking as a supplementary migration system or an alternative to the EU system (Andrijasevic, 2003).

This rendering of the phenomenon of trafficking blurs the image of the trafficker as the evil foreigner who takes advantage of the liberal policies of the EU member states. Trafficking becomes more similar to assisted migration, and research has shown that the business of trafficking is often dependent on the reputation that traffickers establish as well as their success rates (Koser, 1998). While recruitment by a trafficker has been a definitional characteristic of trafficking, this research likens the trafficker to a service provider. By challenging both the description of trafficking and of traffickers, these approaches equally question migration policies. Yet, in formulating 'accusations' against restrictive migration policies, they do not engage with the very limitations that make such normative claims impossible. Without engaging with the problematization of illegal migration in terms of security, it is impossible to understand how such claims are limited in their effects. Interventions to deal with human trafficking have been carefully qualified so as not to act as a pull factor for illegal migrants. In the UK, the House of Commons report on human trafficking repeatedly reassures the government that these issues have been carefully considered and that including (temporary) residence provision for victims of trafficking who testify against their traffickers will not impact upon the management of illegal migration (House of Commons, 2006).

The literature on trafficking which has taken the migration lens has problematized trafficking without being able to engage in the 'problematization of the problematization' (Campbell, 1998b). While different problematizations of human trafficking are poised against one another, their assumptions are not questioned or their taken-for-granted representations and interventions are not problematized. While debating categories of legality/illegality, forced/voluntary migration, this literature has not questioned what the category of illegal migration allows to be done about trafficking and what it excludes. It has assumed that illegal migration is a problem that needs to be fought against, thus indirectly fighting trafficking. The problematization of trafficking concurs largely with the existent ways of dealing with illegal migration.

Moreover, this approach takes as given the security concerns that inform the representations of illegal migration and the interventions to manage the phenomenon. Anti-trafficking policies are just a subcategory of those targeting illegal migrants. Van Impe could therefore argue in favour of preventive measures for human trafficking in order to obstruct 'the considerable misuse of various channels of migration' (2000: 121). Vectoring human trafficking through migration leads to the interpretation of trafficking as illegal migration with a surplus, that is, the exploitative trafficker. While this representation of the trafficker as the evil foreigner makes possible repressive policies targeted at him/her, vectoring has effects on trafficked and non-trafficked migrants that are ignored in this literature.

The problematization of trafficking as an object of knowledge produces categorized identities for the subjects of trafficking. The literature on trafficking intervenes at two levels: at one level, by explicitly promoting policies to tackle the phenomenon of trafficking and, at another level, by fostering the category of trafficked women. These two types of interventions are intimately linked, as the categorization of women limits the policies that are devised to deal with them. Whether women are perceived as rational illegal migrants, powerless deceived victims, illegal prostitutes, irregular workers or, most recently, trafficking survivors influences the policies adopted by authorities. Specific categorizations are governed by specific policies.

Human trafficking as a problem of organized crime

The major threat of organized crime for society is that criminal networks develop a strong economic and 'political' structure in society through legitimate ways. The underlying motive for such criminal penetration is the opportunity to make a profit quickly with little

risk, unhindered by rules or just making use of weak rules, circumstances and 'cover techniques'.

(European Commission, 2001)

The problematization of trafficking as organized crime framework is
largely similar to that of illegal migration in terms of the arguments
it puts forth and the strategies to create a niche for human trafficking as
a specific form of organized crime. As with migration, the link between
trafficking and organized crime raises definitional problems and identification problems. What is organized crime and who are the criminal
organizations which have established themselves as 'travel agents' for
illegal migrants? Defining what organized crime is has proved an
extremely difficult task because of the multifaceted nature of criminal
organizations (Apap et al., 2002). In relation to trafficking, it is necessary 'to identify the new forms of criminal organizations that seem to
be active in this sector . . . We should determine whether the subjects in
question are recycled from other criminal experiences or whether we are
dealing with new organizations' (Pomodoro, 2001: 241).

The answers provided in the literature on the proliferation and categories of criminal organizations are as varied as they are contradictory.
In Phil Williams' interpretation, some organizations are target-specific,
while other well-established criminal groups have simply diversified
their activities into one more profitable area of activity (Williams, 1999).
Trafficking is either the unique profit-making activity of an organization
or an addition to other criminal activities such as drug- or arms trafficking.
For Shannon, criminal organizations frequently conduct trafficking in
conjunction with other illicit ventures (Shannon, 1999). Other authors
see sex trafficking as a 'large scale, highly organized and profitable international business venture transcending state borders and nationalities of
women who supply the commodity of sex and of men who demand it'
(Bertone, 2000: 7). Organized crime is represented as an insidious type of
threat, penetrating the state and destabilizing its functions, while at the
same time surpassing it. Unlike migration, which is a threat that the
state can manage by appropriate strategies that promote legal migration
and deter illegal forms, organized crime is experienced as a very serious
challenge.

The literature on organized crime and trafficking warns against some of
the conclusions which have been reached in the migration literature.
One should beware of the portrayal of organized crime as 'relatively harm-
less, a form of borderline entrepreneurship that feeds on opportunities

provided by various forms of prohibition' (Williams, 1999: 1). Human trafficking cannot be a benign form of business venture when it is linked with organized crime. Organized crime is most often perceived as external, involving 'alien' actors who subvert otherwise orderly, law-abiding, subjects whether these be bureaucracies, corporations, markets or the internal security of the polis itself (Edwards and Gill, 2002: 253).

Despite this disagreement, the debate in the literature on trafficking and organized crime focuses, just like with migration, on creating categories and drawing boundaries. Is human trafficking (partly) synonymous with large-scale organized crime? Research often contests the hypothesis of large-scale organized crime which is supposedly at the heart of the trafficking phenomenon. Vocks and Nijboer see trafficking as 'small networks of recruiters and exploiters, who knew each other' (Vocks and Nijboer, 2000: 385). The consequence they point out is that, through such connections, exploiters can make very real threats to victims and their families. By expanding the conceptualization of organized crime, these authors expand simultaneously the scope of what human trafficking is and entrench the link between trafficking and organized crime. In a trafficking trial in Romania, the judge decided that the eight persons involved in transporting and exploiting women for prostitution in Spain did not constitute an organized group because there was no hierarchy and no precise tasks for each of the members.[3] Such a decision would most likely be considered inappropriate by Vocks and Nijboer.

Some authors have tried to replace the 'bureaucratic' model of organized criminal activity implicit in Mafia-type analyses with a more complex understanding of organized criminality as being developed and sustained through networks rather than omnipotent criminal families or cartels (Taylor and Jamieson, 1999: 259). If the 'Mafia shorthand' is thought to be no longer adequate for the description of transnational organized crime, the concept as such is not questioned. Just like migration, organized crime is considered a natural given whose nature needs to be adequately grasped. According to Finkenauer, human trafficking seems to fall more into the 'crime that is organized' category than it does into 'true' organized crime (Finkenauer, 2001: 172). The IOM has also described an often direct relationship between the women being trafficked and their traffickers. Interviews suggested that traffickers are often 'young criminals, attracted by the possibility of earning easy money even at the cost of profiting from girls/women that were friends, school mates or neighbours in their home town or village' (quoted in Finkenauer, 2001: 174). The literature can, however, accommodate them by creating new categories of organized crime such as middlemen networks.

Kyle and Koslowski have pointed out that some migrant smugglers are more akin to the historical free traders of an earlier era (Kyle and Koslowski, 2001: 48). They denounce existing studies of human smuggling for using a particularly ahistorical concept of organized crime that allows no conceptual space for analysing the organizational sources of transnational human smuggling. What they call for is actually an enriched and expanded definition of organized crime able to accommodate the strategies of human smuggling and trafficking. Rather than the Mafia-type organization which has been stereotypically linked with organized crime, these authors claim a flexible concept which will accommodate various types of structures. Such a concept can also ultimately accommodate individual traffickers. As in the case of migration, these approaches do not question how organized crime has become a threat of such proportions for the EU. Just like illegal migration, organized crime is taken for granted as a threatening reality which can be tackled once it has been properly dissected as an object of knowledge. The main concern of these authors is to distinguish trafficking as another 'reality', to show how it is simultaneously different and related to organized crime.

More than just a form of organized crime, human trafficking is often simply integrated in the looser catagory of crime. As the feminist abolitionist Donna Hughes has put it, without recruiters, traffickers and pimps, trafficking in women would not exist (Hughes, 2000: 10). More generally, human trafficking can only exist and be explained in relation to crime. In this approach, organized crime is no more of a theoretical construct than illegal migration was for the migration literature. What remains unquestioned is the intervening power of its categorizations and the effects these entail upon those who are categorized. By considering organized crime as a natural given to be adequately grasped and problematizing human trafficking in terms of organized crime, this literature implicitly takes up the construction of these problems as threats and the interventions associated with it.

This does not mean that critical engagement with the description of organized crime is lacking. Wijers and van Doorninck have noted that a criminal approach focuses on individual victims and perpetrators, leaving aside structural causes (Wijers and van Doorninck, 2002). Moreover, they warn that a criminal approach can expose women to secondary victimization, risks of retaliation from the perpetrators, harassment by the authorities in the home country or stigmatizing exposure to the home community. However, these critiques are unable to replace a general construction of organized crime as a threat to society by individual concerns of clearly limited groups. Organized crime is already located in a securitized discourse which vectors human trafficking and establishes a logic of suspicion for trafficked women. Trafficked women are continually suspected of not being genuine victims, of taking advantage of the system or, even worse, of being involved themselves in these networks. The cases of victims of trafficking who later on become recruiters themselves are used as examples of the ubiquity of networks and their power of infiltration.

Human trafficking as a problem of prostitution

> The nightmare of human trafficking is upon us ... it is a stain on our culture. [...] We see it in the plate glass windows of Antwerp and Hamburg; it inundates the centres and pavements of Amsterdam, Paris, Athens, and Rome; it is the product for sale in the markets of London and Madrid ...
>
> (Diamantopoulos, 2001)

As this quotation by a former EU Commissioner suggests, human trafficking has also provided a new locale for debates about prostitution. The problematization of trafficking as prostitution is a historical inheritance, which has not been displaced by concerns with other forms of forced labour such as domestic work. The 1949 UN Convention for the Suppression of Traffic in Persons and the Exploitation of the Prostitution of Others states that 'prostitution and the accompanying evil of the traffic in persons for the purpose of prostitution are incompatible with the dignity and worth of human persons and endanger the welfare of the individual, the family and the community' (UN, 1949). The resurgence of trafficking in the 1990s has entailed a fierce debate around the Protocol and its abolitionist approach to prostitution as a social evil.

The 2001 UN Anti-Trafficking Protocol, some feminist activists have argued, has not significantly departed from the idea of prostitution as a social evil (Doezema, 2002). Yet, feminism is radically split on the issue of prostitution and the question of agency: can prostitution be freely chosen? Feminist lobbying on what trafficking is has been quite fierce, with different groups promoting opposite definitions of trafficking. Trafficking has found a niche within the category of prostitution, leading to the subsequent task of deciding what subcategory of prostitution trafficking is and what distinguishes the latter from the former. The debates have mirrored the debates on prostitution led by the Coalition Against Trafficking in Women (CATW) and the Global Alliance Against Trafficking in Women (GAATW). Put in a nutshell, the two positions are prostitution as sexual slavery versus prostitution as labour.

One side, represented by the CATW, has argued that 'trafficking' should include all forms of recruitment and transportation for prostitution, regardless of whether any force or deception took place. This approach is driven by a belief that all prostitution is abusive of women. In the words of its founder, Kathleen Barry, prostitution cannot be a right, as it is 'injurious to women's physical and mental health and well-being' (Barry, 1995: 308) and it abrogates the right to sexual integrity and autonomy.

As prostitution is deemed to be a degradation that no normal woman would consider, the question of voluntary or forced prostitution becomes irrelevant. Prostitution can only be the result of some sort of coercion and violence, with violence understood along a continuum from direct physical violence to violence inscribed in the social and economic structures. This position has been mostly criticized for denying any agency and self-determination to those women who voluntarily engage in prostitution. According to Doezema, it was based on the assumption that a woman's consent to undertake sex work is meaningless, that prostitution can never be a matter of personal choice and a form of work (Doezema, 2002: 21).

The other position, held by GAATW, makes the distinction between 'trafficking in women' as 'forced prostitution' on the one hand and 'voluntary prostitution' on the other. GAATW has taken up a distinction developed in the mid-eighties by the prostitutes' rights movement (Doezema, 1998: 37). Trafficking is reprehensible only inasmuch as it is linked with forced prostitution and abuse of human rights. Since the re-emergence of trafficking in women on the political agenda and the increase in measures targeting all sex workers, this position has met with renewed criticism by sex activists. Anti-trafficking measures, it was argued, did little for the protection of women's rights and could have negative effects for the rights of sex workers. In their comment on the UN Anti-Trafficking Protocol, the Network of Sex Work Projects (NSWP) has argued that

> [h]istorically, anti-trafficking measures have been more concerned with protecting women's 'purity' than with ensuring the human rights of those in the sex industry. This approach limits the protection

. afforded by these instruments to those who can prove that they did not consent to work in the sex industry. It also ignores the abusive conditions within the sex industry, often facilitated by national laws that place (migrant) sex workers outside of the range of rights granted to others as citizens and workers.

(NSWP, 1999)

NSWP and other organizations for sex workers' rights (for example the English Collective of Prostitutes and Legal Action for Women UK) have been at the forefront of this critique of equating 'trafficking in women' with 'forced prostitution' and have argued that the fight against forced prostitution is a fight against prostitution tout court as long as the rights of prostitutes are not protected. The condemnation of forced prostitution has led to a lack of interest in the rights of 'voluntary' prostitutes. Doezema and Wijers warn against the definition of trafficking as forced prostitution, as it supports the distinction between 'native' and immigrant prostitutes as 'voluntary' and respectively 'forced'. This dichotomy also implies a further distinction between guilty and innocent prostitutes (Doezema, 1998: 42). Doezema has argued that the innocence of the victim determines on which side of the dichotomy she will fall, perpetuating an understanding of prostitution as evil and abnormal.

Reports on trafficking as 'forced prostitution' emphasize the deceit, the fact that women did not choose to be prostitutes, or 'poverty as force' (Doezema, 1998). These are strategies of making innocent victims eligible for human rights protection. Turned into innocent passive victims, trafficked women are to be protected at the expense of 'dirty whores' who are to be policed and punished. Doezema's discontent regards the denial of the prostitutes' human rights and the false divisions that representations of trafficking create among sex workers. Alison Murray (1998) has noted that the 'voluntary' prostitute is generally associated with the Western sex worker endowed with agency, while the sex worker from a developing country is considered incapable of making this choice, being either easily deceived or deterministically influenced by poverty.

This image of the passive victim incapable of self-determination has been reinforced by reactivating the myth of white slavery. Doezema has shown how the prostitution approach to present-day trafficking has inherited many of the presuppositions of white slavery (Doezema, 2000). At the turn of the twentieth century, 'white slavery' caused a veritable moral panic about the sexual enslavement of young virgins

(Irwin, 1996). Doezema has argued that, while the myth of 'trafficking in women' or 'white slavery' is about protecting women, it has not displaced the underlying moral concern with the control of 'loose women'. The 'loose women' that Doezema has in mind differ very little from Judith Walkowitz's Victorian prostitute (Walkowitz, 1980). 'An object of fascination and disgust, the prostitute was ingrained in public consciousness as a highly visible symbol of the social dislocation attendant upon a new industrial era' (Walkowitz, 1980: 32).

The feminist approaches that reject the linkage between prostitution and human trafficking argue that it privileges the rights of victims of trafficking at the expense of those of sex workers. In problematizing human trafficking as prostitution, Doezema, Wijers and other feminist writers have analysed trafficking in terms of the influences it entails on sex workers, migrants, asylum seekers, etc. and do not measure it against some standard of 'reality'. For sex activists, anti-trafficking measures have so far incurred more harm than good to sex workers. Repeated raidings by the police have led to detention of all foreign prostitutes under the suspicion of having been trafficked. For instance, sex activists have condemned the police and immigration raids in Soho that had held 60 migrant women under the suspicion of having been trafficked (International Prostitutes Collective, 2001).

The sex activists' position has shifted the discourse of rights from the category of trafficked women to that of prostitutes. While the credo of anti-trafficking NGOs has been that trafficked women must not be subjected to the same treatment as undocumented migrants (Jordan, 2002), sex activists contend that prostitutes should not be submitted to any human rights abuses. Faced with the continual threat of deportation of (illegal) foreign prostitutes, sex activists have argued that trafficking is not prostitution, but forced or bonded labour, in the domestic, sex or any other industry (Adams, 2003: 138). Moreover, human rights abuses should be considered independently of whether those who suffer them have been trafficked or not.

The question, 'what is human trafficking?' has been mobilized by sex workers' movements for critical purposes. If answering this question can make possible the deployment of technologies of government to govern trafficking, it can also activate a critique of 'how not to be governed thus' (Foucault, 1997). The feminist literature has emphasized the agency of migrants who choose sex work. Andrijasevic has shown that prostitution is considered by trafficked women simply as a migratory project. For her interviewees, prostitution was simply a means to an end, a temporary solution they favoured (Andrijasevic, 2003). By pointing out forms of agency, Andrijasevic attempts to loosen both the necessary link between the trafficking subcategory and prostitution as well as that between trafficking and migration. Laura Agustin (2007) has also argued that migrants who work in low-prestige jobs should not be considered by definition passive victims.

However, the 'problematization of the problematization' of anti-trafficking measures through the effects that certain descriptions of trafficking have upon sex workers encounters the limitation of different subjective positions – sex workers, on the one hand, and victims of trafficking, on the other. Sex workers mobilize specific lived experiences to buttress their own narrative. NGOs and the police use other lived experiences for their narrative. Subjective positions and lived experiences are mobilized to make apparent the dangerous effects of anti-trafficking measures either for sex workers or for victims of trafficking.

The subjective positions of sex workers and victims of trafficking become incompatible in a discourse of security. The police are dangerous for sex workers; anti-trafficking measures have dangerous effects. It is important at this point to note that the problematization of the problematization of trafficking takes up representations of insecurity and danger. The feminist problematization of the problematization questions the cultural assumptions in the construction of migration or prostitution as particular social problems. It reclaims migration and sex work as forms of individual agency within constraining social and economic contexts. At the same time, however, these critiques deploy a counter-rhetoric of insecurity and danger. Turning trafficking into a problem of prostitution actually creates vulnerabilities and insecurities for sex workers, asylum seekers and migrants. Yet, the extension of insecurities envisaged in this literature cannot be achieved as these representations of danger appear to be contradictory.

Human trafficking as a problem of human rights abuse

> Imagine if victims of rape or torture could only get medical attention if they agreed to cooperate with the police in persecuting their abusers?
>
> (Pearson, 2002: 56)

The humanitarian approach to trafficking proposes a different problematization of trafficking which emerges from the lived experiences of victims of trafficking. Rather than engaging in debates about the linkages between trafficking and illegal migration, organized crime and prostitution, a human rights approach simply replaces the question of what kind of migrants, prostitutes or criminals these women are by the unquestionable answer: 'they are suffering human beings'. Suffering is read both in the physical and moral sense – human rights activists also endorse the representation of human trafficking as slavery – and in legal terms. The victims' suffering is an abuse of rights, which can only be rectified by reinstating those rights.

Vectoring trafficking through representations of human rights violations is a politically explicit strategy. These representations of trafficking as human rights violations do not offer a theoretical refinement of other representations but engage in emotional narratives about violence, pain and suffering. Numbers, statistics and other social problems are less important from this perspective. What counts here is that 'Each of these numbers [of trafficked persons] is the life of a human being' (Zohreh Tabatabai quoted in Bolton, 2005). The humanitarian approach is concerned with instilling the 'right' way to feel about the group of victims of trafficking. To promote understanding and sympathy for their situation, these advocates have focused on personal stories and psychological explanations of the pain and suffering trafficking causes. The main purpose of these accounts is to promote an identification with victims of trafficking in a way that crosses the divisions preserved by other approaches. The focus is no longer on the specificity of trafficking as a form of migration, organized crime or prostitution, but on the commonality of potential suffering.

The human rights approach tries to use the mobilizing potential of sentimentality and emotions to efface divisions by presenting a one-dimensional image of the trafficking victim as a suffering individual. While being aware that categorizations affect the way in which victims of trafficking are dealt with, the human rights activists do not challenge the existing categories of illegal migrants, criminals and prostitutes. They create a different category of human rights bearers or trafficking survivors. This new category is supposed to transcend all previous categories.

The humanitarian approach is therefore harnessed to restructuring social relations in the sphere of trafficking. It envisages specific interventions, different from the repressive and preventive strategies embraced especially by those concerned with migration and organized crime. By promoting a representation of victimhood that is indifferent to representations of migrants, criminals or prostitutes, the humanitarian approach would appear as the most effective political strategy of vectoring human trafficking. However, as feminist research has pointed out, the universal subject of rights is particularized in a specific categorization of 'victim of trafficking' to the exclusion of the rights of sex workers, migrants or asylum seekers. Moreover, the pursuance of rights for victims risks dismantling the sparse rights that sex workers enjoy. The politics of rescuing victims of trafficking is often based on large-scale raids that 'sweep up everyone present for arrest, interrogation and detention' (Urban Justice Center, 2007).

The rights of victims of trafficking are also counterposed to the rights of women 'to control their body, life, work, and especially to migrate, to decide for themselves whether they want or not to work in prostitution, to be free from coercion and violence' (Wijers and Lap-Chew, 1999: 246). The subject of rights is divided from herself inasmuch as trafficked persons can only be victims but not claimants of rights themselves. The subject of rights is also divided from other subjects of rights. The humanitarian solution to shift the focus from seeing trafficked persons as a category of migrants or prostitutes to 'understanding them as people bearing human rights' (Jordan, 2002: 30) acts as a strategy of identification/dis-identification.[4] Trafficked women are dis-identified from categories of migrants, criminals or prostitutes by the emphasis on suffering. Therefore, women who are trafficked into prostitution should not be deprived of their rights on grounds that they are undocumented migrants. Yet, these rights are only the rights of the victim, an identification achieved through a mode of suffering and a feeling of pain.

The problem with the dis-identification strategy is that it rests on an illusory critique. Victims of trafficking are not embodiments of common humanity, but particular victims. By insisting that trafficked women should not be likened to illegal migrants or prostitutes, the critique does not displace all the other categories and their social construction. The category of human rights bearers does not dispute the previous categories; it only qualifies them. Trafficked women as illegal migrants or prostitutes who have been victimised are entitled to human rights protection. An argument has been put forth that special benefits for women in forced prostitution can act as an incentive to other women to illegitimately claim this status (Home Office, 2006). Despite the attempt to divorce representations of victims of trafficking from those of illegal migrants, prostitutes or criminals, the separation is highly unstable. Rather than exploring the reasons for this conceptual instability, the humanitarian approach translates its emotional rhetoric into a pedagogy. The strategy favoured is one of responsibilization of political elites: instead of being concerned about stopping illegal migrants, Western states should be rather disturbed by the victimization and sacrifices such policies cause (Deimleiter, 2001: 265). Authorities need to be educated on the rights and needs of trafficked persons (Jordan, 2002: 29). The work that human rights advocates are supposed to undertake is that of gathering stories about the fate of victims of trafficking due to governmental policies and stories about returnees who are harmed or retrafficked as a result of summary deportations.

The instability of the subject of human rights and the inability to suspend competing representations needs to be understood in the institutional context in which the problematizations of trafficking are proposed and contested. If the universality of human rights and the subjects it fosters have been intensely criticized for silencing the particularity of cultural subjects, dismissing other forms of political resistance and being intrinsically connected with ideologies of imperialism,[5] there is a different aspect that is most startling in relation to human trafficking. The human rights of one category are counted and assessed against the human rights of another category. The state becomes an arbiter in this allocation of rights. Rights can only be enjoyed by particular groups of people to the exclusion of others. The rights of some are threatened by the rights of others. The delimitation of categories, the representation of some categories as dangerous to others and the divisions among categories of migrants, sex workers and criminals need to be understood in relation to the problematization of (in)security. Danger, threat, exclusion, insecurity and vulnerability are assumptions that subtend the competing problematizations of human trafficking. The next chapter will start to unpack the problematization of security.

Human trafficking and the (absent) problematization of security

This chapter has shown that human trafficking becomes visible politically by being derived from migration, organized crime, prostitution and forms of human rights abuses. Paraphrasing Foucault, one could say that human trafficking exists inasmuch as it establishes relations of resemblance, proximity, distance, difference and transformation in relation to other objects (Foucault, 2002). Human trafficking is construed as a series of variations on illegal migration, organized crime, prostitution and human rights abuses.

Concerned with providing a better representation of the reality of trafficking, this literature often engages in a 'politics of representation/intervention' without paying sufficient attention to the political effects that categorizations of trafficking have. Human trafficking as a problem and trafficked women as a specific category can be made governable through vectored categorization. This literature enters the field of relations of power/knowledge and engages in the politics of representation of human trafficking, without being sufficiently reflexive about how descriptions work within an already structured context. Edwards and Gill have suggested that any alternative strategy with respect to transnational organized crime needs to look at how 'the problem' is narrated and 'how this in turn selects certain strategies of control and their concomitant operational instruments, whilst deselecting others, and then how it organizes the interpretation and appraisal of their effects ...' (Edwards and Gill, 2002: 247).

Their suggestion is especially interesting as human trafficking does not emerge in a void, but in a political field where migration, organized crime and prostitution are already 'narrated' and modes of intervention selected. The vectoring has been already vectored in the field in which trafficking emerges and which is characterized by the representation of illegal migration, organized crime and certain aspects of prostitution as security problems. The literature on trafficking which analyses it at the intersection of migration, organized crime and prostitution has been inattentive to the representation of threat that structures the field in which their discourse is located. Research on trafficking rarely mentions security. Protection appears as a puzzle of who deserves to be protected: particular individuals versus society or the state, but also specific categories of people versus others.

I am interested in this (absent) problematization of security because it appears as the limit that subverts the alternative representations of who victims of trafficking are or what trafficking is. Security influences what can be said and done about human trafficking. Illegal migration, organized crime and prostitution are embedded in a problematization of security. In a speech to the European Parliament before the Seville European Council, Romano Prodi regarded migration as the 'most burning issue' to be dealt with by the EU (Prodi, 2002). While a model for managing migration should not be incompatible with the fundamental values of the Union, he emphasized, it should also attend to 'our citizens' legitimate demand for security'. Similarly, transnational organized crime is the dark side of globalization, threatening and damaging democracy and the economic basis of societies, weakening institutions and confidence in the rule of law (Apap et al., 2002: 6). A report on organized criminality commissioned by the EU starts by defining crime as a threat to the well-being of our societies (Fondazione Rosselli, 1999). Moreover, the paper argues, 'the internationalisation of criminal activities means that no country can feel completely secure within its borders at the same time when the danger of all-out military confrontation has receded with the end of the Cold War' (Fondazione Rosselli, 1999: 5). While prostitution is no longer explicitly constructed as a social evil, the underlying imaginary of threat to public order, public health and community morality has led countries like Sweden to criminalize it. Equally, debates on criminalizing prostitution have recently gained impetus in France as well as other European countries. The feminist literature has also mentioned representations of danger linked with prostitution without specifically tackling this problematization.

The humanitarian approach attempts to displace extant representations of human trafficking. Human rights advocates argue in favour of an approach protecting the fundamental human rights of victims to balance measures of increased border control and punitive measures against carriers and traffickers. Although activists deplore the scant emphasis given to human rights in the problematization of trafficking, the human rights approach has been progressively embraced by different organizations and states. One of the important think-tanks on issues of migration and trafficking, the International Centre for Migration Policy Development (ICMPD), has argued that trafficked women should be granted rights either because it is in the interest of justice to punish traffickers or because it can help the police prevent other cases of trafficking:

> Law enforcement officers should always adhere to this method [human rights], not only because it is the correct and caring thing to do so, but also because it is ultimately in the best interests of the investigation to do so because the cooperating victim will always make a more resilient witness if given time and support to come to terms with her experiences.
>
> (ICMPD, 2002)

This argument is not particular to the ICMPD, but has been taken up by many NGOs in order to buttress the pedagogy that the humanitarian approach advised. Law enforcement officials can therefore be trained to understand the importance of human rights.

The non-contradiction between human rights and punitive law enforcement is even more surprising when counterposed to the contradictions between different representations of rights. Human rights become part of the interventions to deal with the phenomenon of trafficking. Even when security seems to be absent, human rights are mobilized for the purposes of preventing the phenomenon. Rather than subverting existing representations of trafficking, they enrol 'victims' as resilient agents of interventions to tackle human trafficking. The humanitarian approach is no longer contradictory to the other representations of trafficking and the interventions devised to manage it.

The discursive presence of (in)security, threat and danger and the ultimate non-contradiction between alternative problematizations of trafficking require an analysis of what security means and especially what its problematization entails for human trafficking. Even when the representation of danger is mentioned, it is mostly understood as a 'moral panic' and its problematization is not explored. Doezema, for example, has noted various fears and anxieties linked with human trafficking: fears of women's security and independence, of foreigners and migrants, moral fears and fears of disease such as AIDS (Doezema, 1998: 39). When the dangerous effects of anti-trafficking measures are formulated by activists, this discourse of threat appears as incompatible with another discourse of threat, the threat to trafficked women. The problematization of problematization is suspended, as the relation between the two remains unexplored.

2
Problematizing Security: The Presence of an Absence

'Central to the problem of policing THB [trafficking in human beings] is the difficulty in clearly identifying the threat that THB poses to a State'. Thus starts a Europol Report on human trafficking (Europol, 2003). Another Report, this time by the IOM, is more explicit in identifying trafficking as 'the most menacing form of irregular migration due to its ever-increasing scale and complexity involving, as it does arms, drugs, prostitution and so on' (Laczkó and Thompson, 2000: 19). Or, once more, in a different definition of threat, '[t]rafficking ... strips victims of their rights to liberty, dignity, security of person, the right not to be held in slavery, the right to be free from cruel and inhumane treatment' (OSCE, 1999). These reports raise the issue of trafficking as a threat and concern themselves with establishing what is threatened and by whom, or by what. Definitions of what makes human trafficking a threat, whether to the state or trafficked women, are considered important by those involved in governing the phenomenon. The first chapter has argued that the problematization of trafficking as illegal migration, organized crime, prostitution or human rights abuses were important for the same reasons of governing it.

This chapter will explore the (absent) problematization of security and offer conceptual tools to apprehend its effects. I start by unpacking what I have called the security vectoring of trafficking. What is security vectoring for human trafficking? What effects does the problematization of security entail or, to put it simply, what does security do? How does security render contradictions non-contradictory? The effects of security can only be understood by problematizing the problematization of security. What security is has an impact on interventions, on what security does and what it allows to be done. This chapter will unpack the 'there is' of security. Ascertaining whether human trafficking is a security issue has been important for practitioners and analysts alike. At the beginning of an article that reflects on sex trafficking and threat construction in the EU, Jacqueline Berman asks whether human trafficking is a *'grave threat'* to international security or *really* a law enforcement issue (Berman, 2003, emphasis mine). Berman's question (Is human trafficking 'really' a grave security threat?) takes us in the midst of the problematization of security.

Really can be read in different ways. It can be read as opposed to *false*, which has entailed acrimonious debates about what is rightly and what is wrongly defined as a security issue. 'Real' as what pertains to the objective materiality of the world delegitimizes construction as false. *Really* can also be read as opposed to *symbolically* and *imaginarily*. The term 'symbolic' is introduced in relation to the institutional embedding of discourses and practices. 'Imaginary' is a term I introduce here to make explicit the relation that the concept of security creates between the subject and the world. Security has an imagined element rendered as a desirable state to be achieved. Finally, *really* can also be read from a *subjective perspective*: whose version of reality is the 'real real'?

Unpacking the question of the reality of security shows a different relation that the debates on security have towards problematization. While the first discussion of whether security is real or not, whether one representation is false and another not is also a literature of problematization, the other debates formulate problematizations of the problematization of security. All forms of construction, symbolic or imaginary, have effects which are differentiated depending on subjective positions. As the previous chapter has shown, the problematization of human trafficking entails different effects depending on the particular subjects involved and their representations.

Questioning the 'reality' of security

Real versus *false* will be considered here as a particular take on some of the debates about the social construction of security problems. Many of the debates in security studies are concerned with what security means nowadays, which problems are actually threats and therefore legitimate objects of study in the field and, for those in the social constructivist camp, which issues *should* be dealt with as security threats and which not. The opposition of real versus constructed has characterized the debate starting in the 1980s on the proper sphere of security. For strategic studies, or classical security studies, the offspring of American and Western defence policy (Buzan, 1991: 6), threats are objectively given and military in nature. For those who concern themselves with the 'study of threat, use, and control of military force' (Walt, 1991: 212), human trafficking is 'wrongly' conceived of as a threat. Human trafficking is largely indifferent to the state, it is not military in nature and does not threaten national security; one could say that human trafficking bypasses the state.

Threats to a state are objectively given inasmuch as they can be read from the behaviour of other states. States *cum* individuals are intentional beings whose actions are expressive of their goals. The main question that concerns the strategists would be of measures to be taken to pre-empt or neutralize such threatening behaviour by other states. The arms race and theories of deterrence dominated the discourse on security (Buzan, 1997: 6). Established in the conditions of the Cold War, strategic studies were understandably concerned with the territorial survival of the state and attacks to state sovereignty. While 'national security' was strictly defined and limited, given the 'military and nuclear obsessions of the Cold War' (Buzan, 1997: 9), state sovereignty could provide some leeway, bearing in mind that much of the Cold War was 'fought', directly or indirectly, on the territories of third states considered to be essential zones of influence for the two big powers. Military actions outside the national territory could thus count as infringements of sovereignty.

From the possible widening of state sovereignty, the next step for an enlarged concept of national security was the economic dimension. On the one hand, economic power could be transformed into military power as money could buy arms and new military technology. On the other, economics was thought to be a viable substitute for military power (for example, Gilpin [1981]). Economic sanctions are a tool of US foreign policy, as much favoured as investment in military technology. In a gatekeeper article on the meaning of security, Stephen Walt allows for economics only if it relates to military issues. Widening security is limited by two axes: that of the state and that of military appurtenance. Any larger expansion, Walt has argued, would destroy the intellectual coherence of the field and make it more difficult to devise solutions to any of these important problems (1991). Buzan has read in this unwillingness to widen security a 'generally unspoken political concern that allowing non-military issues to achieve security status would have undesirable and/or counter-productive effects on the whole fabric of social and international relations' (Buzan, 1997: 9).

Later on, the concept underwent successive extensions given that other threats, non-military in nature, were seen as endangering the state. Organized crime, to take an example closely related to trafficking, has been considered as a potential entry on the list of 'real' security threats. By weakening state institutions, organized crime is analysed as an objective threat to sovereignty. Organized crime infiltrates the legitimate business and political elites and reaches a 'symbiotic' phase in which it becomes fully integrated into the political structure, as in the example of Italy, where the Mafia became closely connected with the Christian Democratic Party (Lupsha, 1996: 24).

Even if human trafficking does not satisfy the conditions of possibility for a threat, namely it is not of a military nature and it does not threaten the survival of the state, it can be integrated in a loose definition of national security. Myron Weiner for example has provided an account of migration as a threat to the state. Weiner has undertaken an analysis of 'how, why and when states may regard immigrants and refugees as potential threats', of the conditions under which migration is legitimately dealt with as a security threat (Weiner, 1992/1993: 104). He has identified five ways in which migrants can become a security threat to the state: when refugees and migrants are working against the regime of their home country; when they pose a risk to their host country; when immigrants are seen as a cultural threat; when they are perceived as a social or economic threat; when the host country uses immigrants as instruments to threaten the country of origin. In the same vein, refugee crises can spill over and cause destabilization of states (Zimmerman, 1995: 107).

Weiner's analysis would be the appropriate response to a demand to qualify the type of threat that human trafficking represents, as required by the Europol Report quoted at the beginning of this Chapter. Post-9/11, one of the main concerns with the threat of human trafficking was that, similarly to arms- and drug trafficking, it yields huge sums which can be used by terrorist groups. In his discourse justifying the war on Iraq, George Bush has included trafficking as one of the most important threats we are facing today (Bush, 2003).[1] Therefore, trafficking could potentially become a crucial security issue for the state, even given a commitment to security threats as objective givens.

In the post-Cold War world, security appeared to be driven to almost automatic self-expansion: environmental problems, ethnic problems, migration problems, etc. A so-called widening debate has endorsed an expanded concept of security and has shifted the boundaries of the security realm to include all sorts of threats to the state and other forms of political communities. It has however resulted in simply adding adjectives, as Huysmans has put it (Huysmans, 1998c: 227); for example, environmental, political, economic, societal security. For Krause and Williams too, broadening has turned security into a 'grab bag of different issue areas' (Krause and Williams, 1997: 35). Wideners have discovered a proliferation of threats that need to be analysed and dealt with. Human trafficking as connected with organized crime would be analysed as a cluster of threats: political, economic and societal. Wyn Rees has looked at organized crime and the security construction from a conventional widening perspective (Rees, 1999). Organized crime is an 'indirect' political threat inasmuch as it is linked with political corruption which may exercise a pernicious effect even within relatively stable countries. Economically, organized crime groups may establish microeconomies within the boundaries of the state. On the societal dimension, organized crime can contribute to the breakdown of the cohesion of a society by promoting high levels of violence and intimidation.[2] A widening approach would limit itself to telling us 'how things are' and extending the limit of 'real' security threat. Some wideners would say that human trafficking is 'really' a security threat and should be analysed as such. Others would add a constructivist proviso to the analysis of issue areas.

The opposition between 'real' and 'false' means that, in certain locales, things are made into security threats and/or unmade. There are particular processes that turn issues into security problems. Yet, the main disagreement is about the processes that vector particular issues along security lines. In Lene Hansen's formulation, the main dividing line is between security as a discursive practice, rather, and security as a direct representation of an objectively threatening reality (Hansen, 1997: 376). Reality can change, but can discourse change reality? In this latter approach, discourse becomes the real. What is interesting is no longer the debate about whether security issues are rightly or wrongly so, truly or falsely, but the understanding of the processes which make security real.

Constructing security: the real of symbolic practices

This section will consider two modes of opening up processes of security construction. The first one – though not necessarily chronologically the first – has been offered by the Copenhagen School of security studies (CoS). Ole Waever has labelled the process by means of which issues become naturalized and gain 'ontological hardness' securitization. The second approach, linked with the Paris School of security studies, focuses on the symbolic power of discourse.[3] It emphasizes the role of the speakers and of their positions of authority for the success of discourses.

The CoS has expanded the concept of security to provide better tools to understand the 'proliferation of threats' on the political agenda. Their theory combines a taxonomy of sectors in which issues can be securitized with an understanding of the process by which issues are raised above the 'haggling of normal politics' (Buzan et al., 1998). In the 1998 *Security Framework*, the CoS identified five sectors of security: military, political, societal, economic and environmental. Later on, Lautsen & Waever argued for another possible sector of security, religion (Lautsen and Waever, 2000). Sectoral differentiation serves to distinguish between referent structures of securitization (societal securitization will tackle identity, while military security is concerned with state survival).

However, it is with the notion of securitization, inspired by Austin's theory of speech acts, that the CoS becomes truly innovative (Huysmans, 1998b). Issues are securitized by virtue of discursive construction or, as Buzan and Waever have put it, '[s]ecurity is a quality actors inject into issues by securitizing them, which means to stage them on the political arena ... and then to have them accepted by a sufficient audience to sanction extraordinary defensive moves' (Buzan et al., 1998: 204). Human trafficking would be discursively constructed as a threat rather than as a labour issue. Alongside the speech act, securitization is characterized by three other elements: political actors (with the state as the ultimate securitizing actor, as it is the state that needs to take up the security claims), the audience that accepts the speech act and the sanctioning of extraordinary measures.

The most important debates around securitization have concerned the relation between speech acts and political actors, on the one hand, and that between speech acts and exceptional measures, on the other.[4] Didier Bigo has criticized the CoS for reducing symbolic practices to linguistics, at the expense of analyzing institutional practices and actors. One tradition of analyzing securitization has been to look at discursive representations of dangerous others in the media. Many articles on human trafficking look extensively at media representations of what human trafficking is and how others are depicted. When other discourses are considered, it is generally those of major political actors, like the EU commissioners, government officials and party leaders. Often these discourses are selected depending on their previous selection by the media. There is little critical assessment of how these discourses have attained the prominence that makes them relevant for securitization.

The concept of problematization has already indicated that representations are embedded in institutional locales. The objects of discourse, Foucault has pointed out, can only be analysed in a complex group of relations between institutions, economic and social processes, behavioural patterns, systems of norms, techniques (Foucault, 2002: 49). To analyse the institutional conditions of security, Bigo draws on Pierre Bourdieu's analyses of the positions from which discourses are uttered. Not everybody has the power to turn human trafficking into a threat or even represent the issue of human trafficking. For Bourdieu, the efficacy of speech acts cannot be separated from the existence of institutions that confer authority upon the speaker/utterances (Bourdieu, 1991). Successful speech acts are uttered from positions of authority. As Michael Williams has concisely put it, 'Performing the discursive speech act of security ... is a *social accomplishment* which can only be effective in the context of a corresponding constellation of social forces' (Williams, 1997: 299). The question that hovers is how to discriminate between various actors, and decide which actors and discourses to privilege.

Drawing on Bourdieu's theory of symbolic power, Bigo has considered the constitution of authority to speak security. The 'constitution of authority' (for example, the authority the police gains in dealing with security matters normally reserved for the military) is to be understood in terms of Bourdieu's convertibility of capital, with the proviso that Bourdieu's types of capital (economic, social, cultural) are replaced by types of knowledge (Bigo, 2000: 87). Practices of security exist in a specific field, formed by actors with particular know-how and technologies, namely the 'security professionals' (Bigo, 1996, 2000, 2002). As not any speech act is felicitous and depends on conditions both internal and external to discourse, practices of securitization can only be undertaken by those endowed with the knowledge to do so. Those who speak security must have the capacity to produce a discourse on the figure of the enemy and impose their own definition on what constitutes a threat (Bigo, 1996: 51, 2002: 75–6). The success of voices which speak of security depends on the positions actors hold and on the symbolic capital these are endowed with, as well as on the capacity to produce a discourse which supports and reinforces a particular reading of reality.

In response to Bigo, Waever has reiterated the importance of the performative speech act at the expense of what he calls, following Austin, the 'conditions' of a felicitous speech act. The three main conditions that Waever lists are (i) the internal construction of the security speech act as a plot with an existential threat, a point of no return and a possible way out; (ii) the position of authority of the securitizing actor and (iii) conditions historically associated with the threat (Waever, 2000: 252–3).

Although Waever, following Butler's insight that it is possible to speak with authority without being authorized to speak (Butler, 1997a: 157), claims that authority is not essential for the success of a securitizing act, he lacks a theorization how unauthorized agents can disrupt authoritative discourses.

Butler has criticized Bourdieu for linking the 'authority' of speech acts exclusively to institutional positions, so that only those who are legitimate actors in the field can successfully 'do things with words' (Austin, 1975 [1962]). Unlike Bourdieu, she is concerned with discourses that can be authoritative in relation to a particular subjective position. Such authoritative practices as Rosa Parks' (the black woman who famously refused to give her place on a bus to a white person) can only happen from an *abject* position, those who have a different *habitus*. Butler's indebtedness to Foucault makes her account of performative speech acts interested in the power effects of discourses in constituting subjects and abjects. A Bourdieuean approach to speech acts focuses rather on the emergence and reproduction of discourses and practices, on the constitution of subjects who are authorized to speak rather than abjects to whom legitimate speech is denied and whose words come to count as less than words. 'In laying claim to the right for which she had no prior authorization', Butler says about Rosa Parks, 'she endowed a certain authority on the act, and began the insurrectionary process of overthrowing those established codes of legitimacy (Butler, 1997a: 141). Yet, Butler has been the target on of acrimonious criticism for having divorced the Rosa Parks' act itself from the social and legal context of mobilization that had been going on.[5] Butler lacks an account of what makes this unique individual act a rupture of the regime of truth in a situation.

Waever's example of environmental movements, having performed unauthorized speech acts, also leaves open the question of practices which are able to account for the success/failure of a speech act (Waever, 2000: 286 n7). On which arguments do environmental movements base their discourse? How have they entered the institutional realm in which authoritative discourses are formulated? Environmental movements often employ alternative knowledge to counter already 'authorized' knowledge; yet, the CoS lacks the tools to allow for this possibility as securitization is limited to the act of uttering. Williams has formulated this issue of authorization in a Bourdieuean voice against the CoS approach:

A key element in understanding the politics of security is thus not simply the linguistic and conceptual structures involved, but their position within a specific institutional setting. The ability to 'speak security' effectively involves the ability to mobilize specific forms of symbolic power within the specific institutional fields in which it operates.

(Williams, 1997: 298)

The savoir faire of the police can be made applicable to other issues. NGOs, for example, can be incorporated in the regime to govern human trafficking inasmuch as they have made their expertise indispensable by 'liaising with the authorities on ... behalf [of victims] and intervening to protect the rights of trafficked persons' (Anti-Slavery International, 2002: 32). Chapter 4 will expose the mechanisms at work that have allowed NGOs to enter the institutional field for governing trafficking in human beings.

The securitization of human trafficking is articulated from various institutional positions and institutional interests are at work in the constitution of a 'regime of truth'. A regime of truth refers to how knowledgeable representations and interventions about human trafficking are rendered legitimate given that relations of power that support it. Truth, Foucault pointed out, is linked in a circular relation with systems of power which produce and sustain it (1980: 133). As at the European level human trafficking was initially thought to fall under the aegis of the Europol, to be dealt together with drugs- and arms-trafficking (den Boer, 1998), other institutions are now involved in the management of human trafficking: border police, internal police, customs, migration services, international NGOs, human rights NGOs, etc. These institutional actors do not only mobilize resources, but create particular forms of knowledge to 'fabricate the threat migration represents (for example, a statistical representation of asylum seekers or of illegal migrants in a discourse on social instability, or, categorizing migration together with drugs trafficking, international criminality, and terrorism)' (Huysmans, 1998a: 572).

The CoS has not denied a Bourdieuean actor-oriented approach to language; they do not analyse 'floating' discourses and agree that securitization is spoken from positions of authority. In a sense, they are closer to Bigo in their understanding of security than to Butler's emphasis on the effects of power relations. Waever has seen securitization as 'articulated only from a specific place, in an institutional voice, by elites' (Waever, 1995). Where, for example, Waever and Bigo part ways is in their respective delimitation of the 'security field'. For Waever securitization is a political spectacle where the main actors are the political elites. For Bigo it is bureaucracies that are important in the securitization process.

The CoS has focused on political actors as speakers of security, given their understanding of what politics is. As liberal democratic politics has electoral responsibility at its core, the dynamics that the CoS has in mind is that between political actors and their electoral 'audience', those who need to be convinced of the legitimacy of a security threat. Such an approach equally sanctions an analysis of securitization in the media, if media is seen as the intermediary, the medium through which representations are circulated between political elites and the audience.

Media representations have been extensively used by sociologists to explain the creation of 'moral panics'. Securitization, although mediated, reinforced or even spurred by media representations, remains very much the premise of institutions. Bigo has remarked that '[j]ournalists often repeat and summarise what they hear from their information sources: security bureaucracies' (Bigo, 2001a: 126). The media discourse on trafficking tends to mirror two types of discourses, one endorsed by NGOs and anti-trafficking campaigners who see trafficking as a human rights violation and the other one upheld by law enforcement. An article from *The Spectator* quotes Andy Felton, who has worked on Project Reflex, a unique British/Romanian initiative to stem illegal migration to the UK, who argues that victims of trafficking, far from being gullible peasant girls, as portrayed by the IOM, were seasoned prostitutes before they left (*The Spectator*, 25 April 2003). 'Happy hookers of Eastern Europe', as the journalist calls them, are the opposite of the victim image promoted by other media reports and the NGOs.

Sociological analysis would shift the centre of gravity of securitization behind the bureaucratic closed doors rather than relegate it to political actors and the media. Their concept of politics looks at complexly structured fields which interact and which actors endowed with various forms of capital and particular habitus enter. The dichotomy that the CoS preserves between political elites and the audience tends to reproduce either an image of cynical politicians or of unawareness on the part of elites and ignores the role that knowledge plays in creating a 'regime of truth' about threats, whose veridicity is taken for granted by politicians and electorates alike. The analyses of security which have turned a sociological eye upon practices have been mainly concerned with the emergence of practices in specific institutional loci. In such an analysis, human trafficking would be the result of a contingent combination of practices that links it with other threats such as illegal migration, drug trafficking, organized crime and even terrorism. An understanding of this *security continuum* would require extensive interviewing and monitoring of police officials entrusted with the management of human trafficking.

As the first chapter has suggested, the securitization of trafficking is not necessarily a discourse that utters security in relation to trafficking. It is by being represented as a form of organized crime, illegal migration and prostitution that human trafficking acquires the threat connotations of the former. It is by drawing lines of division and exclusion that interventions in the field of human trafficking are securitizing. Representations that take up other categorizations are subject to vectoral transformations. These representations are directed and modified by the initial categorizations. Yet, vectoring does not only happen through linguistic cohabitation or transference, but takes place in a field where professionals place these issues together, interlink them and devise interventions to manage them. At the same time, the first chapter has also shown that the field of human trafficking is variously configured by different forms of knowledge beyond those that belong to the 'security professionals'. The 'authority of statistics' that Bigo mentioned as instrumental in establishing a regime of truth is only partial, always in need to be supplemented by other forms of knowledge.

While the CoS restricts the ambit of security to the model of war, Bigo has made explicit the heterogeneity of practices which do not fit the militarised logic of friend/enemy making, but are 'policing' practices in the Foucauldian understanding of the word (Bigo, 1996).[6] As the securitization scenario was played on the stage of 'panic politics' – as opposed to 'normal politics' (Buzan et al., 1998: 34), the distinguishing feature is internal to discourse, the specific rhetorical structure of survival and urgency. In a Bourdieuean approach, securitization is a matter of everyday technologies that the 'professionals of security' employ. Biometrics, databases or surveillance do not immediately entail questions of survival. As the police are one of the actors involved in securitization (cf. Bigo, 1996), 'policing' human trafficking is different from practices of the military, for example. Bigo has claimed that security practices and technologies are more important than public policies and political discourse, if one is to understand what is at stake (Bigo, 2001a: 121).[7] An analysis of practices disentangles securitization from the logic of war to find practices of security that work 'through everyday technologies, through the effects of power that are continuous rather than exceptional, through political struggles, and especially through institutional competition within the professional security field' (Bigo, 2002: 73). In his analyses of policing, Bigo has argued that the link between the migrant and the criminal is the result of the techniques that the police have used against migrants, techniques previously used against criminals (Bigo, 2001a: 134). He has turned upside down an interpretation of discourses which would point to the slippage from 'clandestine/illegal immigrants' to 'criminals' or from the criminalized movement of drugs and arms to the criminalized movement of people. While discourses remain important for ensuring the continuity of practices and providing rationales for certain practices, Bigo sees practices as ontologically prior to discourses.

However, it is less important to decide whether it was first that border officials transferred practices from dealing with illegal migrants to trafficking, whether the police first considered trafficked women as illegal prostitutes, having thus committed an offence or whether it was a discursive construction that entailed certain practices. The relationship between discourse and practice is more complex, a relationship of co-dependence rather than 'implementation' (Rose and Miller, 1992; Valverde, 1996). It entails an analysis of heterogeneous practices that place certain issues in a field defined by security professionals. Yet, the interests of the security professionals are always surpassed by concepts and principles that are not exclusively given in a field. If Chapter 4 will expose the structuration of the situation of trafficking through forms of knowledge that are mobilized to represent victims of trafficking as objects of knowledge, the remaining chapters (5, 6 and 7) will look at principles that hold together the social. Just as a field of security is held together by an imaginary of security, the social is held together by universal imaginaries. Jacques Rancière's question, how would the dominated enter a field where their actions are limited by the volume of capital to be placed on the symbolic market? (Rancière, 2003: 193) already points to the necessity to think of what transgresses the forms of knowledge and authority that constitute representations and devise interventions upon human trafficking. Beyond the particularity of interests that define the professionals of security, concepts and principles need to address those who are 'outside' the field. If Bourdieu suggests that domination functions with the 'unknowing' complicity of agents (Bourdieu, 1990: 70), then these agents need to be co-opted by the regime of truth. They can only be co-opted if the truth that security professionals construct by virtue of their *habitus* is also apparently in the interest of the dominated.

Discovering security: the real of imaginary (in)security

Is security all about institutional interventions, knowledge and representations? Zygmunt Bauman, Anthony Giddens and Ulrich Beck link security with the imaginary of modernity and an ontology of the subject. This section is devoted to ontological security to explore how an imaginary of security functions beyond real and symbolic practices or rather consonant with those. Ontological security suggests that security's regime of truth is rooted in the subject's desire. On the one hand, ontological (in)security provides an explanation for the quasi-pervasive securitizing practices and, on the other, it challenges an analysis of practices inasmuch as it functions like an invariant of postmodernity. Ontological security can be read as posing a challenge to the analysis of practices; if we know the underlying reason for securitization, it is no longer necessary to study practices, but to come to terms with our ontological (in)security.[8]

The phrase 'ontological security' was coined by Giddens, in the early 1990s. 'To be ontologically secure' is, according to him, 'to posses ... "answers" to fundamental existential questions which all human life in some way addresses' (Giddens, 1991: 47). There are four existential types of questions: questions about *being, finitude and human life,* questions concerning the existence of *other persons, self-identity* (Giddens, 1991: 50–5). This general philosophical argument becomes a sociological argument of 'ontological insecurity' in modernity, characterized by the intrusion of abstract systems and the de-skilling of day-to-day life, an 'alienating and fragmenting phenomenon so far as the self is concerned' (Giddens, 1991: 137). Anxiety about self-identity is one of the characteristics linked with modernity. What Giddens has called 'ontological security' could more aptly be called 'epistemological security', as it is closely bound with the limits of knowing, with asking questions about the nature of being, of self and others and the impossibility to provide answers. Huysmans has looked at the 'double fear' in security stories as both the 'fear of death' and an 'epistemological fear – a fear of not knowing' (Huysmans, 1998c: 234–5).

Bauman has also located three ingredients of *Unsicherseit* (security, certainty and safety) as 'conditions of self-confidence and self-reliance on which the ability to think and act rationally depends' (Bauman, 2001: 17). As a writer of postmodernity, Bauman argues that the conditions of globalization produce continuous uncertainty; they do not allow any risk-free, secure spaces and in the process encourage fear about threats to personal safety. As institutions are no longer capable of offering security and certainty, all they can do is shift anxieties to one ingredient of *Unsicherheit*, individual safety. Bauman combines a meta-narrative of human civilization and its 'essential' propensity towards security, with a large-scale narrative of globalization. Bauman was not a singular figure to point out that the unresolvability of large-scale uncertainty/insecurity brings about an exclusive focus on personal safety. Such a strategy is seen as politically appealing, given that 'the roots of insecurity are thrust in anonymous, remote or inaccessible places' and 'it is not immediately clear what the local, visible powers could do to rectify the present afflictions' (Bauman, 2001: 50–1). In this account, the pervasiveness of security practices is due to state failure. Other authors have also emphasized how the state, confronted with the globalization of economic life and its inability to control or provide a secure space for its citizens, takes up a 'compensatory expression of state efficacy and accountability' (Connolly, 1999b: 129). 'Under these circumstances', Connolly goes on, 'signs of state inadequacy in other domains become transfigured in the realm of criminal punishment' (Connolly, 1999b: 129).

For Beck, a division between first and second modernity introduces risks to parameters previously unknown. Beck's risks are attributable to the inability of social institutions to control the risks they have themselves created. Risk and insecurity are the technological offspring of modernity itself. The industrial society of the first modernity is no longer able to control the risks to which it has given rise (environmental, technical) and the risk society of the second modernity becomes the era of incalculable, unaccountable and unlimited risks.[9] Control is no longer possible in risk society, which instead 'balances its way along beyond the limits of insurability' (Beck, 1999: 32). In conditions of extreme uncertainty, decision makers are no longer able to guarantee predictability, security and control; rather, 'the hidden central issue in world risk society is how to *feign* control over the uncontrollable – in politics, law, science, technology, economy and everyday life' (Beck, 2002: 41, emphasis added). For Beck, too, security has become a feigned imaginary.

Beck's risk society, Giddens' late modernity or Bauman's postmodernity are characterized by changes in the forms of lives, types of connections, ties, communities that exist and which have anxiety and insecurity built at their heart. Despite the limited resonance of Giddens' ontological security, the idea of an insecurity that is explainable in the context of the larger process of modernization has appealed to security studies. By integrating 'ontological insecurity' in such a metanarrative of modernization, all security constructions are shown to be equally flawed. Different constructions of security have Girardian undertones, in which all 'others' become arbitrary objects of (in)security, scapegoats of modernity (Girard, 1986). The problem with such an approach is that it does not account for how security problematizations function in concrete contexts, except as expressions of the unfunctional imaginary of security.

Every form of insecurity is therefore amenable to a grand insecurity, the insecurity of postmodernity, late modernity or globalization. In contrast to ontological (in)security, the problematization of security emphasizes concrete analyses of representations and interventions. Rather than assuming a form of risk or disorientation characteristic of (post)modernity, problematizing the problematization of security focuses on the heterogeneity of representations and shows how interventions are made up of and assembled from various elements. Human trafficking is not simply expressive of a *malaise* of the state under the conditions of globalization, but is constituted as a particular assemblage of representations and interventions.

Opposing the grand narrative of 'risk society', the governmentality literature has advocated a concrete and empirical analysis of specific types of risk representations and interventions. Contra Beck's metanarrative of risk, Dean has pointed out that '[r]isk and its techniques are plural and heterogeneous and its significance cannot be exhausted by a narrative of a shift from a quantitative calculation of risk to the globalization of incalculable risk' (Dean, 1999a: 191). In the case of trafficking in women, risk functions mainly as a strategy for assigning people into categories of risk. Typical risk profiles of victims of trafficking would read along these lines:

Most (Central and Eastern European) victims of women trafficking are between 18 and 25 years of age, unmarried and without children. Relatively often, victims of women trafficking, especially Central European victims, come from problem families – single parent families, alcohol abusing parents, incest, mistreatment, financial and housing problems, psychological problems.

(Vocks and Nijboer, 2000: 383)

A study by the IOM office in Romania has found that 38 per cent of girls between 15 and 18 years of age in orphanages were ready to 'emigrate to a foreign job', putting them at risk of being trafficked. The same study has found that 38 per cent of single women and girls aged 15 to

25 and 20 per cent of women and girls who lived with their parents were ready to emigrate to a foreign job (US State Department, 2002). These practices of profiling are part of the strategies and techniques of pro-active policing and prevention and they are important inasmuch as they create specific exclusions which cannot be understood from an invariant account of 'ontological security'.

The ontologization of insecurity has also informed analyses of the constitution of the modern subject that security practices invoke. Practices of security are grafted upon the constitution of the modern subject in need of security. Bauman has defined 'the typical modern practice, the substance of modern politics, of modern intellect, of modern life, is the effort to exterminate ambivalence' (Bauman, 1991: 7). Dillon has shown that (in)security is tightly bound with metaphysics, inasmuch as the 'metaphysically determined being has a foundational requirement to secure security' (Dillon, 1996: 27). The metaphysical being is the Enlightenment being, driven by a desire to security and secure identity, but doomed to eternal ontological insecurity. Ontological insecurity bears the name of the other, the difference that cannot be eliminated but is constitutive of the modern being. It is not the conditions of (post)modernity that create insecurity, but the metaphysical definition of identity. Identity can only be constituted and re-enacted as identity/difference. As Connolly has famously put it in his groundbreaking *Identity/Difference*,

> Identity is ... a slippery, insecure experience, dependent on its ability to define difference and vulnerable to the tendency of entities it would so define to counter, resist, overturn, or subvert definitions applied to them. Identity stands in a complex political relation to the differences it seeks to fix.
>
> (Connolly, 1991: 64)

This is the predicament of the modern subject. Campbell and Dillon have argued in the introduction to their co-edited book that 'the political subject of violence, rapaciously invoking security, comes in a variety of guises, however, depending upon where its particular idiomatic expression happens to locate the centre' (Campbell and Dillon, 1993: 28). The imaginary of security is consonant with the variety of security practices through which the modern subject attempts to make herself secure. Given the metaphysical necessity to secure the identity of the modern subject, they conclude, alongside Der Derian, that 'the enemy of the politics of security is the very heterogeneity, difference and otherness' (Campbell and Dillon, 1993: 28).[10] Taking up Connolly's analyses of identity/difference, poststructuralists claim that an identity is made insecure or threatened 'not merely by actions that the other might take to injure or defeat the true identity but by the very identity of its mode of being as other' (Connolly, 1991: 66). Securitization therefore conceals 'the inherent insecurity in any referent object ... the *impossibility* of security' (Edkins, 2002: 75).

Ontological (in)security adds a double aspect to the problematization of security. First, representations and interventions do not function at the microlevel, but are also linked with larger systems. Even if some of the literature attempts to derive micropractices from the metanarratives of (post)modernity or globalization, they also point out the need to consider interrelated fields of practice. To remind ourselves once more of Žižek's question, what holds micropractices together are imaginaries about the world, its processes and the subjects that inhabit the world. However, this literature derives practices directly from these imaginaries and equates macro- and micropractices of security. Their importance for analysing problematizations of security is that of providing an imaginary framework within which symbolic practices can be deployed. It is an imaginary of ontological and epistemological security that confers consistency and holds together heterogeneous practices. The imaginary of ontological security holds these (micro)practices together. The institutional positions of security professionals and discourses of elites are embedded in a shared imaginary of security that can create a consensus about and acceptance of security practices.

Experiencing (in)security: the real of the subject/abject

If security constructions invoke an imaginary of ontological security, an imaginary of expectation that security can deliver, they do so by a long historical process that has constituted the modern subject. Understood as problematization, security representations and interventions attempt to foster forms of subjectivity and agency, aligned with the purposes of government. Yet, the constituted subject of security has been ignored by the CoS. In the CoS definition, securitization is a *topological* move from the realm of normal politics to extraordinary politics, made possible by the construction of an existential threat to a *referent object*. Referent objects are 'things that are seen to be essentially threatened and that have a legitimate claim to survival' (Buzan et al., 1998: 36). A similar separation between performative speech act and audience makes the concept less useful for grasping the constitution of the subject.

Although Bourdieu has offered a sophisticated tool for analysing subject constitution, I have shown that sociological analyses in security studies are more interested in institutional actors rather than in understanding the constitution of abjects.

A lot of the critical literature that accepts the imaginary promise of security has tried to modify the problematization of security by proposing individuals instead of states as its subjects. Critical scholars have challenged the disqualification and abjectification of life that security entails and have counterposed the human being to the state, asking the question of primacy: Who is the primary referent object of security? '[I]s it states, or is it people? Whose security comes first?' (Booth, 1995: 123). Critical Security Studies (CSS)[11] and feminist security studies have promoted the individual as the legitimate referent object of security and tackled the issue of inclusion/exclusion and concurring versus competing securitizations. These schools emphasize a normative concern with the individual driven by the concern that state security is not synonymous with the security of everybody living within the state. CSS introduce the question of 'whose security', promoting the individual as the legitimate referent object of security. They take seriously the injunction that security should be about 'real people in real places' (Booth, 1995: 123) and add that one cannot separate individual security from the wider social context (Wyn Jones, 1999: 117). As Wyn Jones has pointed out, Booth is not concerned with an abstract liberal individual, but understands the individual in her corporeal, material existence and experiences (Wyn Jones, 1999: 115).

The previous chapter has shown that accounts of human trafficking as 'human rights violations' attempt to bring to the fore women's suffering and portray real-life victims who would be able to support a different representation of human trafficking. Women's experiences of violence and exploitation are supposed to buttress an alternative account of security, promoting them as legitimate referent objects.

If Tony Blair took a short stroll from Downing Street to Soho, the heart of London's sex trade, he'd find human rights abuses right under his nose every bit as terrible as those in Iraq. Increasingly, coercion, human trafficking and violence dominate the UK's sex industry. Yet strangely, this domestic human rights issue fails to arouse crusading zeal.

Stories surfacing from these women are barely credible in 20th-century Britain. Last year 'Natasha' gave evidence against a pimp. Aged 15, she had been forced to have sex with customers for 20 hours a day, earning her 'owner' pounds 500 a day. She'd come from a broken and impoverished home in Romania, been tempted by offers of a better life, and ended up trafficked via the Balkans to sex slavery in London. A similar recent prosecution of two Albanians for trafficking, rape, indecent assault and drug possession revealed another Romanian girl, 16-year-old Anna, who had been sold at 12 and trafficked via Macedonia to London.

(Coward, 26 March 2003)

Faced with stories of victimization and human rights violations, the answer to 'whose security?' seems straightforward: trafficked women. This question only makes sense if it is fully formulated, 'against whom are women to be secured?' Formulated as a security issue, human trafficking sets competing referent subjects against each other. Women are to be secured against the 'evil' trafficker, but cannot be secured against the state which chooses to deport them. Moreover, women might need to be made secure against other individuals and groups.

CSS have not been concerned with the problem of 'which individual' is to be considered in relation to security. Krause advocates human security as the security to be analysed, given that the 'new security threats' are actually threats to the material well-being of individuals rather than to states or large human collectivities, as the CoS has claimed (Krause, 1998: 310). Nonetheless, in the edited book on critical security, Krause and Williams refine the understanding of the individual and consider three possibilities (Krause and Williams, 1997: 43). The first one takes 'individuals as persons' as the object of security and to focus on the promotion of human rights, protecting persons from each other and from state institutions. The second concerns 'individuals as citizens' and sees threats to individuals coming from the institutions of their own state. The third analyses human security in terms of membership in a 'transcendent human community with common global concerns'. In the face of threats such as environmental ones, the individual can be secured only by securing humankind as such (Krause and Williams, 1997: 44–5).

Feminist security studies have also assumed that security should be rethought from the standpoint of those who cannot voice their security concerns, those 'whose experiences of danger and violence are written out of the account' (Pettman, 1996: 98). They have either set out to make such concerns audible from specific loci or have advocated, more generally, the diminution of all forms of violence (Tickner, 2001: 143). They have tirelessly interpellated those whom Cynthia Enloe metaphorically calls the 'margins, silences, and bottom rungs' (Enloe, 1993: 186). Christine Sylvester has argued for privileging the 'profoundly mundane' and women's experiences of insecurity (Sylvester, 1994, 1996). The little mermaids with silent security dilemmas, to paraphrase Lene Hansen's famous critique (Hansen, Lene, 2000) of the CoS, is the phrase that sums up those who have been ignored, those who cannot utter their security concerns. They are the ones that need to be brought into the limelight of security.

The proponents of a 'human security' approach place common humanity rather than raison d'Etat at the core of normative concerns, implying that security of the state is not necessarily synonymous with the security of everybody living within the state (Poku and Graham, 2000: 13).[12] In a human security approach, trafficked women would be granted rights to shelter, justice, food and medical assistance. The human security paradigm attempts to take security beyond the limits of the state. Unlike the feminist analyses of the limited remit of security and locations of numerous sites of insecurity, human security applies to a generally abstract subject. A concept of human security would restrict, for example, the possibilities of understanding the insecure and inse-curing status of trafficked women in relation to the state. While all women would be granted shelter, food and medical assistance if they contact the police, it would be for a limited period until deportation. Other rights would only be granted if women are supportive and give evidence against their traffickers. These contradictory techniques are dependent upon the contradictory status that trafficked women hold within the state.

Berman has captured an interesting dichotomy, the split condition of the trafficked women between 'as if' citizens and not-citizens. As 'white women', East European sex workers are at once identical to the 'white' women that the state is supposed to protect. As illegal immigrants and workers, they are 'different' from citizens and therefore to be deported (Berman, 2003: 54). She also provides the other facet of the relation between state and individual as referent objects of security, when she argues that the discourses on human trafficking result in an attempt to 'reinvigorate the state as the defender of the "white" women, punisher of illegal immigrants and criminals and protector of the political community' (Berman, 2003: 64).

Foucault has accounted for this dilemma of the subjects who are to be protected at another's expense. The modern state does not only assign membership in the political community and ensure the survival of the community, but is also in charge of the well-being of individuals (or of categories of the population). The governmental practices of the state are to reach citizens in their individuality and totality, *omnes* and *singulatim* (Foucault, 2000b). Yet, as part of this process of securing the individual, the state permanently draws boundaries, creating categories of individuals who are to be protected at the expense of the exclusion and elimination of others. In Dillon's formulation, the 'continuous biopolitical assaying of life proceeds through the epistemically driven and continuously changing interrogation of the worth and eligibility of the living across a terrain of value that is constantly changing' (Dillon, 2005: 41). National Socialism was an extreme example of how the protection of the population, its good and fit life entail the disqualification of other forms of life and the elimination of other individuals.

Poststructuralist analyses of security have exposed the constitution of subjectivity, its reproduction and iteration through practices of security. Security practices reproduce an unstable identity at the level of the state, and the containment of challenges to that identity (Campbell, 1992: 78).[13] As identities are performatively constructed in the securitizing process, poststructuralism moves away from the traditional concern with the a priori assumptions of agency and pre-given subjects *to* the problematic of subjectivity and its political constitution (Campbell, 1998a: 222). Security and subjectivity are intrinsically linked, given that securing something requires its differentiation, classification and definition (Campbell, 1992: 253).

Poststructuralists, however, remain evasive on the subject that they consider. Many emphasize, in the wake of Connolly and Campbell, the constitution of identity/self through the exclusion of difference/other and the reproduction of identity. However, the 'other' they envisage is mostly a derivative of the constitution of 'us'. Even assaying the worthiness of life by biopolitical practices appears as a consequence of the plight of modernity and the constitution of the state as the form of political organization par excellence. In Campbell's analysis of how American identity is reproduced through rewritings of dangers, the others who are written out as dangerous, abnormal, risky are 'faceless faces', substitutable to one another. Different others succeed one another, subjected to the need of identity reproduction. The long march of others is not without effect on the constitution of identity. The others who are excluded and made abject create – by means of negation – a specific imaginary of identity. Others are not random others, but those who, in certain historical configurations, negate the imaginary of the self. The identification of the self takes place 'through a repudiation which produces a domain of abjection' (Butler, 1993: 3). It is this imaginary of the self, of the modern subject that poststructuralists have challenged. For Rob Walker, it is only in the context of the *subject* of security that

> it is possible to envisage a critical discourse about security, a discourse which engages with contemporary transformations of political life, with emerging accounts of who we might become, and the conditions under which we might become other than we are now without destroying others, ourselves, or the planet on which we all live'.
>
> (Walker, 1997: 78)

Subjects of security would therefore need to take up the challenge of difference and re-evaluate their discourses and imaginary of security.

Such an account is vulnerable to the critique that it cannot discriminate between dangerous and non-threatening others. The other is arbitrarily constituted as dangerous by the identitary requirements of the self, it is made abject, relegated to the '"unlivable" and "uninhabitable" zones of social life which are nevertheless populated by those who do not enjoy the status of the subject' (Butler, 1993: 3). The abject only exists as a constitutive outside (Butler, 1993: 3), as the limit to the domain of subjectivity. And if the other voices her own security concerns as feminist security studies have suggested, this only serves to perpetuate a dynamics of insecurity. Security functions by explicitly securing the self/us (with the ambiguity implied in the impossibility of achieving a secure identity) and implicitly relegating others to spaces of abjection.

Conclusion

This chapter has engaged with an extensive field of approaches to security to gauge their complexity, their problems and impasses. Traditionally, security was considered as an objective problem, similarly to how other literatures have read migration or organized crime. The only question that remains is how to deal with threats. For those who have problematized security as a matter of construction, security can be read as an assemblage of representations and interventions that foster subjects and project an imaginary of future certainty. The CoS has emphasized discourses and the importance of 'speaking' security, while the Bourdieuean-inspired Paris School has embedded discourses in institutional positions. Security has also been seen as a problem of how individuals relate to the world, how they imagine their position in the world and how the world can fall short of this imaginary. Ontological

security has appeared as a useful explanation for the inflationary problematizations of security. Although the imaginary of security makes
possible certain practices and discourses to be formulated and to thrive
in the present context, it cannot be divorced from specific discourses
and institutional struggles. The promise of security activates a certain
understanding of order and of ordering things and people. This imaginary of ordering appears most explicitly in relation to the subject of
security who is to be rendered secure and made part of such an ordering.

Yet, this promise of security is made possible to the extent that other
subjects are excluded from this ordering. Security practices create abject
bodies, shadowy others are already prepared for elimination or neutralization. Butler has summarized this contentless image of the other:

> I have seen it [the abjection of bodies] in the German press when
> Turkish refugees are either killed or maimed. Very often we can get
> the names of the German perpetrators and their complex family and
> psychological histories, but no Turk has a complex family or psycho-
> logical history that *Die Zeit* ever writes about ... So, we get a differ-
> ential production of the human and a differential materialization of
> the human.
>
> (quoted in Meijer and Prins, 1998: 281)

The ordering of security based on a dynamics of abjection and of exclusion exposes the very promise of security as an impossible promise.
The abjectification that security does depends on the very imaginary
of ontological security instantiated in symbolic practices, both institutional and non-institutional. The limit of security is the limit of the
order that it defines, it is the limit of otherness. The conceptualization
of security with which analyses will work depends on the immanent
relation between symbolic and imaginary practices which make possible
the creation of spaces of abjection, of the indeterminate and shadowy
limit of order and of all ordering processes. Can these spaces of abjection be undone? The next chapter will go on to explore how desecuritization, emancipation, and ethics can reformulate the relation to the
other and how they expose the fallacies of the promise of security.

3
Unmaking Security: Desecuritization, Emancipation, Ethics

The previous chapter has shown that security is a problematization deployed at the imaginary horizon of a promise of ontological and epistemological certainty. This promise rests upon the exclusion and abjectification of another, who is repudiated as dangerous or risky, turned into life which is not life and 'materiality' which does not matter (Meijer and Prins, 1998: 281). The question that has emerged out of this conceptualization of security – given the exclusionary effects of security in the ordering of subjects and abjects – was how to unmake these practices. Spaces of abjection are created through symbolic practices (institutional and non-institutional, mobilizing technologies, knowledge and language) and an imaginary of security as desirable *stasis*. Critical approaches to security do not share either the conceptualization of security or the diagnosis of its effects. However, in grappling with the heterogeneous understandings of the effects of security practices, these approaches have transformed the conceptualization of security. Here, I shall interrogate them for the purpose of exploring the impasses and insights that a politics to unmake security needs to consider.

The discontents with security can be understood in terms of its symbolic effects (as with the CoS), its partiality, its limited and arbitrarily exclusive remit (CSS) or the specific relationship to the other that it instantiates ('the ethical turn'). For the CoS, securitization triggers a particular dynamics out of the normality of politics, a dynamics of urgency and immediacy. Therefore, the symbolic practices of security cannot be simply analysed in their performative emergence, but must be gauged in light of the effects they entail for the political community. CSS see security as unequally allocated to just some. Against the constructions of security that privilege the state, Booth and his students argue for a focus on the individual as the subject of security. The security of the individual demands critical attention to a large array of issues which affect the prospects for a free life. The 'ethical turn' can be loosely said to share an understanding of the effects of security as making-abject. The ethical discontent with security is similar to that formulated here, namely relationality to the other that security entails as the horizon of political action.[1] However, their understanding of ethics-out-of-security will be shown to be problematic due to their conceptualization of both security and politics. Ethical approaches have not created a 'school', but have rallied different poststructuralist writers at different times – ethics is not a constant in their research, but a theoretical engagement with the question of subjectivity. Campbell, for example, has been mostly concerned with analysing security discourses. His ethical turn has led to a book and a series of articles inspired by the work of Jacques Derrida and Emmanuel Levinas (Campbell, 1998b, 1999). Similar encounters can be found in the work of Dillon (Campbell and Dillon, 1993), Connolly (1999a) or Jenny Edkins (2000).

The ethical turn reconfigures the relation between self and other in terms of responsibility and ethics becomes integral to subjectivity (Campbell, 1998b). The ethics that I consider here is of Levinasian and Derridian inspiration. In his book on ethics, Alain Badiou has distinguished two types of ethical approaches: the first one of Kantian inspiration, with a conception of the subject of moral law as universal and context free and the second promoting an ethos of the other (Badiou, 2002a). While human security approaches can be seen as partaking of a Kantian 'ethics of the same', sameness is problematic for security. As security creates and repudiates spaces of abjection, sameness is a priori ousted from its relationship to the other. For security practices, sameness is an imaginary of *stasis* where threatening differences have been eradicated and insecurities eliminated. An ethical approach able to unmake security practices can only be an 'ethos of the other', an ethics that radically reshapes the self/other relationality.

This chapter will locate the theoretical insights of these three approaches in the context of the humanitarian approach to trafficking. Based on their theoretical positions, these approaches will be made to speak to the problem of trafficking. While the three approaches discussed in this chapter, desecuritization, emancipation and ethics, are not the only forms of thinking politics out of security, I consider them together as they all run into an impasse when conceptualizing the failure of the humanitarian approach to trafficking. The humanitarian approach was imagined as an alternative representation of human trafficking to ground different political interventions from those of illegal migration, prostitution and organized crime. How can these three approaches speak to the failure of the humanitarian approach? I argue that desecuritization, emancipation or ethics can only make sense of this failure by exposing theoretical flaws in their own conceptual toolbox.

Although a classical human rights approach would appear at first sight to partake more of what Badiou has called an ethics of sameness, the humanitarian approach to trafficking can be analyzed as partaking of performative speech acts, an imaginary of emancipation and an ethics of the other. The subjects of trafficking are not abstract subjects of rights. Human rights approaches have put forth a strategy that can only make them equal through dis-identification from categories of dangerous abjects. This strategy of dis-identification requires an alternative discourse that represents trafficked women as a different category. In formulating an alternative discourse to the discourse of illegal migration, this strategy can be read as an attempt at desecuritization. Similarly, the focus on the plight of trafficked women shifts interest away from the state – at least potentially. Trafficked women become part of a process of emancipation as defined by CSS. With the help of NGOs and other specialized organizations, women can build another future, a future of security away from exploitation and vulnerability. The new identification of trafficked women with bodies in pain reconfigures the self/other relationality. How does one relate to the suffering other? One can pose this question in terms of an ethos of the other. If the first three sections of the chapter are dedicated to a theoretical exploration of the premises with which desecuritization, emancipation and ethics work, the last section will show how these approaches speak to the failure of the humanitarian approach. Their theoretical problematique will be brought to speak to the particular situation of trafficking in women. How can these theoretical strategies orient themselves to practice?

Desecuritization and alternative discourses

The CoS strategy of desecuritization can be read as the most immediate and direct theoretical engagement with the practices employed by NGOs and human rights activists. They attempt to contest and replace the security speech act by other speech acts that emphasize the suffering of victims of trafficking and their particularity. Although it is important to analyse the reconfiguration of the security field that allows them to enter the field of security professionals, for the moment I shall limit the analysis to the speech act, the consistent discourse that they formulate. The next chapter will explore their role and the impact of their practices upon the field of security professionals. This chapter engages with the discourse of suffering whose veracity and poignancy has led to increased attention to the well-being and life of victims of trafficking.

The CoS have, however, an ambiguous theoretical position about whether/when desecuritization should replace securitization, despite some of their concerns with the effects of securitization. For Waever, the choice between the 'dubious instrument of securitization' and desecuritization is not altogether clear (Waever, 2000: 285). Securitization appeared at times as a very effective tool to make sense of several developments in the field of migration, refugee and asylum policy and even environmental policy. More often however, the CoS have expressed a preference for desecuritization as being '*more effective* than securitizing problems' (Waever, 1995: 57, emphasis in original). Although Waever has not specified the grounds which motivate the choice of desecuritization over securitization, Huysmans has read 'effective' in instrumental or utilitarian terms (Huysmans, 1998a: 572–3). Yet, it remains unclear in exactly which sense desecuritization is more effective, especially given the attention-catching potential of securitization that they emphasize. Arguments of effectiveness have also been made in favour of securitization. In a recent discussion of the ethical issues raised by the securitization versus the desecuritization of HIV/AIDS, Stefan Elbe has listed as the first advantage of a security approach the mobilization of more political support and economic resources for addressing the HIV/AIDS pandemic (Elbe, 2005). The few misgivings that Waever has expressed about the 'ensuing effects' (Buzan, et al., 1998: 32) of securitization have, however, been counterpoised to the attractions of securitization. Rhetorical strategization takes over concerns with democratic politics:

> In some democratic perspective, 'de-securitization' is probably the ideal, since it restores the possibility of exposing the issue to the normal haggling and questioning of politicization, but if one is actually concerned about something, securitization is an attractive tool that one might end up using – as a political actor.
>
> (Waever, 2000: 251)

The ambiguity about the need for desecuritization appears to me to reside in the analytical duality of the concept of securitization. Firstly, in line with the 'linguistic turn' in social sciences, securitization is a performative speech act. Moreover, successful securitization is a felicitous speech act such as the felicitous naming of ship or performing of a marriage. As a speech act, it is defined by a specific structure internal to discourse (survival, priority of action 'because if not handled now it will be too late, and we will not exist to remedy our failure') (Buzan, 1997: 14). Secondly, securitization is also defined by the 'extraordinary defensive moves', the emergency actions undertaken by institutions and various security actors. Successful securitization implies extraordinary measures, a breaking of the 'normal political rules of the game (e.g., in the form of secrecy, levying taxes or conscription, placing limitations on otherwise inviolable rights, or focusing society's energy and resources on a specific task)' (Buzan, et al., 1998: 24).

In the CoS assessment, securitization is *at best*, 'a kind of mobilization of conflictual or threatening relations, often through emergency mobilization of the state' (Buzan, et al., 1998: 8). Thus, securitization invokes a spectre of violence that hovers in the shadows of political communities. Violence becomes a permanent possibility in a society that defines itself in terms of conflictual relations, reminding us of the contradictions of the promise of security. The imaginary of security does not sustain the identity of the community, but necessarily places it in a dynamics of violence. However, securitization entails other effects beyond the spectre of violence. Without the element of exceptionalism that securitization brings about, speech acts could not be closed off, their contestation suspended. Moreover, the exceptionalism of securitization reshapes politics along the lines of friend/enemy or rather friend/foe, as the 'foe' is the dangerous other whom Schmitt tries to exclude from the realm of politics, the true name for the abject (Aradau, 2006; Schmitt, 1996). In a Schmittian reading of the exceptionalism of security, the pernicious effects of security are deeply political, or rather depoliticizing: securitization makes abjects whom it banishes from the realm of politics (cf. Agamben's reading of 'bare life').

The concrete and specific measures that are involved in successful securitization raise the issue of normal versus exceptional or extraordinary politics. It is in relation to the procedural 'normalcy' of democracy that the 'exceptionalism' of securitization can be theorized.[2] The element of urgency takes securitization out of the realm of normal politics. Securitization reinscribes issues in a different logic, a logic of urgency and of extraordinary measures, a sibling of the logic of 'political realism' (Huysmans, 1998a). This approach takes securitization on a different path than the more benign one to which the CoS were attracted, namely the 'tactical attractions' of securitization. Security does not simply function as a way to obtain sufficient attention (Buzan, et al., 1998: 29). It is rhetorically modelled upon war and it instantiates politics as exceptionalism.

As securitization means 'that an issue is presented as an existential threat requiring emergency measures, and justifying actions outside the normal bounds of political procedure' (Buzan, 1997: 14), desecuritization becomes an ethico-political choice which upholds the values of democracy. Andreas Behnke has read the CoS preference for desecuritization in similar terms: 'Given that this move suspends the usual democratic process, securitization constitutes a highly problematic strategy which should be avoided' (Behnke, 2000: 91). The 'anything goes' for a higher common good can only be dangerous for a political tradition of freedom and democracy. Waever has, however, rejected this location of securitization in a democratic context, claiming securitization as a more general tool.[3] Contra Waever, I argue that without a normative assumption about what politics is, the effects of securitization cannot be gauged. Moreover, without this normative distinction, securitization would lose some of the elements that constitute its specificity. The decisionistic and exceptional moment of securitization could no longer be the limit of 'normal politics', but its normality. Why securitization and not just a normal practice of an authoritarian regime? Or illiberal practices of liberal regimes? The specificity of securitization they want to preserve cannot be disentangled from a specific understanding of normal politics as democratic.[4]

Mike Saward has identified political equality, inclusion, expressive freedom and transparency among the contested principles that make up a democracy (Saward, 2003). He has also emphasized the proceduralism of these principles, the fact that they need to be embedded in practical institutions and processes (Saward, 2003). In an incidental definition of politics, Buzan and Waever also remark that '[i]deally, politics should be able to unfold according to routine procedures' (Buzan, et al., 1998: 29). Huysmans has commented that security institutionalizes speed against the slowness of procedures and thus questions the viability of deliberation, contest of opinion and dissent (Huysmans, 2004b). While the securitizing speech act has to be accepted by a relevant audience and remains within the framework of the democratic politics of contestation, the exceptionality of procedures is its opposite. The speed required by the exceptional suspends the possibilities of judicial review or other modalities of public influence upon bureaucratic or executive decisions. Securitization reinscribes issues in a different logic, a logic of urgency and exceptionalism.

As securitization is not simply a speech act that stages a narrative of survival in order to attract attention, but a performative enactment of exceptionalism in political life, questions about what type of politics we want need to be asked. The exceptionalism and decisionism of securitization activate a Schmittian politics. The specificity of security as a 'particular kind of speech act in the work of the Copenhagen School is underpinned by an understanding of the politics of enmity, decision, and emergency which has deep roots in Schmitt's understanding of political order' (Williams, 2003: 515). Huysmans has also forcefully argued that securitization leads to a reordering of social relations according to the logic of 'political realism' and has defined it as a 'technique of government which retrieves the ordering force of fear of violent death by a mythical replay of variations of the Hobbesian state of nature' (Huysmans, 1998a: 571).

Although securitization and its numerous interpretations depend on an externalized opposition of liberal democracy and exceptionalism (see Huysmans, 2006: 127–44), analyses of the exception have shed light on the intrinsic relationality and dependence between liberal democracy and exceptionalism. Exceptions are not only the limit moment of liberal democracy, which make it verge onto a different mode of politics. Exceptional moments are inbuilt in the functioning of democracy and liberal law when they govern the social (Aradau, 2007). The opposition between universality and particularity can be used to show what is at stake in this externalization of liberal democracy and the exception. Exceptionalism is closely entwined with concrete situations that need to be governed and the particular necessities that arise out of these situations. Re-embedding exceptionalism within practices of governing the social rephrases the difference that Bigo had noted between the exceptionalism of securitization and the ordinary continuity of routine interventions in the social. Bigo has recently tried to make the exception part of sociological analyses of security. The concept of 'ban', he argues, links the sovereign exception to exclusion and normalization (Bigo, 2006: 35–43). At the same time, exceptionalism has been seen as entwined with a different conceptualization of democracy. In this definition, democracy is not about procedural norms, universal principles and slow decisions, but about constant revolutionalizing from the standpoint of those who are rendered as foes or abjects.[5] This redefinition of democracy and democratic politics would need to also think its relation to practices of security.

However, for the CoS, the duality of securitization as a speech act and extraordinary measures entailed by a procedural understanding of democracy creates a tension at the core of the concept of securitization. Which politics would desecuritization uphold – a politics of contesting and contestable speech act or a politics that needs to seriously consider the concept of the exception and its political implications? Williams has located the political potential of the CoS in the discursive construction of security: an ethics of argumentation would be the antidote to securitization (Williams, 2003). Speech acts, whatever their structure, are in a certain sense ordinary in their functioning: they need to be reiterated, are open to contestation and can be replaced. Desecuritization becomes a matter of different speech acts, which one could privilege depending on external, pragmatic criteria, for example, how much attention we want to capture for an issue. Such contestation of a securitizing speech act would be consonant with the democratic politics of transparency and public scrutiny. However, when one takes into account the extraordinary measures and exceptional politics that securitization is steeped in, desecuritization can only be regarded as a political choice restoring democracy. The question of desecuritization becomes one about the kind of politics we want and the definition of democracy to be upheld. The critics of the CoS have usually formulated this dilemma as: do we want a politics of exceptional measures or do we want a democratic politics of slow procedures which can be contested? As I have already intimated and as I shall explore at length in Chapters 5 and 6, there are modes of politics that need not be subjected to this formulaic dichotomy. We need more than a formal definition of politics, as the ambiguities of procedural democracy versus exceptionalism cannot be resolved at a formal level. The dichotomy liberal democracy versus exceptionalism leaves no room for critiques of democracy which do not, however, partake of a Schmittian politics of the exception.[6]

Emancipation and the democratization of security

Unlike desecuritization, the concept of emancipation is overtly political. In the CSS definition, emancipation promises to enact a radical democratization of security. It tackles the concept of democratic politics in claiming a voice for the silenced, the 'security have-nots' (Dunne and Wheeler, 2004), those who have been excluded from the remit of security. Critical Security Studies have tried to conceptualize emancipation as an alternative to predominant constructions of security. Even if CSS do not engage with the concept of desecuritization, the two concepts are definitely related if only for their potential in establishing alternatives to particular social practices.

While for the CoS desecuritization remains the prerogative of the political actors who 'speak' security and can formulate alternative discourses, emancipation is harnessed to those who are made insecure.

Feminists are concerned with the emancipation of women and with uttering women's security concerns which have been silenced. CSS attend to those who are continuously being made insecure, be they women, refugees, or the poor. Although they do not explicitly consider the effects of security and the particular relationality that security brings about, I am interested in the political consequences of a call to 'democratize' security.

The concept of emancipation is associated with the intellectual tradition of the Frankfurt School and a critical tradition of thinking social change and resistance. Despite this intellectual tradition, Ken Booth claims it is impossible to say 'what emancipation looks like, apart from its meaning to particular people at particular times' (Booth and Vale, 1997: 110; Wyn Jones, 1999: 121). Normatively, emancipation is intimately linked with the idea of moving towards a better world (Wyn Jones, 1999: 120). For CSS, it remains a very general notion which can only be fleshed out by considering 'real people in real places' (Booth, 1995: 123) and their insecurity predicaments. Booth is worth quoting at length here as he has written the first manifesto of CSS and formulated the concept of emancipation to be endorsed by his fellow critical security analysts:

> Emancipation means freeing people, as individuals and groups, from the social, physical, economic, political, and other constraints that stop them from carrying out what they would freely choose to do, of which war, poverty, oppression, and poor education are a few. Security and emancipation are in fact two sides of the same coin. It is emancipation, not power and order, in both theory and practice, that leads to stable security
>
> (Booth, 1997: 110)

The 'generality' problem of emancipation is solved by CSS not through recourse to various theories but by making it the equivalent of security. When equated with security, emancipation becomes problematic, as it can no longer envisage social transformations outside the logic of security. CSS want a radical alternative to state-centred security and propose another type of security, defined as emancipation (or emancipation defined as security) at the level of the individual. The struggle for security is restyled as a struggle for emancipation, without unpacking the links between emancipation and security.

Critical scholars like Booth and Wyn Jones endorse both constructivist and normative approach to security, where security is a value to be fought for. Booth has acknowledged that security has enormous political significance and to place an issue on the state agenda means to give it priority (Booth, 1997: 111); on the other hand, security is emancipation as an ideal to be achieved. Or, in Wyn Jones' formulation, '[s]ecurity in the sense of the absence of the threat of (involuntary) pain, fear, hunger, and poverty is an essential element in the struggle for emancipation' (Wyn Jones, 1999: 126). In line with this second meaning of security, Booth has pointed out that 'security studies need to engage with the problems of those who, at this minute, are being starved, oppressed or shot' (Booth, 1997: 114). This understanding of security has steered their critical project towards the 'realities of security' that have been made invisible by 'the traditional mindset of those have dominated or disciplined International Relations' (Booth, 2004: 8). Uncovering the realities of security (or rather insecurity) entails locating human rights abuses, the oppression of minorities, the powerlessness of the poor, and the violence against women (Booth, 2004: 7).

These uses of security forget that security itself institutes a particular kind of ordering political communities and that it is important to be aware of the politics one legitimizes by endorsing security. The equivalence of security and emancipation suspends the project of making the effects of securitization explicit, of analyzing its political effects and assumes security should be the concept that defines politics. Although Wyn Jones limits security to a list of issues (pain, fear, hunger, poverty), the logic of security is part of the constitution of order and deployment of power. Rather than the 'other' of power, security practices buttress institutional arrangements and legitimize forms of domination and exclusion. CSS inadvertently endorse the exclusionary logic of security and the politics that is instituted by doing security, independent of which/who is the referent object or subject.

The dual usage of security makes the CoS partly right in arguing that CSS 'will often try to mobilize other security problems – environmental problems, poverty, unemployment – as more important and more threatening' (Buzan, et al., 1998: 204), thereby reproducing the traditional and objectivist concept of security. The charge of 'objectivist security' is partly wrong because it fails to acknowledge that the CSS project is a political project, be it a normative one. It is not a question of saying what security is, but of claiming security for those who are deprived of it. In this sense, CSS share a radically democratic political project with feminist scholars.

The security that is to be privileged, emancipatory security, is life preserving. Both CSS and feminists often endorse the valorization of life beyond the violence of security, a 'realism' of life that would surpass the social constructivism of practices. Ann Tickner in the feminist camp has argued that 'we can no longer afford to celebrate the potential death of hundreds of thousands of our enemies; the preservation of life, not its destruction, must be valued' (Tickner, 1992: 138). This valorization of life can be read as a discourse of survival, as a biopolitics of the state that makes live and lets die. The valorization of life as 'survival' suspends questions about 'how not to be governed thus' and lets the subject be captured by biopolitical practices of security.[7] The life of refugees and asylum seekers can be valued as they are provided with food, shelter, even medical assistance, but are in principle excluded from the political community. They are to be saved from sinking boats only to be deported to their countries of origin. By bringing the conditions of politics upon the precondition for acting as a political subject, the discourse of life preservation closes down struggles about the kind of life that people can live. The Foucauldian question 'how not to be governed thus' is also neutralized by a biopolitics of survival.

The exclusion and abjectification constitutive of security have not raised many concerns as it seems obvious that vulnerable women would utter their insecurities against existing security articulations privileging the state or patriarchal power relations. In a feminist reading of the CoS, the problem with securitization was the inattention to the structural impossibility of speech that women can experience (Hansen, 2000) and not the effects of speaking security itself. While it has appeared almost self-evident to activists to point out these insecurities of trafficked women and to try to obtain protection for them (Jordan, 2002), such a move of 'securing' the victims of trafficking has led to spiralling insecurity for prostitutes (now subjected to increasing raids, interrogatories, and incarceration) as well as for asylum seekers and refugees (suspected of having been trafficked or of being exploited). As security practices reproduce exclusion and abjection against 'other others', feminist security studies and CSS would need to formulate a concept of politics in relation to which security is defined. Democratic politics as an all-encompassing universality is incompatible with the politics of security as we cannot all be equal sharers of security.

Reclaiming security as both critical and feminist security studies do functions rather as 'counter-securitization', as this move leaves intact the logic of security that shapes social relations. Equated with security, emancipation only shifts the remit of (in)security within the social realm and shuffles various categories of security have-nots. Individual or human security cannot be the answer of emancipatory politics, as this would trigger the question of whose individual security is supposed to be sacrificed. Who is to be made dangerous so that others can be made secure, what forms of life are to be disqualified? On which grounds can one privilege such a construction of security, the security of migrants over the security of racists, the security of HIV-positive people over those at risk of being infected? This line of inquiry could be prolonged by many other examples.

This insight was present in Booth's early accounts of emancipation. Emancipation, he then argued, needs to take precedence over concerns with power and order exhibited by security research given the inherent fragile nature of formations of power which are always at the expense of somebody (Booth, 1991: 319). Although Booth did not take his formulation any further, the question that arises is whether emancipation can be at nobody's expense. Emancipation, as Laclau has formulated its traditional meaning, presupposes 'the elimination of power, the abolition of the subject/object distinction, and the management – without any opaqueness or mediation – of communitarian affairs by social agents identified with the viewpoint of social totality' (Laclau, Ernesto, 1996: 1). Would the security that Booth equates with emancipation not be insecuring other others? The desired universality of security is not only foreclosing particular forms of (in)security, but is also inherently dependent upon the reproduction of insecurity. Practices of security constitute and reproduce insecurities, vulnerabilities and fear in the subject to be secured and the abject to be neutralized, disciplined or even eliminated. While Booth's insight that the problem with privileging power or order is that they are at somebody else's expense, willing power away from security will not lead to emancipation. Security cannot be the remedy to (in)security.

Like CSS, feminist security studies have raised pertinent questions about security practices and have advocated the need to reorder unjust practices. And similar to CSS, they have also succumbed to the appeal of 'security' as the organizing principle of this reordering (for example Tickner, 2001). Rather than questioning the effects of security, many feminists have tried to use security for an emancipatory purpose. The literature is significantly concerned with bringing women into the limelight of security practices, to supposedly yield more concern and therefore increase the possibility of extraordinary measures being taken to rewrite the script of the world in their favour. Even when the exclusionary and abjectifying effects of security are explored and the promise of security deconstructed,[8] it is a dominant practice of security that is targeted. The question is whether, in having 'security' as the reordering principle of social relations, both feminists and critical theorists can account for the continuous insecuring of others, for the governmental practices that divide and categorize subjects.

If one considers the emancipation of trafficked women, the disruption of their insecurities is an admirable goal. Nevertheless, turning trafficked women into referent objects often perpetuates a dynamics of 'insecuring' another. And if the other is taken for granted as being the trafficker (morally blameable), when 'other others' made insecure in the process of securing trafficked women are prostitutes or asylum seekers, the necessity of an ethical-political principle to contest these practices is even more evident. Shifting subjects of security from one category to another does not suspend the problematization of security. The limit which desecuritizing or emancipatory approaches confront is that of security as universal. Security would normatively be something which we can all partake of or share in. It is only by opening up its process and interventions that one can see how security functions and what kind of social dynamics it brings about.

Ethics and abject others

Contra the abjectifying effects of security, ethics highlight difference and heterogeneity; they bring otherness into a relation of interdependence with the self and reshape relationality on an ethical basis. In an early work, Campbell and Dillon formulated this 'ethical turn' as a response to challenges by the world we live in: 'We live in a time of doubt, paradox and difference' (Campbell and Dillon, 1993: 161). An ethical approach would acknowledge that the world is other than what we are ideologically induced to believe. Their preference for difference is to be read in the same worldly terms, because 'the modern globalization of human existence allows no one an escape from continuous encounter with otherness, however much the encounter seems to have intensified attempts to efface difference' (Campbell and Dillon, 1993: 161). In a world of pervasive difference, the securing of the self against the other, the drawing of boundaries, needs to be replaced by the recognition of and an opening towards difference. Later on, Campbell's encounter with Levinas' philosophy located ethics in ontology instead of the 'reality' of the world. Together with Michael Shapiro, he argued for an *'ethical relation* in which our responsibility to the other is the basis for reflection' (Campbell and Shapiro, 1999: x). Ethics as opposed to security would constitute the relation to the other, on a different principle from fear. For Campbell and Dillon, for example, this principle is derived from Levinas' philosophy.[9]

The transformed relationship to the other is based on a Levinasian infinite ethics of responsibility: '[r]esponsibility for the Other, for the naked face of the first individual to come along ...' (Levinas quoted in Campbell, 1999: 32). In a Levinasian world, security becomes an onto-logical impossibility, given that the subject is constituted by the relation to the other, called into being by the prior existence of the Other (Campbell, 1999: 33). Such an ethic is resonant with Campbell's con-cern with Bosnia, as it implies responsibility for the plight of Bosnians, responsibility for the ones who are not immediately dangerous and who could be conceptualized as 'our neighbours' at the margins of Europe.

How does such ethics respond to dangerous others? Campbell himself has remarked that the Levinasian logic is restricted to the neighbour, to an other defined by 'proximity'. Such proximity is defined by Levinas in terms of *Gemeinschaft*: 'my next of kin are also my neighbours' (Levinas quoted in David, 2002: 85). Given the organic proximity of the other, the question of dangerousness is suspended. When faced with the idea of threat, Levinas is adamant that '[i]f self-defense is a problem, the "executioner" is the one who threatens my neighbour and, in this sense, calls for violence and no longer has a Face' (Levinas, 1998: 105). The ethics of responsibility can be suspended when faced with dangerous others. Simon Critchley has formulated a sort of taxonomy of problems that Levinas' ethics entail: fraternity, monotheism, androcentrism, fil-iality and family (Critchley, 2004). As it is impossible in the space of this chapter to thoroughly engage with the problematique of Levinas' ethics, my remarks will be limited to two aspects of ethical engagement: its relation to the dangerous other and (non-)embeddedness in power relations.

Richard Kearney has sharply formulated the theoretical impasse of the encounter with a dangerous other:

> [H]ow are we to address otherness at all if it becomes *unrecognizable* to us? Faced with such putative indetermination, how could we tell the difference between one kind of other and another – between (a) those aliens and strangers that need our care and responsibility, no matter how monstrous they might first appear, and (b) those others that really do seek to destroy and exterminate ...
>
> (Kearney, 2002: 10)

Although one can debate Kearney's meaning of 'really', the dilemma he voices cannot be tackled from within Levinasian philosophy, given that his other, as the 'Altogether Other' which transcends mere finite experience, is the name for God.[10] The Levinasian ethics is 'the ultimate name of the religious as such' (Badiou, 2002a: 23) and the ethical relation to the neighbour is modelled upon a theological relation with God. How can one interact with God or what happens if God is dead? What does this limit-interaction mean for politics?

Derrida has formulated an answer to this dilemma with the limit concepts he has devised for ethics. The role of such limit concepts (one could say, similar to Levinas' other) is to preserve the gap between politics and ethics, and always make room for a more generous form of politics. Radical concepts such as pure hospitality, forgiveness or justice expose and challenge the limitations of a politics of migration or war, for example. Any form of particular politics is a form of violence that distorts the 'unconditional' of politics. Beyond the restrictive understanding of hospitality as evinced by Kant's *Perpetual Peace* or by state practices that differentiate and divide among those who can be welcome and those who need to be expelled, there is a concept of pure or unconditional hospitality.

The term 'Levinasion/Derridean ethics' as it has been used in IR has ignored Derrida's self-avowed 'political impracticability' of his absolute concepts. Derrida would simply claim that 'any politics which fails to sustain some relation to the principle of unconditional hospitality has completely lost its relation to justice' (Derrida, 1994: 35). Democracy and justice are always 'to come', always differed by the impossibility of the ultimate encounter with God and the limit. Derrida's unconditional principles for politics cannot be restricted by any conditions, but they can also never be inscribed in the structures of the world and can never come to be.

Such a conclusion does not directly shed light on any concrete situation. It does not speak to requests of a particular context and its injunctions need to be translated politically. Unconditional principles should not be contaminated by 'the historically restricted concepts of humanity, ethics, and democracy under which we presently labor' (Caputo, 1997). Given, however, the 'unworldliness' of Derrida's concepts, such work of translation is arduous and has remained minimal in international politics.[11] Edkins' concluding remarks on an ethico-political decision against the technologization of famine are that

[t]he decision itself is a terrifying nontime or nonplace, where there is no subject and where we are facing the traumatic real ... We have to make a move for which there are no secure grounds. This moment

is, nevertheless, something that we must face: the fact that it is undecidable is not an excuse for inaction.

(Edkins, 2000: 157)

Undecidability avoids the closure of a situation. It avoids its ordering
and thus also the horizon of security. What happens to change and
transformation if we are caught in a permanent state of undecidability?
While her remarks would be valid for any political decision, it is unclear
whether there is no politics of famine, where there are no ethico-political
decisions taken in this situation. In this sense, any political engagement
in the situation of trafficking would always already fall short of the
radical principles of politics. Yet, the situation of trafficking needs exactly
those decisions that reconfigure and take politics out of the grip of
security.

Besides the injunction to become political, politics seems to be
completely absent and impossible. As with Derrida, all decisions are
doomed to fall short of the ethico-political requirement. And we remain
unable to gauge whether one decision is preferable to another. Yet
politics is always a matter of decision. As my discussion of Badiou in
Chapter 5 will show, a political decision has to be made from the point
of view of the undecidable. In a situation of undecidability, a decision
is always necessary. What counts is what decision is taken – it is not the
form of undecidability that is constitutive of politics, but the content,
the substance of the political decision.

From within a Derridean approach it is impossible to bridge the
undecidable and the decision. Without some way of understanding
how decisions can be taken 'ethically' when faced with the undecidable,
decisions become simply a matter of power. The question of decision is
folded back either upon the Schmittian question of sovereign power
revealing itself through the decision or upon the inescapability of
power – any decision would be just part of the system of power relations
and therefore depoliticizing. Dillon is right to note that the political
is always taking place in a space of undecidability which allows decisions to be taken without being certain which decisions are correct, as
'correctness' cannot be thought from within the situation (Dillon, 1996:
199). Yet, when exploring a political situation, it is possible to say that
some decisions are 'correct'. We know what the right decision is.

What does undecidability mean in a fight for national liberation, in a
struggle for women's rights or against exploitation? What does radical
hospitality mean in the fight against fascism or racism? Critchley has
defined political action, following Derrida, as 'the taking of a decision

without any determinate transcendental guarantees' (Critchley, 2004: 178). The impossibility of distinguishing between decisions appears even more strikingly when one encounters a concrete other and needs to distinguish between various others. As Žižek has made clear, Levinas himself succumbs to 'to vulgar commonsensical reflections' (Žižek, 2004: 106) when asked to make this translation in relation the Palestinian/ Israeli relations:

> My definition of the other is completely different. The other is the neighbour, who is not necessary kin, but who can be. And in that sense, if you're for the other, you're for the neighbour. But if your neighbour attacks another neighbour or treats him unjustly, what can you do? Then alterity takes on another character, in alterity we can find an enemy, or at least then we are faced with the problem of knowing who is right and who is wrong, who is just and who is unjust. There are people who are wrong.
>
> (Levinas quoted in Žižek, 2004: 106)

The same quote appears in David Campbell's book on Bosnia. Campbell sees the 'potential limiting of responsibility ... in the passage from ethics to politics' (Campbell, 1998b: 180). That is why Campbell needs to supplement Levinas by Derrida, to 'fold the ethical relation into the social effects of the ontologies of politics that harden skin and feign presence, so that the relationship with the Other that makes those effects possible, the state among them, is never elided' (Campbell, 1998b: 182).

Contra the 'too transcendent' (Kearney, 2002: 11) ethics of relationality/of pure hospitality, William Connolly has advocated a more mundane form of ethical relation, based on the recognition and reaction to the other's suffering. Connolly revisits an obligation to respond to suffering as formulated by John Caputo in *Against Ethics*: 'Obligation means the obligation to the other, to one who has been laid low, to victims and outcasts. Obligation means the obligation to reduce and alleviate suffering' (Caputo quoted in Connolly, 1999a: 127). In this reformulation, unlimited responsibility becomes a tractable obligation for politics.

Ethics is no longer ontologically given, but is derived from an 'encounter with the world' and the other's suffering. Connolly's turn to suffering is extremely interesting as a possible engagement with the consequences of security practices. If security is seen as suffering inducing, can an ethical relation that prescribes an obligation to alleviate suffering unmake security? Connolly is aware of the tenuous relation between the obligation to diminish suffering and the dangerous other.

> Some of the most difficult cases arise when people suffer from injuries imposed by institutionalized identities, principles, and cultural understandings, when those who suffer are not entirely helpless but are defined as threatening, contagious, or dangerous to the self-assurance of these identities, and when the sufferers honor *sources* of ethics inconsonant or disturbing to these constituencies.
>
> (Connolly 1999a: 129)

It is exactly these 'limit cases', these difficult cases for his ethics that Connolly leaves aside. Even when he argues that a mode of suffering needs to be moved 'from below the reach of justice to a place within its purview ... [so that] the language of injury, discrimination, injustice and oppression can apply more cleanly to it' (Connolly, 1999a: 143), his historical examples are carefully chosen: slaves, women, homosexuals. The status of slaves, women, homosexuals has not changed due to an obligation to alleviate suffering that became manifest at some point in time, but through their political struggles, through their irruption on the political scene and a claim to politics that was a formulation of the injustice to which they had been subjected.

If an obligation to alleviate suffering is to inform an ethical approach, a more radical question could be asked: what happens to the terrorist, the sexual abuser and the illegal migrant? Or to Badiou's famous 'religious-corrupted-terrorist-polygamous' (1999)? Although Connolly chooses 'others' who have experienced suffering and domination in specific relations of power, the ethical relation does not engage with issues of representational politics or power relations. Ethics function as an avoidance of power relations rather than as a direct confrontation with them. If an ethical approach presupposes a radical reconstitution of the world which would reshape politics, it is unclear how such a move can happen without an engagement with power relations. Yet, Derrida's messianic future can never arrive, and unconditional principles can never be embodied in political communities.

Connolly's approach points to an ethics that can be processed in the world. How would the obligation to alleviate suffering function in a particular situation like trafficking? One can imagine that this obligation is mediated, fostered, processed differentially. Pity can be one of the means through which the alleviation of suffering becomes necessary and evident. Luc Boltanski has noted that certain types of sufferings have surfaced at various epochs, while others have passed unnoticed, and has translated this insight into a practical task of those who convey suffering: to make it recognisable, to include it in a so-called *repertoire of recognisable suffering* (Boltanski, 1999). Pity for certain categories of oppressed people could only be experienced at particular historical moments and not at others. 'Within the realm of political struggles the conflict of beliefs supporting pity ...', Boltanski points out, 'corresponds to a conflict over the identification of the unfortunates whose cause is to be judged politically worthy' (Boltanski, 1999: 155). Here we are faced again with Connolly's difficult cases, those who are dangerous, those who would be deemed unworthy of pity. According to Boltanski, pity cannot work on those who are deemed responsible for the ills that have befallen them or those who are considered dangerous to the community. Suffering must be undeserved and pity cannot be experienced towards the culpable and the dangerous. Only some forms of suffering and its bearers can be recognized as 'the other in me'. If pity can function as an ethical injunction to reconfigure the abject other, it has to become political, to engage in contestations over the representation of its object and promote a credible and emotional depiction of suffering.

The next section will explore the humanitarian approach to trafficking as a form of ethical injunction (pity), an alternative discourse (desecuritization) and a concern for the vulnerability and insecurity of individuals (emancipation). As the unconditional principles of ethics cannot inform the world, I am interested in how a more practicable ethics that emphasizes suffering can be processed and I shall focus on the strategies of pity as they have been formulated in the situation of trafficking. I shall argue that all three approaches are surpassed by the requirements of knowledge, by the governmental impulse that demands more and more knowledge about the 'abject others' than any of these strategies can offer. The space of abjection is not a space of shadows, a constitutive outside as Butler has suggested. It is actually a space of detailed knowledge about those who are governed as abjects.

Dividing strategies

The humanitarian approach to human trafficking can be addressed from within the three approaches discussed (desecuritization, emancipation and pity). The human rights discourse has been an alternative discourse to security, human trafficking as migration, organized crime and prostitution. It has proposed a different problematization of human trafficking, in which women should become a subject of security rather than its abject. This problematization is purportedly emancipatory for trafficked women, who become the subjects of security, where security is understood in Tickner's life-preserving terms. At the same time, this strategy entails a new relation to the other, a relation that is being advised upon law enforcement and other authorities, as well as clients or generally the public who could encounter trafficked women.

Pity functions as an alternative discourse that would dis-identify women from the abject, the dangerous other, to re-identify them as bodies in pain. Dis-identification entails a reconstruction of security where women are subjects to be secured. Re-identification means the reconfiguration of the relationship self/other which can make the voice of the other audible as 'the other in me' rather than as the dangerous other. Reshaping the relation to the other is, however, a minute work of details and representations. In the case of human trafficking, responsibility for the suffering other (in this instance, trafficked women) was supposed to ground a different politics from politics of (in)security. Thus, pity is a direct confrontation with representations of the dangerous other, which it tries to dismantle.

The alleviation of suffering has been advocated and practised by various NGOs involved in anti-trafficking campaigns with the explicit purpose of challenging practices that considered trafficked women as illegal migrants and foreign prostitutes involved in illicit affairs. Victimization (in the sense of representing women as 'victims') was supposed to challenge what NGOs called the 'law enforcement' approach to human trafficking, which considered trafficked women as illegal migrants and quickly deported them, subjecting them to renewed suffering. Due to practices of re-victimization by the state, victims of trafficking were thought either to fall an easy prey to traffickers all over again or to experience suffering and stigma when returned. Victims of trafficking, NGOs argued, were much more in need of rescuing rather than punishing; their suffering should be alleviated and not reinforced.

Suffering was thought to disrupt the securitization of human trafficking, which turns women into dangerous others as illegal migrants, prostitutes and/or criminals; it was harnessed to a restructuring of social relations in the sphere of trafficking and envisaged specific interventions, different from the repressive and preventive strategies embraced especially by those concerned with migration and organized crime. Being intrinsically linked to emotions, to sentiment, the suffering of the victim is supposed to trigger direct reactions in the spectator, beyond other rational calculations. Pity has to engage in a detailed reconstruction of the object of pity, a different representation of the victim in order to instil the 'right' way to feel about the group of trafficking women.

To promote understanding and sympathy for their situation, these advocates will focus on the pain and directly physical suffering that trafficking causes. The main purpose of these accounts is to promote identification with victims of trafficking in a way that crosses divisions preserved by the other approaches, to create an 'emotional contagion which transmits the *sociable* from interiority to interiority' (Boltanski, 1999: 82, emphasis in original). Sentimentality is in principle open to any form of distress. Although universalizable, suffering needs to be rooted in common sensibilities to create what Boltanski has called a community of 'visceral' reactions, which pre-exist their principled justification (Boltanski, 1999: 54). The physical suffering of trafficked women is meant to trigger such visceral reactions, to function as a 'solidarity-inducing denominator' (Boutellier, 2000: 68) and anti-trafficking campaigns have made extensive use of a symbolic of the body in pain, pierced, bleeding, defenceless. The suffering of victims of trafficking is made directly physical, linking up with the imaginary of bodily suffering. As Didier Fassin has remarked in relation to immigration policies in France, the recognition of the body becomes the ultimate site of political legitimacy (Fassin, 2001: 7). The women's suffering bodies supplant all other justifications for how trafficking should be dealt with.

Amnesty International, like many other NGOs involved in anti-trafficking, has pointed out that women are 'systematically subjected to torture, including rape and other forms of cruel, inhuman and degrading treatment' (Amnesty International, 2004). Women's confessional stories of the experience of trafficking are also intended to signify their suffering to an imagined audience. 'He beat and raped me constantly for three days', confesses a victim of trafficking, 'to the point while I was lying in blood and urine while tied to the bed. He then brought two of his friends who raped me, put out cigarette butts on me, and cut me with razors' (Barbir Mladinovic, 15 June 2006).

Anti-trafficking campaigns – which interestingly are both targeted at changing the problematization of trafficking, but also at preventing the phenomenon – visualize this imaginary of suffering in bodies that are naked, impaired, pierced, fragmented, or bleeding. Rutvica Andrijasevic has aptly deconstructed the gendered imaginary that anti-trafficking campaigns deploy and attempt to fix (Andrijasevic, 2007). The IOM campaign in the Baltic States, in 2001, has offered one of the more controversial representations of the suffering body (IOM, 2000). A woman is shown in the image of a string puppet controlled by an invisible puppeteer.

The strings have hooks that penetrate into the woman's skin and body. The text that accompanies the image sends a chilling warning 'You will be sold like a doll'. Explicitly used to convey the suffering of the body, this image is also used to convey the image of the trafficked woman as an inanimate object (Andrijasevic, 2007). Immobilized by hooks and watching away from the spectator, the woman stands for passivity and painful containment. As the director of IOM Vilnius pointed out, the image was used to convey the situation of victims of trafficking – 'manipulated, coerced, helpless and in pain' (Sipaviciene, 2002).

In an ad by the Poppy Project in the UK, the (potential) victim of trafficking is represented as an encaged doll (Poppy Project, 2004). A transparent Barbie doll box exposes a terrorized and bruised face, a face separated from the rest of the body. Although the body is invisible, made absent, the woman's terrorised face renders visible the trauma of an absent body. Next to the doll box, another absence imaginarily recreates the invisible scene. A pair of male trousers unmistakably relate terror, trauma and violence with prostitution. Images of dolls or of bodies to which sale tags have been attached – and are sometimes shown to also pierce and impair the body – represent women as entirely passive, deprived of any agency, simply objects of trade. These images are not simply used to convey an emotional pedagogy as anti-trafficking activists claim. They are also representations that fix representations of who the victims of trafficking are.

Although fixing the representation of women and 'hooking' their experiences onto the signifier 'Woman', as Andrijasevic aptly remarked, these strategies remain unable to unambiguously fix the representation of victims of trafficking. Through the bodily inscription of suffering, these images are supposed to function as a strategy of dis-identification. Trafficked women have been subjected to cruelty and their undeniable suffering at the hands of traffickers makes them extraordinary, beyond the ordinary identifications with illegal migrants and prostitutes. Where their trajectory might have coincided with that of a migrant or prostitute, suffering is redeeming. Trafficked women are dis-identified from categories of migrants, criminals or prostitutes by the emphasis on physical suffering. Women who are trafficked into prostitution should not be deprived of their rights on grounds that they are undocumented migrants. To attract pity, women are to be made 'innocent' and not 'culpable', undeserving of suffering. The imaginary of dolls, little girls, or puppets reinforces the innocence and passivity of victims. How could victims of trafficking be dangerous when they are passive subjects to the mercy and violence of others?

If universalizable physical suffering attempts to suspend the official distinction between innocent and guilty women present in official discourses, particular representations continuously undermine this strategy. For Willy Bruggeman for example, former deputy director of Europol, only a restricted category of victims are 'sex slaves in the truest sense' (Bruggeman, 2002). Other victims have not been entirely coerced or deceived. Although some would never have imagined the slave-like conditions under which they would have to work, they knew they were going to be employed in the sex industry. Others thought they were recruited to work in the service or entertainment industry, but were instead forced into prostitution. As many of these women signed on to be illegal migrants or even to work irregularly as prostitutes, they are seen to be not (entirely) innocent and not deserving of pity.

Moreover, not all victims have been redeemed by physical suffering, by the 'baptism of brutality' (*The Evening Standard*, 10 October 2002: 16) that has turned them into embodiments of human suffering. Despite the unifying representations of inflicted pain, not all victims have been physically abused, abducted and then repeatedly raped, beaten up, bodies burnt with cigarettes ends. If some women are 'innocent victims', others would almost fit scenarios of receiving 'just deserts': their suffering incurred as a result of their reckless actions, undertaking a(n) (illegal) migration project. The ambiguities or impossibility to objectify pain – increased by the emphasis on consent and prior knowledge – also render victimhood ambiguous. As Elaine Scarry has concisely captured the dilemma of the body in pain, having pain is a certainty, while hearing about pain is always shrouded in doubt (Scarry, 1985).

The question of subjectivity does not receive a final answer in the representation of bodily pain and physical suffering. Governing human trafficking requires knowledge of the individuals whose conduct it is supposed to steer. Who are the women upon whom pity should be bestowed? The confessional answer the women themselves provide, or the NGOs' semi-confessional answers need to be backed up by expert knowledge. The stories of women's suffering relayed by the media and the intense imaginary of gendered, passive, impaired bodies-in-pain used by the NGOs need to be supplemented by the solidity of knowledge.

The question, 'who are you?' can never be completely answered by the individual confession. Although the 'psychiatrisation' of criminal danger was based on procedures of confession, self-examination and revelation, as Foucault has demonstrated at length, it also involved an expert assessment of the future risk that the individual could pose.

Such a doubling of confession by the knowledge of risk was linked to the shift from thinking that punishment should answer the crime, to thinking of it as a mechanism in the 'defence of society' (Foucault, 2000a). The question 'who are the trafficked women?' needs a supplementary answer, an answer that would turn women into subjects that can be known and therefore dealt with on the basis of this knowledge.

I have already suggested that an ethical approach encounters the limit case of those concrete others who are dangerous. Similarly, desecuritizing and emancipatory strategies also set a limit concerning the danger that the other can pose. If 'otherness' is at stake in these strategies to unmake security, then otherness must be disentangled from any risky or insecuring connotations. As Connolly has rightly pointed out, the limit of ethical relationality is also represented by dangerous others. Desecuritization, emancipation and ethics continually need to negotiate the boundaries between danger and non-danger, between insecuring otherness and non-threatening others. However, in negotiating these boundaries, the discourse of victimization, the insecurity of women and the ethical injunction to alleviate suffering are supplemented by scientific representations of who trafficked women are. Their confessional stories are not enough to legitimate suffering and the NGO images of gendered passive bodies are not reliable vehicles for reshaping the problematization of trafficking. Particular victim representations and victim stories continually fall out of these dominant discourses and imaginaries.

The failure of humanitarian approaches is thus essentially a failure to fix the border between who counts as dangerous and who counts as non-dangerous. Alternative discourses encounter the limit of exceptional practices – the majority of women are still deported, even when deportation is restyled as 'voluntary return'. They are also subjected to forms of confinement, placed in shelters for rehabilitation and reintegration that appear more appropriate for the containment of danger than care for the life of women. The insecurity of women is an ambiguous construction that does not cancel the need to establish the boundaries of danger and non-danger. Moreover, the emancipatory promise of security always leaves out particular others: victims of trafficking who do not fit the imaginary of physical suffering, passivity and impairment. The insecurity of victims of trafficking also leaves out the insecurities of other categories of people it immediately affects. Anti-trafficking campaigns have been shown to create insecurity for sex workers, illegal migrants and asylum seekers through raids, increased surveillance and continual suspicion of being a trafficked person. Pity tries to ground different modes of relationality to the other, independent of the other's particularity. The reconfiguration of relationality is possible for a whole array of subjects, excluding the dangerous ones. Recasting trafficked women as suffering victims deserving of pity cannot function until the question of dangerousness has been elucidated. Bodies in pain cannot be dangerous. Yet, bodies in pain do not tell much about the subjects to be governed and their actions. Particularity and representation are the premises of any governmental intervention. Particularity and representation are the substance of security, which makes possible the deployment of technologies and practices of control and risk management. Ethical principles need to be translated back into governmental technologies. Victims cannot remain pure presence, they must be known as subjects of government.

Conclusion

This chapter has discussed three strategies for unmaking practices of security, desecuritization, emancipation and ethics. I have placed these strategies together as they all attempt to contest existing securitizations or constructions of danger and propose another mode of political/ ethical engagement. Desecuritization means an alternative discourse to security. Emancipation would entail the universalization and democratization of security. Ethics radically reconfigures the self/other relation. These three strategies encounter a theoretical and practical impossibility. Alternative discourses do not disturb the exceptional measures taken to deal with trafficking. They are also uninterested in the effects of security in terms of practices of abjectification. Desecuritization tries to locate alternative discourses, on the model of Butler's non-authoritative subjects who can speak with authority. Butler's model remains however inadequate in the CoS framework as securitization is restricted to a discourse about referent objects. The speakers of security are also located among the elites, be these political or the new humanitarian elites. The abject who was Butler's model for resistance and 'speaking with authority' is absent from their definition of securitization.

Emancipation makes the abject its concern and argues for the democratization of security to all those who are outside its remit. It works with an assumption of the imaginary of security that can be stretched to encompass everybody. Yet, security embodies the promise of an always already limited universality. Groups, individuals, societies, states etc. can enjoy security only at the expense of others who either pose a risk to or disturb their normality. The emancipatory promise of security is translated into a competition between particularities: trafficked women or sex workers, illegal migrants or trafficked women, trafficked persons or asylum seekers. All these categories can become contradictory subjects of security constructions. Anti-trafficking strategies can infringe the rights of sex workers. Rights for trafficked women mean more surveillance of illegal migrants or asylum seekers. A strategy that would replace expertise with silenced knowledge and lived experiences would seem to at least replicate a boundary and a limit of 'danger'. Moreover, it is only in translating ethical principles to concrete situations that one can gauge their disruptive potential or the rather unsettling possibility that they may be hijacked and rearticulated within existing relations of power. As the problematization of security exists within an assemblage of symbolic representations and interventions and are 'held together' by an imaginary of a universal promise of security, knowledge is an important element of the 'truth' of representations. Knowledge is required to disambiguate the subjectivity of victims of trafficking and to specify them as non-dangerous.

The next chapter will unpack the knowledge that is mobilized about the victims of trafficking. What is to be done about trafficking depends upon clear specifications of the subjects involved. Confessional stories are insufficient and need to be buttressed by the solidity of knowledge. Particular insecurities do not counter the potential for danger and alternative humanitarian discourses do not replace existing practices. Can the knowledge about victims of trafficking reshape the configuration of security practices?

4
Subjects, Knowledge, Resistance

The previous chapter has shown that the formulation of desecuritizing, emancipatory and ethical strategies to unmake security leads to a theoretical and practical impasse. The representations of victims of trafficking proposed by the humanitarian discourses, the representation of suffering and continuous insecurity that trafficked women experience do not fulfil the requirements of knowledge. Are trafficked women non-dangerous? The specification of non-danger is essential to all three strategies. Moreover, theoretically, it remains unclear how desecuritization, emancipation or ethics could unmake the exceptional and the extraordinary practices that security entails. Anti-trafficking NGOs have been unable to challenge the imaginary of the border and its liminal position as a boundary between the security of the community inside and the insecurity that comes from outside. Returning women to their home country remains the main strategy to which other practices need to be adjusted.

A holistic approach to human trafficking, as promoted by many NGOs, connects the representations of victimhood to strategies of prevention which include voluntary repatriation. Trafficked women are to be rescued only to be later on returned home, 'humanely' deported even against their manifest wishes.[1] The rights of trafficked women do not entail a more democratized security, but have pernicious effects upon other subjects (prostitutes or asylum seekers, for example). The ethical approach that places pity at the heart of a different discourse of trafficking engages with representations of the potentially dangerous trafficked women. Women, however, need to be assessed as non-dangerous; detailed knowledge about them is required to support the premise that humanitarian NGOs and activists try to promote. Unmaking security needs therefore to consider how the knowledge about who trafficked women and the relation to what they do and who they say they are relates to the imaginary and symbolic practices of security.

This chapter will explore how anti-trafficking NGOs create representations of who trafficked women are consonant with the practices of security. What does the representation of who they are mean for unmaking security? I have shown that desecuritization, emancipation and ethics are unable to specify the abject other as undubitably non-dangerous. If security is a process of ordering social problems, of governing 'problematizations', it does so by attempting to conduct the conduct of people. Michel Foucault has called this social *dispositif* of governing social problems by working upon the actions of the people involved 'governmentality'. I have already defined governmentality as the description/representation of social problems and interventions to remedy them. Governing human trafficking through representations and interventions (or rationalities and technologies, as Foucault calls them) needs a third element, that of agency. Women's agency does not only encounter these representations of who they are and how they should conduct themselves, but can radically contest or definitely confirm the knowledge and practices deployed. A *dispositif* of security attempts to affect behaviour and construct forms of ordered agency and subjectivity in the population to be governed, as part of the social problem identified. The abjectifying effects of security are thus a form of ordering agency, taming subjectivity and excluding those who are irremediably 'disordered'.

Analysing security as 'governmental' is not new in IR. Bigo (1996; 2002), Campbell (1992), Dillon (1995b), Dillon and Lobo-Guerrero (2008, forthcoming); Der Derian (1992), Huysmans (2004a; 2006), for example, have used concepts from Foucault's work on governmentality, to creatively explore security practices.[2] In a governmental approach, representations of social problems can be thought of as a permanent incentive for interventions that will tackle these problems. If problematization refers mainly to representations and interventions to manage human trafficking, these representations and interventions are deployed in relation to a subject to be governed. The concept of a *dispositif* of security captures these three main lines: power, knowledge and subjectivity. Representations and interventions are deployed according to a game of power, the mobilization of knowledge and the constitution of subjects. The concept of *dispositif* captures the dynamics of a problematization that is inscribed in the real and the effects that this inscription causes.[3] The deployment of a *dispositif* depends on the knowledge about who trafficked women are. Resistance is at the heart of the notion of a *dispositif*, given the latter's propensity for instability. Politics out of security cannot therefore be restricted to the institutional mediation of practices and representations, but also needs to be considered through practices of subjective resistance. This chapter will unpack what resistance could mean for unmaking practices of security. The possibilities of resistance will be explored through a close engagement with the practices of security that govern human trafficking and the mobilization of different forms of knowledge about who victims of trafficking are.

The first part of the chapter will focus on security as a governmental *dispositif*. It will show what the failure of subjects to be recognized as non-dangerous entails for the reconfiguration of relationality. Rather than non-dangerous, trafficked women are governed as subjects that embody a continuous risk. If practices of security are made possible by the description of subjects, the subject's resistance is a direct and immediate attempt to unmake practices of security and challenge representations of who the subjects are (and implicitly of who/how they should be). The second part will explore what the concept of resistance is and analyse what it can mean for women who resist security practices that govern human trafficking. The constitution of women as risky beings will be shown to depoliticize their agency in resisting the *dispositif* of security.

The security *dispositif*: preventive interventions

The second chapter has shown that security has been mostly seen as part of the logic of war, survival, emergency and exceptionalism. To limit the expansion of the concept, the CoS has framed a different domain of security from the political – one linked with emergency and exception (Bigo, 2002: 73). Yet, this limit of security is a non-sustainable limit. Securitization is not necessarily framed as survival, but can also be cast as prevention of undesirable events. Prevention is, for example, an important element of trafficking, even if trafficking spans various practices. The survival of trafficked women is often at stake; yet, the threat of trafficking is not primarily about the danger to the other's life, but about its subversive effects upon societies and states. Restricting security to the sovereign logic of exception and war would mean endorsing what Der Derian has called the 'onto-theology of security; that is, the a priori argument that proves the existence and necessity of only one form of security because there happens to be a widespread, metaphysical belief in it' (Der Derian, 1992: 74).

Governmentality unpacks security practices beyond the sovereign 'discernment and implementation of inclusions and exclusions ..., and, paradigmatically, according to the modern Hobbesian Carl Schmitt, with the friend/enemy distinction' (Dillon, 1995b: 328). Understood as a form of ordering the social, security means the 'positing, ordering, and placing of all beings, here especially human beings as population, at the disposal of an enframing mode of representative-calculative order ...' (Dillon, 1995b: 330). Individuals or populations are ordered according to a norm against which deviations can be measured. Security implies 'counter-measures to deal with the danger which initiates fear, and for the neutralization, elimination or constraint of that person, group, object or condition which engenders fear' (Dillon, 1995a: 161–2). Governing human trafficking as a problem of security would entail the regulation and ordering of the behaviour of (suspected) victims of trafficking, traffickers, smugglers or other categories that could either become victims of trafficking or could encounter the former.

The analysis of the *dispositif* of security can be harnessed towards its three constitutive elements. It can focus on representations, as the previous chapter has done. It can also analyse, as Bigo has suggested, a 'topology of security' harnessed to an analysis of 'practices of coercion, protection, pacification, static guard, control, surveillance, information gathering and sorting, information management, grid-like security cover, calming, dissuasion, locking up, turning back, and removal from the territory that are deployed by security agents (private or public, police, military police, or army)' (Bigo, 2001b: 99–100). The third mode of analysis focuses on how these representations and interventions attempt to steer conduct. In order to act upon the other's actions, clear knowledge about who the other is is needed. All these modes of analysis unpack security as a specific type of ordering of the *polis*, an ordering based on practices of inclusion and exclusion and imbued with a mimetic desire to make its members conform to ideal images of what they should be (Hindess, 1998: 59).

However, by focusing on one mode of analysis, one runs the risk of ignoring the tensions between the elements constitutive of the security *dispositif*. Interventions do not immediately or directly translate representations, but could potentially contradict those. Knowledge cannot be considered at a distance from the institutional routines and practices that make it possible. Subjectivity is also in tension with representations and interventions that try to define, steer and limit it. The concept of securitization cannot theoretically integrate these tensions as it verges towards either speech acts or exceptional measures. It also takes out the question of how security makes up subjects and the forms of agency, which practices of security encounter. As a reader of Bourdieu, Bigo analyses security practices deployed in a field by actors with a particular know-how and technologies, the security professionals. Although his more recent analyses point out exclusion and normalization as the effects of security, he has been primarily concerned with the genesis of practices.

A *dispositif* of security considers the triad of representation, intervention and subjectivity. The *dispositif* makes it possible to analyse how a diversity of actors intervene on the problematization of human trafficking and understand the role that NGOs play in a field dominated by security professionals. Although having adopted discourses that challenge the securitization of human trafficking, they appear as partners in the larger field of prevention (variously named as anti-trafficking, counter-trafficking or the struggle against human trafficking). To understand how these various interventions affect the subject to be governed, I shall start by locating the role of NGOs regarding the problem of human trafficking.

The definition of human trafficking as a risk to be prevented has allowed NGOs to enter the field of EU professionals, law enforcement, police and immigration and to propose different interventions to minimize and eventually eradicate the phenomenon. Prevention can be ambiguously read as preventing human trafficking from happening and preventing the insecurities of victims. How does prevention work and what does it entail for the NGOs? Prevention creates a specific relation to the future, a future defined by potential 'dangerous irruptions in the future' which can be minimized or neutralized by intervening in the present (Castel, 1991). Risk requires the monitoring of the future, the attempt to calculate what the future can offer and the necessity to control and minimise its potentially harmful effects. Risk is important for understanding how security practices function, because it has always been a way of ordering reality, of rendering it into a calculable form (Dean, 1999a; Ewald, 1986, 1991). It is exactly the calculability of risk that makes it interesting for governing society, as a strategy for managing societal problems. Risk introduces a particular expert knowledge in the field of security, the knowledge of preventing dangerous irruptions. Enlarging the definition that François Ewald has given of insurantial risk, risk is a 'specific mode of treatment of certain events capable of happening to a group of individuals' (Ewald, 1991: 199).

Ewald's (1986) and Jacques Donzelot's (1984) genealogical analyses of risk have shown that risk provided a response to the problematization of specific social and historical problems. Insurance provided an answer to the 'scandal of the poor' in the post-revolutionary French *République*, where neither political equality nor capitalism could (Donzelot, 1984). Despite equality before the law and equal sovereignty, the poor had no property and were therefore forced to sell their labour. Yet, free access to work did not mean the end of indigence. The resolution of the social question – impossible through either political claims or economic measures – was given in the form of mandatory insurance. The wage system was the first form of collective risk insurance, guaranteeing rights, giving access to benefits outside work and protecting workers from the peril of indigence. In this context, other social problems of industrial modernity became governed by technologies of risk insurance. Insurance could render contentious work accidents as something inherent to work, against which workers could be protected through insurance. Insurance risk becomes social and is deployed as a 'technology of solidarity' which makes accidents, unemployment and other social problems collectively borne through insurance (Dean, 1999b: 140).

Yet, Ewald adds another side to the reparation and compensation that insurance offers, namely prevention. The problem of compensating losses is inseparable from the problem of reducing the probability of their occurrence. The solidarity that insurance risk was supposed to foster in a collectivity was simultaneously undermined by the division and classification of populations in high-risk/low-risk groups. The marketing of insurance has led to a process of 'underwriting security' by means of which an insurer analyses the levels of risk that a potential client represents and decides whether an insurance policy can be written (Lobo-Guerrero, 2006). The moral hazard that a client can pose for an insurer is translated in a form of prevention in relation to social risks. If insurers take the moral measure of the individual they insure (Baker, 2000: 569), risk prevention takes the moral measure of groups which appear to be at risk. The insurance industry depends on other institutions to police society and high-risk groups so as to reduce risks and make them profitable.

As an intervention to govern social problems, risk management combines insurance and prevention. Prevention is based on practices of dividing and categorizing social groups, while insurance is primarily a form of the statistical computation of probabilities. As risks are the effect of a 'combination of abstract *factors*, which render more or less probably the occurrence of undesirable modes of behaviour' (Castel, 1991: 287), risk is doubly related to social problems and subjects. Prevention entails individual and group profiling, based on 'procedures for the allocation of individuals to risk groups, on a genealogical basis, in terms of a family history of illness or pathology, and/or on a factorial basis, in terms of combinations of factors statistically linked to a condition' (Rose, 2001: 8).

Formulated to tackle problems posed by 'dangerous individuals', delinquents and criminals, prevention has borrowed heavily from the expert knowledge provided by psychology and psychoanalysis. The clinical practices of risk initially focused on the likelihood of a person (in particular, a mentally ill person) committing a violent act. If psychological knowledge was taken out of the asylum and the clinic to govern the risk of dangerous behaviour of criminals, mental defectives, sexual perverts and psychopaths, it has been extended to more and more 'marginal' categories, such as alcoholics, drug addicts and children with learning disorders. As the authors of *The Psychiatric Society* have aptly put it, psychology colonized social life (Castel, Robert, Castel, Françoise and Lovell, 1982). Psychology and psychiatry have gradually taken up and transformed political, economic and social problems, and have made these problems thinkable in new ways and governable by different techniques (Rose, 1989: ix).

Robert Castel has documented the mutation of social technologies that have minimised direct therapeutic intervention, supplanted by an increasing emphasis on a preventive administrative management of populations at risk (1981). Strategies of prevention are based on the assumption that if prevention is necessary, a danger exists, even if only in a virtual state before being actualized. As these correlations remain arbitrary and can only be proven *a posteriori*, dangerousness becomes 'a quality immanent to a subject' (Castel, 1981: 146). The virtuality of danger is related to specific individuals and groups who are to be categorized as 'high risk'. Although linked with the management of risk groups and populations, preventive risk also involves a therapeutic objective in the administration of individuals diagnosed as pathological (Weir, 1996: 374). This double aspect, individualizing and categorizing, of risk technologies appears most explicitly in clinical risk management.

Clinical risk breaches the distinction between governing individual bodies and governing populations (Weir, 1996: 382). It implements population-based calculations, forming risk groups by applying risk categories that divide the population and subsequently place groups 'at risk' under surveillance or treatment. These risk technologies are based upon a combination of the characteristics of individual case studies and observation of patterns in a population and the identification of associated risk factors (Lupton, 1999: 63). Some groups are to be defined as 'high risk', with risk being defined as internal, due to their behaviour or biography, rather than external.

Clinical risk management mobilizes psychological expertise to create risk profiles and contain the risk of various categories of people deemed to have mental and/or emotional problems. To statistical calculation, psychology has added a more important promise 'to provide inscription devices that would individualise such troublesome subjects' (Rose, 1998: 74). Psychological expertise is needed to invent diagnostic categories, evaluations, assessments; it is needed to provide an individuated answer to the question at the heart of all acts of government: 'who are you?' Subjects of risk are constituted through a combination of therapeutic interventions, pathological categorizations and a statistical calculation of the incidence of certain factors in a population group.

Risk prevention reveals an interesting dynamic between the groups 'at risk' and the calculation of 'high risk'. Clinical risk first locates a series of abstract factors that are responsible for the emergence of certain behavioural patterns, diseases and mental disorders. According to this logic, it is possible to say that children of alcoholic parents are also 'at risk' of being alcoholic. By being 'at risk', they also pose a potential risk to the community, a risk related with all the 'disorders' of alcoholism. Those judged 'at risk' of being a danger to the community are subjected to therapeutic (e.g., counselling, self-help groups, support groups) and disciplinary (training and retraining) practices in an effort either to eliminate them completely from communal spaces (e.g., by various forms of confinement) or to lower the dangers posed by their risk (Dean, 1999a: 189).

What does the *dispositif* of security as risk management mean for unmaking security practices? The *dispositif* of security relies upon forms of knowledge that are contested among various actors. Change happens through contestatory interactions between fields and institutional actors with diverging *habitus*. Yet, the rules of knowledge acquisition in the field of security short-circuit any type of amateur interventions. The security professionals' institutional knowledge about threats and the technological means to deal with those makes them relatively impermeable to the criticism of 'amateurs' such as NGOs, associations, churches, spokesmen and other types of ad hoc organizations. Bigo speaks of an 'ethos of shared knowledge between the professionals, a knowledge beyond the grasp of people who do not have the know-how about risk assessment and proactivity' (Bigo, 2002: 74). Amateur actors can only enter the field of shared knowledge by proposing useful or similar knowledge.

As society is a complex structuration of fields, claims of knowledge, authority, etc. can clash with claims from other fields. Without an overarching epistemic authority, claims to knowledge remain irreconcilable.

The very struggle over the representation of a social problem can make institutional space for various actors. As it is unclear in what sense exactly migration, for example, is a threat, it can be integrated in a whole series of practices that allow for the intervention of the police, border officials, judiciary, politicians or NGOs. Migration is simultaneously connected with terrorism, smuggling, crime (more or less organized), allowing interventions from different fields and by various actors. Similarly, the ambiguous definition of what the prevention of trafficking means legitimates supplementary interventions and practices proposed by different institutional actors.

NGOs have been able to enter the field of trafficking alongside law enforcement by proposing forms of knowledge that would be useful for the management of trafficking. Many trafficking NGOs in Europe already had expertise in working with sex workers or victims of domestic violence.[4] NGOs have offered first-hand, in-depth knowledge about victims of trafficking. Speaking at an OSCE conference, Stana Buchowska from La Strada has emphasized the role of NGOs as a valuable source of information for the authorities, information which would be otherwise unobtainable (OSCE, 2004). The European Commission also recognized early on the importance of NGOs in anti-trafficking programmes and has integrated NGO representatives in its 'Experts Group on Trafficking in Human Beings', mandated to develop a plan for best practices, standards and mechanisms to prevent and combat trafficking in human beings (European Commission, 2005b). Although NGOs have managed to enter the field of security professionals, their approach to human trafficking has proven less of a challenge to existing technologies of government. To understand how a 'victimization' approach could become part of the security *dispositif* to govern human trafficking, it is important to focus on how interventions can be moved in different directions, realigned to new representations and reappropriated by different institutions. As the next section will show, practices can be reappropriated and moved in different directions, independent of the actors' interests or initial agenda.

Governing human trafficking through risk

> REIW [Regional Empowerment Initiative for Women] ... will help prevent trafficking in the countries of origin as at-risk women are vested with the skills, knowledge and confidence to successfully pursue safe and fulfilling opportunities in their home countries and avoid trafficking schemes.
>
> (International Research & Exchange Board, 2003)

Compared to the more straightforward examples of securitization such as migration, trafficking is a peculiar case, as it has witnessed a move from state security to a humanitarian approach. An analysis of the *dispositif* of security allows us to see how such an approach becomes enmeshed in the securitization of human trafficking (beyond the constraints imposed on amateur actors such as NGOs, by their presence in the security field). Pity towards trafficked women becomes enmeshed with preventive strategies of risk and women are 'constituted' as specific categories of victims, pathological beings that are themselves risky rather than exposed to risks.

Despite the injunction to tend to the victims, the humanitarian approach is reconfigured when it becomes a mechanism for dealing with social problems. The representation of the 'victim' and of the abuse of rights made possible by her vulnerability activates technologies of prevention. The recurrence of such experiences needs to be stopped and detailed knowledge of the phenomenon and those involved is required. NGOs are urged to work together with law enforcement in a more holistic approach to human trafficking.[5] Although victims of trafficking often reach NGOs through the mediation of the police and after an initial screening to ascertain whether they are genuine victims has been undertaken, NGOs have drafted memoranda of understanding with the police that detail the process of identifying and transferring victims of trafficking to their assistance (see Danish Red Cross, 2005). In Romania, one institution which is part of the police service is responsible nationally both for the prevention of trafficking and the protection of victims.[6]

Victims of trafficking cannot remain pure presence; their risk identity needs to be specified for the purposes of preventing human trafficking. Preventing trafficking relies on interventions that delimit and categorize 'high risk' groups, groups which are at risk of being trafficked. Trafficked women are profiled for preventive purposes, and it is these specific profiles, developed in conjunction with psychological knowledge, that make possible the constitution of these women's identity as a subject of the governmentality of human trafficking. This representation of vulnerability is at first sight consonant with the unifying representations of victims as suffering bodies, as the risk of trafficking is taken to be a risk to women's well-being. Yet, the representation of trafficked women insidiously mutates into a risk to the state/society, as a group at risk thought to embody a permanent virtual danger that could irrupt in the future.

The identification and calculability of risk depend on the construction of risk profiles. Studies of risk practices have emphasized the construction of biographical profiles of human populations for risk management and security provision (Ericson and Haggerty, 1997). Victim profiles have also become ubiquitous in trafficking reports and studies of the phenomenon. If the Council Framework Decision on combating trafficking in human beings identifies trafficked women as victims of coercion, force or threats, including abduction, deceit or fraud, abuse of authority and vulnerability (Council of the European Union, 2002), these terms become psychologized in other reports and documents. Coercion, abuse, deceit and vulnerability need to be explained. A report by the European Parliament explicitly defines and limits vulnerability as specifically due to 'poverty, lack of education and professional opportunities' (European Parliament, 2001). Yet, the explanation that unfolds from these initial details is not located at the societal level, but is entirely internal to the individual. The flaw is not with society, but with the disordered individual that needs to be reformed.

Foucault has noted that in the nineteenth century the psychiatric knowledge summoned by courts reconstituted an 'absolutely ambiguous series of the infrapathological and the paralegal, or of the parapathological and the infralegal, which is a kind of reconstruction of the crime itself, a scaled-down version, before it has been committed' (Foucault, 2004a: 20). The links between the 'desire to leave one's country', which studies of trafficking invariably locate with trafficked women, and the infra- or parapathological factors that lead to it, both pathologize and indirectly criminalize the process of migration.

In NGO analyses, socio-economic conditions are being translated at the individual level as 'a strong desire to seek employment abroad', shifting emphasis from questions of inequality to vulnerability factors (El-Cherkeh, Stirbu, Lazaroiu and Radu, 2004). Other reports employ a similarly psychological redefinition in terms of the victim's 'wish for a better life'. These redefinitions are not limited to the NGO sector, but are taken up by the EU and other international organizations. A Europol overview of trafficking redefines poverty and the hopes or expectations of a more prosperous future as the vulnerabilities that are exploited by the traffickers (Europol, 2004). Even when economic and social factors are concerned, a shift towards individualization and psychologization becomes apparent. An IOM study of vulnerability factors to trafficking in Romania discards the hypothesis of 'an objectively poor environment as a characteristic of vulnerability' (IOM, 2003). While poverty is acknowledged as a 'push' factor, calls for eradicating poverty remain highly impractical. Another, more feasible, way of tackling the issue of poverty is by changing individual psychological reactions to poverty. Prevention will be deployed by action upon the actions of individuals.

Even if socio-economic risk factors such as poverty, lack of job opportunities and gender inequalities are enumerated in the various reports on trafficking, their role is not only redefined under the influence of psychologization, but also limited in practice. In interviews with the IOM and three other NGOs in Romania working for the reintegration of trafficked women in the country of origin, I found that, as the economic aspect of the risk governance is very difficult to tackle, it is eclipsed by the more easily addressable concerns with psychological rehabilitation and recovery.[7] NGOs have liaised with EU actors by providing psychological expertise that could be more easily translated into practice, compared to large-scale economic and social interventions. Psychological counselling counts as one of the most important methods for victim assistance and reintegration. A report on trafficking in South Eastern Europe cites medical care and psychological counselling as the first two strategies of integration, while expressing concern about the scant emphasis placed on educational assistance and lack of vocational and training programmes in transit and destination countries (Counter-Trafficking Regional Clearing Point, 2003).

In the general assemblage of risk factors used to govern specific groups, trafficked women become mostly an assemblage of psychological risk factors. From the NGOs' perspective, this shift to psychological profiling is not surprising, given that trafficking is understood as a traumatic experience for women. For psychological expertise, a traumatic experience is also linked with specific factors in the victim's past. Animus, the main NGO involved with returned trafficked women in Bulgaria, warns that it is important to consider the predispositions that exist in the personal history of women and girls (Stateva and Kozhouharova, 2004). Typical risk profiles of victims of trafficking will therefore include past biographical details deemed important by the experts. Significantly, victims are shown to have often experienced 'exposure to violence at home or in a state institution' (Limanowska, 2002). Most victims have been abandoned by parents, friends, and/or husbands, and many have been sexually abused (Centrul pentru prevenirea traficului de femei, 2002). They often come from dysfunctional families (La Strada).[8] Animus also indicates that the groups most at risk of being trafficked are women and adolescents who have suffered traumatic experiences, e.g. victims of domestic violence, sexual assault, children from orphanages, and children with a large number of siblings and only one parent (Zimmerman, 2003). Among the returned women at Animus, 26 per cent had been victims of incest or childhood psychological abuse and all of them had untreated psychological trauma (Stateva and Kozhouharova, 2004: 112).

The victims of trafficking emerging from these reports appear as doubly traumatized, both by the experience of trafficking and by earlier, childhood experiences of abuse. The experience of trafficking is doubled by forms of conduct and ways of being that become integrated in a logical profile that accounts for the cause and origin of trafficking. This continuity of trauma is not surprising for the psychological expertise. A classic of psychological trauma and an oft-mentioned reference in NGO documents, Judith Herman's *Trauma and Recovery* states that adult survivors of child abuse are at great risk of victimization in adult life (Herman, 1997: 111). The experience of trafficking is thus a repetition, an almost fateful reliving of earlier traumas. Diana Tudorache, from the IOM shelter on Kosovo, clearly connects the two types of traumatic events. In her words, '[t]he feelings of vulnerability and emotional pain that are experienced by the VoT [victims of trafficking], combined often with a background of childhood abuse and mistreatment, play a significant role in the occurrence and severity of the acute reactions' (Tudorache, 2004: 23). Within a short period (2001–4), IOM Romania commissioned and published two studies of the vulnerability of the 'young female population in Romania' (IOM, 2001, 2003). Based on interviews with women who have been trafficked, IOM has produced victim profiles which emphasize their past traumas.

The past, however, especially the location of a traumatic event in the victim's past (such as childhood abuse, dysfunctional family environment, domestic violence and institutional abuse) activates another scenario of psychotherapeutic practices. As Julie Brownlie has noted in her article on the 'young sexual offenders', victimization is not only an indicator of further abuse but equally an indicator of future risk (Brownlie, 2001). Studies on victims of sexual abuse suggest that adult females who were sexually abused as children experience a variety of long-term sequelae including sexual disturbances, depression, anxiety, fear and suicidal ideas and behaviour (Schaaf and McCanne, 1998: 1119). Victims of sexual abuse, psychological studies have shown, are likely not only to be re-victimized, but they might well become 'perpetrators' themselves. In cases of child abuse or violence, the necessity of abused children to defend themselves at an early stage in life might evolve into offending behaviour later on (Romano and De Luca, 1997: 86). In a less extreme formulation, women who have been sexually abused as children and those who have been traumatized are more likely to engage in future risk-taking behaviour than those who have not experienced abuse (Zimmerman, 2003). Even those who claim that survivors of childhood abuse, for example, are more likely to be victimized than to victimize other people cannot deny a connection with adult antisocial behaviour (Herman, 1997: 113).

These insights activate technologies of risk management which attempt to limit the possibility of a risky offender to reoffend. 'Distressing behaviour', Vanessa Pupavac has noted, is 'conceptualized as inducing traumatic responses leading to dysfunctions, in turn, fostering future vicious cycles of trauma, violence and injustice' (Pupavac, 2004: 204). The spectre of potential offences, whether understood as antisocial, risky or even criminal behaviour, surreptitiously infuses victimization scenarios. If the continuity of trauma could be thought as consonant with victimization, which could still construe sexual exploitation as the undeserved surplus of earlier, also undeserved, abuse and violence, the riskiness inscribed in the women's biographical profiles ends up by subverting pity. Strangely reminiscent of the governmentality of drug- and alcohol addictions, 'rehabilitation' is the motto for practices of victim assistance. The expert knowledge mobilized by NGOs with the purpose of helping trafficking women becomes 'hijacked' by a politics of risk which is based on risk minimization and containment. The women 'at risk' insidiously metamorphose into 'high risk' groups and risk technologies are deployed under the banner of therapy not just to help victims of trafficking overcome their trauma and ease their suffering, but also to limit the possibility of risky actions in the future.

What are these risky actions, what is the potential offending behaviour of trafficked women? The EU documents are unambiguous on this point. If trafficked women are to reoffend, offence is to be understood as immigration or 'retrafficking'. The EU Council Proposal for a decision to combat human trafficking has explicitly stated that helping victims of trafficking or smuggling is a way of preventing them from lapsing into an illegal immigration situation (Council of the European Union, 2002). The joint EU-IOM-NGO Brussels Declaration also sees victim reintegration as a means to reduce the risk of retrafficking (IOM, 2002). While trafficked women are involved in psychological therapy (together, for example, with victims of domestic violence and rape), it is important to remember that these programmes are seen by the EU as part of prevention strategies and therefore need to be supplemented in most cases by return to the country of origin.[9] A Commission discussion paper on granting short-term residence permits can even unproblematically conceive of the fight against human trafficking as two-pronged: by dismantling the networks or by helping victims get out of their illegal situation and avoid lapsing into it again (which would also be linked with psycho-social measures) (European Commission, 2002a).

These preventive measures can only be read as the risk management of illegal migration which subverts the humanitarian approach and subsumes the NGO discourse to the logic of security practices. The potential risk of women migrating and being retrafficked is to be contained and prevented; they will be surveyed and disciplined, subjected to trauma therapy with the purpose of turning them into subjects able to monitor their own risk. Risk technologies have made possible the specification of the victim – previously object of pity – as inherently and continuously 'risky' and have modified the emotional promise of pity into an abstract suspicion of risk. Based on the aggregate of risk factors, vulnerability is traversed by *imputations of dangerousness* (Castel, 1991: 284).

Women remain risky beings, always 'in danger' of being retrafficked, and thus embody in themselves the danger of illegal migration. Rather than rights-bearing individuals, women are dealt with as risk-bearing ones, subjected to a logic of risk which is focused on how to limit the opportunity of the 'risky' offender to offend. The risk of women being retrafficked is a risk which paradoxically dwells 'in' the subject even though it has not manifested itself in the act (Castel, 1991: 283).

The humanitarian approach to trafficking becomes complicit in a politics of security that uses risk technologies for the purpose of preventing human trafficking. This analysis of practices exposes how the two approaches are interconnected and traversed by a logic of risk. Yet, what does this mean for unmaking security practices? The realization that the prevention of human trafficking and the 'protection' of trafficked women are geared towards a concern with stopping illegal migration does not challenge the problematization of human trafficking as essentially a form of illegal migration. As a complex social problem, human trafficking can be split between concerns for the victims and 'legitimate' concerns with illegal migration. While risk prevention and the technologies associated with it make apparent their imbrication and interdependence, what also needs to be challenged is the representation of who the victims are, which allows for the constitution of authoritative forms of knowledge.

Without challenging the knowledge that holds together representations and interventions and makes their deployment possible, humanitarian concerns can be reappropriated and reformulated. Their reappropriation is made possible not simply through field effects (the amateur actors yield to expert knowledge, the EU finances many of these organizations),[10] but through the redeployment of risk interventions and knowledge. While one can attempt to think of change along the first two lines – how would struggles among actors challenge dominant constructions rather than entrench them – the more urgent question is how to tackle the reappropriation of interventions and the redeployment of knowledge. This redeployment can either settle various struggles or obscure the real stakes of struggles. The following section will explore possibilities of challenging the reappropriation of knowledge and the redeployment of risk management.

Resistance against security

The redeployment of risk interventions and risk knowledge is made possible under the description and specification of who the victims of trafficking are. Practices of risk management and prevention create specific subjects at risk or risky abjects. Knowledge can be gathered and interventions made effective only in relation to subjects and their actions. Do victims of trafficking resist the abjectifying effects of practices? The question of the subject/abject is to a certain extent the other side of the institutionally contested genesis of practices. Focusing on the genesis of practices exposes their contingency, their arbitrary reification into the taken-for-granted, the familiar and the natural. Yet, this exposure needs to tackle the paraphernalia of subjects, interventions and discourses. Although I do not want to claim that such change is impossible, the constitution of such practices in relation to the subjects whose conduct is to be steered in the appropriate direction is also its utmost point of instability.

Governing trafficking can only attempt to foster forms of subjectivity that are reproduced by means of these descriptions. Yet, such descriptions have been often rejected by the victims of trafficking. Foucault's insight on the recalcitrance of the subject, the resistance that is immanent to power appears in the trafficked women's refusal to accept these descriptions. Many women refuse to become subjectified as victims of trafficking. NGOs have devised guidelines that would name women as victims independent of their personal decision (OSCE, 2004). 'Victims of trafficking' often refuse to return to their countries of origin and follow programmes of rehabilitation. Yet, can they extricate themselves from these practices? The question of unmaking security practices could therefore be rephrased as the 'opposition to the effects of power linked with knowledge, competence, and qualification ... [and] also against secrecy, deformation, and mystifying representations imposed on people' (Foucault, 2000c: 330).

Having defined security as 'the generative and immanent principle of the formation of [the] political subject' (Campbell and Dillon, 1993: 29), Campbell and Dillon found themselves in the midst of a larger theoretical field in which the relation of the subject and social practices was being debated. If the subject is 'constituted' by regimes of power/ knowledge, the only possible extrication is by un-forming or de-forming the subject. For Campbell, security and subjectivity are intrinsically linked in a twofold way: securing a subject requires its differentiation, classification and definition (Campbell, 1992: 253); security also functions 'to instantiate the subjectivity it purports to serve' (Campbell, 1998a: 199). Security practices attempt to reproduce a secure subject by abjectifying others. Linking security and subjectivity is assumed to have an insurrectional effect. Campbell's formulation of the subject insurrection is 'how do we orient ourselves to danger ...? Do we have an alternative to the continued reproduction of sovereign communities in an economy of violence?' (Campbell, 1998a: 203). His answer is inspired by the Foucauldian 'ontology of freedom', which makes possible the rearticulation of different modes of being and forms of life. Although a more thorough discussion of subjectivity is beyond the ambit of Campbell's book, it is unclear how such a rearticulation could occur. The subject of security is promised ontological and epistemological certainty at the expense of another's vulnerability. Even if this promise of security can only take shape out of subjective insecurity, its imaginary form projects it in the future, thus separating the inherent relation between security and insecurity along temporal lines.

However, the subject who resists can be both the *subject* and the *abject*. As Hinrich Fink-Eitel (1992) has argued, Foucault's theoretical trajectory can be considered as the bifurcation of a history of the other and a history of the self that have continued the lines sketched in *Madness and Civilization* and *The Order of Things*, respectively. If *Madness and Civilization*, Fink-Eitel goes on, dealt with the philosophy of the other, *The Order of Things* is concerned with a philosophy of the other's opposite, of the human being as a finite being on the verge of a break-through to the other (Fink-Eitel, 1992: 31). The bifurcation between the dominance of the self and the dominance of the other in Foucault's work has led to a dualistic approach to the question of subjectivity. The subject who resists her subjectification through practices of security can be the self or the other.

The focus on the self, on the subject of modernity or on the multiple institutional locations of subjects runs into the impasse of accounting how the subject's 'passionate attachment' (Žižek, 1999b) to one's subjectivity is to be unwrung and reworked. Žižek follows the line of psychoanalysis, where subjectivity is unwrought through a traumatic encounter with the Real. Butler on the other hand weds psychoanalysis to the subjectivity of the abject. There is an implicit assumption in Butler that the undoing of subjectivity happens at the site of the other-subject, the one that security practices constitute through exclusion as the abject. Those who encounter power relations most directly and oppressively resist most immediately and directly.

The governmentality literature has de-differentiated the self and the other in its understanding of resistance against power relations. I have already discussed governmentality as an 'art' for acting on the actions of individuals, taken either singly or collectively, so as to shape, guide, conduct and modify the ways in which they act (Burchell, Graham, 1993: 267). Combining the meanings of 'to conduct', 'to conduct oneself' and 'conduct' as a noun, government refers to any attempt to shape with some degree of deliberation aspects of our behaviour, the management of possibilities (Dean, 1999a: 10; Foucault, 2000c: 341). Resistance therefore is a question of 'counter-conducts' of the self and other. In the later Foucault, there is an emphasis on ethics or 'aesthetics of the self' as a modality of engagement against the shaping of conduct. What interests me, however, is the second penchant of his theoretical trajectory, the other, whose resistance is at best silenced if not suppressed. While one could speak of the relation between the resistance of the self and the resistance of the other, of the congruence and reso-nance of their forms of resistance, the emphasis on the other, the infamous or the abject speaks to a political tradition that has seen in the oppressed the makers of their own emancipation. Resisting counter-conducts happen at the site of those who experience governmentality as oppressive and unjust.

The subject that disrupts, transcends and challenges is the oppressed subject or the abject. Oppression is not a question of personal feelings, but is inscribed in power relations. The subjective position of the abject replaces – in this reading – the concern with the modern subject who is constituted through the exclusion of abject others. It is after all an ethics of the self along Foucauldian lines that is envisaged by Campbell. His later engagement with Levinas and responsibility for the other attempts to create an ethical injunction from the site of self. Although both subjects and abjects function within relations of power and both could resist, the abject is directly and immediately captured within these power relations and resists oppression and domination.

The related issue that arises with the resisting subject is whether counter-conducts or insubordination are able to displace the existing socio-symbolic network. Žižek argues, contra Butler, that

> one should maintain the crucial distinction between a mere 'performative reconfiguration', a subversive displacement which remains *within* the hegemonic field and, as it were, conducts an internal guerrilla war of turning the terms of the hegemonic field against itself, *and* the much more radical *act* of a thorough reconfiguration of the entire field which redefines the very conditions of socially sustained performativity.
>
> (Žižek, 1999b: 264)

Butler has actually raised the question of resistance that only manages to undermine (thus determining the failure of the constitution of the subject), but does not have the power to rearticulate the discourse and the normalizing practices (Butler, 1997b). Think, for example, of the sovereign deportation of undesirable asylum seekers or illegal migrants. The subject's insubordination is often acutely violent. Such reactions are not interpreted as political and new technologies are devised to remove the struggling migrants from the view of other passengers at the airports. What few changes are made concern more effective, less visible technologies, but not the principles, the logic of representing asylum seekers or illegal migrants as dangerous, bogus, criminal, and in a word, undesirable.

Or – even more perversely – resistance can be reappropriated by the regime of power/knowledge and technologies of security. The strategy of representing trafficking as the victimization of women is reappropriated in a *dispositif* of risk prevention, according to which women remain risky beings. Resistance to security practices does not mean proposing a less threatening representation of the other, but challenging the very imaginary and symbolic practices of security. It is interesting that the refusal of representations of danger concerning asylum seekers or migrants generally focuses on their artistic side: poetry writing, drawings and music. This artistic side silences their political claims, the disturbance that they cause to the existing 'regime of truth' about migration and asylum. Their integration through art takes away the economic and political implications of migration which security practices try to neutralize through the constitution of danger or risk. Is such an emphasis on the artistic side of migrants not the tacit awareness that other challenges could be truly unsettling? Moreover, the artistic display of migrants' craftiness does nothing by way of challenging the representation of other migrants as bogus refugees, welfare cheaters, criminals or potential terrorists.

The dilemma of resistant subjectivity is that it can be consonant with dominant practices (such as the migrant-as-artist) or it can reproduce representations of danger (the migrant who violently struggles against procedures of return). Representations of bodily suffering that victims of trafficking confess can also be thought as a strategy to resist deportation, rehabilitation and reintegration (coupled with repatriation) in the countries of origin. Narrating suffering bodies or exposing them in their physical impairment creates 'bio-legitimacy', a social recognition of last instance when all other modes of legitimation have been exhausted (Fassin, 2004: 240). However, this recognition only reinforces the governing of human trafficking through security. It allows for more boundaries between the few whose bodies can be 'exposed' to create bio-legitimacy and the numerous others who cannot draw upon their embodiment as a source of political legitimation. The next section will analyse this dilemma of subjectivity in relation to the reproduction of dominant practices or their disruption by looking at how trafficked women refuse practices of subjectivation. Victims of trafficking often refuse to expose their suffering bodies and make them part of the bio-interventions of the humanitarian approach.

Making risky subjects

> 'Psychological pain' does not by itself seem to me to be a definite fact, but on the contrary only an interpretation – a causal interpretation – of a collection of phenomena that cannot be exactly formulated – it is really only a fat word standing in place of a skinny question mark.
> (Nietzsche quoted in Hacking, 1995: 197)

Security practices attempt to eliminate, expel or modify the abject other that appears as an intrusion into the political order. The disorderly conduct and risk potential of trafficked women permeates concerns for their suffering. The psychological knowledge that makes possible such linkage is also deployed for making sense of the women's behaviour in the post-trafficking situation. Psychological knowledge supplements the narration and exposure of the body by a consistent story of the mind.

Body and mind are to be correctly aligned and coherently connected. No contradiction between bodily experience and psychological reactions is allowed. I argue that, through this alignment of body and mind, psychological knowledge depoliticizes women's resistance, and integrates it in a regime of power/knowledge that 'speaks the truth' about them and deprives them of the political clout of ordinary citizens.

Hindess has distinguished three broad categories of subjects in need of different technologies of government, depending on the understanding of the subject's (lack of) capacity for self-government and risk management (Hindess, 2001: 101). The first category concerns those people who are far from acquiring the necessary capabilities and should be cleared out of the way. They are the hopeless cases, the incorrigibles or as Dean calls them, the 'permanently delinquent' (2002: 48). The second category is that in which the capacities for self-government can only be developed through compulsion, through the imposition of more or less extended periods of discipline (Hindess, 2001: 101). The third category concerns those subjects who lack the capacity for self-government due mainly to external reasons – for example, ill health, poverty, or inadequate education.

Trafficked women are the paradoxical case in which the three categories overlap. As illegal migrants, trafficked women are still to be deported. As delinquents, they are to be subjected to disciplinary technologies. As victims of trafficking, women still have to abide by restrictive criteria defined as part of their 'reintegration and rehabilitation' programmes. As psychologically vulnerable, women are to be helped through education and various forms of psychological counselling to become self-sufficient and autonomous subjects who act in accordance with governmental premises. As Carol Harrington has argued, the purpose of therapy is to 're-constitute subjects who autonomously make appropriate (from the point of view of international governance) decisions' (Harrington, 2005: 193). Victims of trafficking are expected to develop a new image of themselves, testify against their traffickers, return to their countries of origin and undertake productive work. Many of these NGO initiatives take place in the countries of origin, where women can be allocated to particular NGOs after having been returned. In Romania, for example, women who are returned by the IOM are subsequently allocated to NGOs which have integration and rehabilitation programmes. In Ukraine, IOM has set up an NGO partnership which includes NGOs which work directly with victims of trafficking and other civil society organizations involved in prevention (IOM Ukraine, 2007).

There is a double inscription of the psychological upon the subjectivity of trafficked women. On the one hand, this inscription leads to the construction of vulnerability and riskiness that accounts for trafficking and allows for the deployment of preventive technologies of risk management and on the other the experience of trafficking is itself constructed as a traumatic. In a report by the Minnesota Advocates for Human Rights, an NGO which has funded anti-trafficking programmes in Ukraine and Moldova, the post-trafficking psychological reactions comprise 'severe mental or emotional health consequences, including feelings of severe guilt, post-traumatic stress disorder, depression, anxiety, substance abuse (alcohol or narcotics) and eating disorders ... self-mutilation or suicide' (Minnesota Advocates for Human Rights, 2005). A study financed by the World Health Organization to analyse the health effects of trafficking reaches similar conclusions:

> The forms of abuse and risk that women experience include physical, sexual and psychological abuse, the forced or coerced use of drugs and alcohol, social restriction and manipulation, economic exploitation and debt bondage, legal insecurity, abusive working and living conditions, and a range of risks associated with being a migrant/marginalised. These abuses and risks impact women's physical, reproductive, and mental health ...
>
> (Zimmerman, Cathy, 2003)

Most NGOs involved in victim assistance have adopted this psychological approach to the 'trauma of trafficking'. This is the case with many anti-trafficking NGOs in Romania, both due to their earlier or concomitant work with victims of domestic violence, their formation as social workers or psychologists/therapists, and the publication of manuals of good practices for the assistance of victims of trafficking. While I do not intend to downplay the exceptional role that the experience of trafficking has for women's lives, I argue that the double psychologization of trafficking depoliticizes their agency by re-reading it as pathological. 'Women as risky' functions as the primary depoliticization of migratory projects and victims of trafficking. Although many women list finding work or working, as the reason for their migratory projects, work remains the illegitimate element in the problematization of trafficking.[11] Work is understood either as prostitution or as any form of work but not prostitution.[12] 'Women as traumatized' is the second depoliticizing move in the governance of trafficking. As they are traumatized and disordered subjects, their actions cannot be considered as endowed with political meaning.

Trafficked women react against the constitution of their subjectivity as abject, as undesirable: women are to be removed from the territory of the country of destination and returned to their country of origin or made useful as witnesses against traffickers. When returned, women often refuse to start rehabilitation programs with the NGOs (Limanowska, 2002). All the women whose testimonies appeared in a 2004 legal file at the Galati Court of Justice had either attempted to return or returned to the country of destination (Italy) to resume sex work. In a personal conversation, one of the judges remarked that in another trafficking trial it had been difficult to obtain testimonies as most women are working in Spain and do not want to return.[13] NGOs also report victims of trafficking returning to their countries of destination and take measures against such misbehaviour. The women who return to sex work are disqualified from receiving any further help by the IOM.[14] In a discussion of anti-trafficking programmes in Nepal, John Frederick has noted that participation in institutional programmes is minimal, 'the girls' voices concerning their institutionalisation are unheard, and the frequency of girls escaping from confinement is not mentioned by NGOs or donors' (Frederick, 2005: 141). The refusal of victims of trafficking to start programmes of rehabilitation and reintegration, as well as the return of victims to sex work, being retrafficked immediately after their repatriation or after rehabilitation programmes are problematic for NGOs and their representation of the victim of trafficking. Both the return to sex work and the refusal to start rehabilitation programmes are interpreted as due either to incomplete psychic recovery or to trauma. Migration also becomes reinterpreted as a dysfunctional decision, taken at a moment which coincides with a family crisis (IOM quoted in Harrington, 2005: 189). Prostitution also becomes pathologized: 'unless compelled by poverty, past traumas or substance addiction, few women would voluntarily engage in prostitution and are thus victims of trafficking' (Donna Hughes quoted in Agustin, 2005: 105).

The reading of trauma and psychological disorder into women's actions suspends critical considerations of their situation, their relation to the 'rehabilitation and reintegration' programmes or to the prospects for the future that such programmes define. Although several NGOs have gradually started to realise the importance of work for 'reintegration programmes', women remain in a zone of labour precariousness, hardly different from their pre-migration situations. Given time and financial constraints, NGOs in Romania are able to offer three-month qualification courses for hairdressing or tailoring.[15] In my discussions with one of the social workers from ADPARE – an NGO working with returned women, as part of the IOM victim assistance strategy – it has become evident that they struggle to help women make ends meet.[16]

Rather than raising difficult questions, psychologized disorderly behaviour 'normalises' resistance and integrates acts of refusal by trafficked women into a cycle of traumatic experience-traumatic effects. A report by a Swedish NGO emphasizes that it is 'normal for the woman victim of trafficking to be aggressive to the whole world as well as to the consultant. Her feelings are mixed anger, guilt, joy, helplessness, sadness' (Kvinnoforum, 1999: 17). In guidelines for shelters that would accommodate trafficked women, the Romanian NGO Alternative sociale has annexed a short description of the psychological disorders that victims of trafficking can manifest: acute stress reaction, adaptive reaction, post-traumatic stress reaction and, the most severe, Stockholm syndrome (Alternative sociale, 2005a). The Stockholm syndrome refers to the victim's emotional attachment to the abuser. Any reaction that the victim might have or the refusal to identify or acknowledge a trafficker can be read as a form of traumatic empathy with the abuser.[17] Moreover, the Stockholm Syndrome as the creation of an emotional bond with the abuser can account for women beginning to work with traffickers and becoming 'complicit in the trafficking process through such activities as supervising other trafficking victims and even engaging in the recruitment of women into the commercial sex industry' (Minnesota Advocates for Human Rights, 2005).

In Romania, a recent overview of human trafficking, circulated to judges and other professionals who deal with human trafficking, dedicates a whole chapter to the psychological consequences of trauma. This chapter was prepared by the director of Alternative sociale, one of most active NGOs on anti-trafficking in the eastern part of the country (Alternative sociale, 2005b). NGO reports now draw up statistics of the psychological disorders that victims of trafficking suffer from: psychological traumas, poor sleep, sleeplessness, fears, anxiety, depression, suicidal thoughts, frustration, self-recrimination, feelings of guilt, nightmares, poor concentration, low physical/intellectual working capacity, low self-esteem and loss of life perspectives. To these psychological disorders are added other medical conditions and different forms of alcohol dependency. An ICMPD training manual for judges and prosecutors in South Eastern Europe provides case studies that identify symptoms of traumatic disorders in victims of trafficking. Masha, the imaginary name for a victim of trafficking in this scenario, exhibits the complete alignment of bodily and psychological reactions.

> Masha is a Russian woman arrested in a raid in a brothel in Germany. She has many bruises and burns on her body. Several of her teeth are missing. Masha does not speak any German but is very hostile towards the police. When a male translator is brought in, she either refuses or is unable to speak. She begins to visibly shake. Later, a female translator is brought in. Masha says that she is not a prostitute and that her bruises and burns were entirely her fault. When pressed on the issue, she says she knows that some girls in the brothel have been raped or beaten but that she does not know who they are. Masha says she is the girlfriend of the man who owns the brothel. She refuses to identify any of the owners or known associates by name. When Masha is told that the owners of the brothel are connected with an international criminal network, she refuses to acknowledge that she knows them.
>
> (ICMPD, 2004: 141)

Although the training manual does not provide any answers, Masha displays symptoms of the Stockholm syndrome. The psychological symptoms disqualify her actions as traumatic reactions and the non-acceptance of reality. Psychological expertise also reinforces gender boundaries and stereotypes and suspends any claims made by women as pathological.

> Victims of trafficking have been perceived to communicate through seduction. Seductiveness appears to be their only way to make requests. If we accept this to be true, we must not judge or condemn the women's actions, because the reasons for this behaviour are to be found in the psychological exploitation of the victims.
>
> (Tudorache, 2004: 20)

Therefore, trafficked women cannot be seen as speaking or acting politically, but only clinically. Governing trafficked women through risk technologies not only constitutes them as risky, or as vulnerable categories able to pose renewed migratory risks, but it also deprives their actions of political potential. What can their refusal to undertake NGO programmes, to return 'voluntarily' to their countries of origin or to testify in court against their traffickers mean when these refusals are only forms of temporary disorders entailed by a trauma?

The pathologization of the subject allows for the reincorporation of resisting forms of agency within the dominant modes of governing. Several researchers have attempted to challenge the representations of trafficking and of trafficked women as victims to be deported by providing different narratives of the women's experiences. They have shown that women are agents of their own destiny. Andrijasevic has analysed trafficking as a migratory project, which women undertake as autonomous agents (Andrijasevic, 2003, 2004). In viewing trafficked women as migrants and not as victims, she argues for women's agency in the trafficking process (Andrijasevic, 2004: 10). The constitution of victimhood is a gendered representation of women as innocent and passive (see also Agustin, 2005). Yet, these narratives that give voice to silenced subjects fit the representation of migrants who are not victims of trafficking but have undertaken autonomous migratory projects. Trafficked women are dis-identified from the category of migrants by suffering as well as psychological risk factors. Autonomous migrants who undertake such risky projects can only be illegal migrants to be deported. The recapturing of women's agency in the process of trafficking and the 'serious thinking and planning that [they] put into migrating' (Andrijasevic, 2004: 10) fit with the representation of migration as rational actors, calculating their chances of success and failure.

Narrating women's subjective experiences risks shifting the representation of trafficking as victimization towards the illegal migration discourse. Moreover, the narratives of specific subjects are always partial, unable to provide a 'universal' point of view. As researchers discover stories of migratory projects and autonomy, NGOs and other authorities tell stories of victimhood and suffering. Yet, in trial archives for example, it is clear that both stories are always already there: women's narratives would contain both elements of autonomous actions and elements of victimization and exploitation.[18] Through the institutional encounter with the police, attorneys and judges, different elements are filtered out. The element of autonomy is discarded, as a certain understanding of victimization is drawn out of the complexity of situations of exploitation.

While one can be critical of the message that narratives of victimhood convey,[19] it is important not to dismiss these narratives, but to understand how they are filtered out of a multiplicity of elements and the complexity of women's stories. One cannot simply deny that stories of exploitation and severe physical and psychological abuse simply happen. One cannot also deny that migratory projects which view 'trafficking' as part of a larger project towards gaining financial autonomy are also real experiences. We are here in a situation that Badiou has defined as 'indiscernibility of knowledge' (Badiou, 2004a: 147). All these subjective experiences are equally real and equally true. By disentangling them from their situations, women as victims and women as autonomous migrants buttress different technologies of government. These experiences can be mobilized for specific institutional interests (for example, the IOM project of orderly migration or the EU policy for reducing illegal migration or the punitive logic of criminal law).

Knowledge of women's subjective experiences can become integrated in the governmentality of trafficking through risk assessment. The mobilization of subjective experiences for the purposes of governing trafficking does not render these experiences untrue. If women are re-identified as risky beings, this does not disconfirm their experiences of suffering. Reformulating this experience as one of migratory projects cannot be universalized, and is limited by the very experiences of those who have encountered forms of violence. These different narratives cannot also be seen as simply subjective experiences of violence, as it is impossible to decide which violence counts as violence and which one is integrated by the subject's adaptive capabilities. As long as we remain captive to different narratives and different subjective experiences, the 'indiscernibility of knowledge' is made discernible in different expert accounts of what counts as trafficking, its victims and the interventions necessary to govern this phenomenon. Experts, practitioners and academics will keep disputing which category of victims is representative of what human trafficking means.

How are we to find a way out of these disputes about expert knowledge? The next chapter locates resistance in relation to political events. Political events cut across the various accounts of subjective violence and the multiple subjective experiences. Resistance to forms of knowledge and technologies can be reappropriated within the dominant modes of governmentality. Women's resistance to return or inscription in programmes of rehabilitations has been rendered pathological through a construction of psychological disorders that would dispose women to abnormal conduct. Other narratives that attempt to undermine this pathological subjectivation of women cannot unmake the construction of trafficking and the representative category of suffering and traumatized victims. Stories of autonomous and rational migrants are the 'other' of trafficking, against which trafficking has been defined from the beginning, by means of dis-identification from illegal migration. These narratives attempt to reverse the situation and claim autonomous migration as the normal, while trafficking speaks of the abnormal practices and violence that states inflict upon migrants.

Subjectivity is therefore what is challenged and contested by governmental practices. On the one hand, different institutions attempt to represent and subjectify trafficked women and, on the other, women themselves challenge these forms of subjectivity as abjection. Yet, I have shown that the psychologization or pathologization of subjectivity is problematic for the possibility of political action. Similarly, reclaiming rational action risks falling back upon existing categories of willing and forced migrants. The situation of 'indiscernibility of knowledge' appears as a situation of indiscernibility of subjectivity. What form of subjectivity could traverse this situation of indiscernibility?

Conclusion

By continuing the critical engagement with the humanitarian approach to human trafficking, I have shown that reducing governmentality to an analysis of fields obscures the way practices have a logic that can function independently of actors. While NGOs strive to impose specific representations of women and victimhood, these representations cannot be divorced from the cohort of institutional practices that represent women for the purposes of risk prevention. Women can never remain pure presence, but need to be known for the purposes of governmentality. If governing a social problem requires knowledge of the phenomenon and of those involved, descriptions of trafficked women mobilize clinical and psychological knowledge for the purposes of prevention. Women's biographies always show them as already predisposed to trauma and victimization, always already victims of a violent past (family abuse, domestic and institutional violence, incest, alcoholism, lack of education, etc.). Yet, a traumatic and violent past also bears the stigma of potential delinquent behaviour in the future. The clinical and psychological knowledge will buttress the hypothesis of such reoffending behaviour, namely of women undertaking migratory projects. Trafficked women appear as risky beings, whose behaviour needs to be controlled and directed away from the future of illegal migration or retrafficking. Prevention is therefore not only targeted at potential risk groups in countries of origin, but particularly at the group of victims who could be retrafficked.

As the representation of the problem of trafficking and of the future actions devised to manage it depends upon the subject's actions and the detailed knowledge about who the victims of trafficking are, the subject/abject has been placed at the core of unmaking security. The point of coherence, but also of instability in the interventions to govern human trafficking is the victim of trafficking. The question of unmaking security practices has been rephrased as a question of the form of subjectivity that can support such practices of resistance. Governmental practices foster and depend upon a certain representation of the subject, on forms of subjectivity and conducts that are consonant with the interventions deployed. The possibility of unmaking security practices has related the subject's resistance to the direct and immediate practices which attempt to define her and direct her actions. Yet, the victims' resistance appears only as pathological reactions, as traumatic irrational actions. The psychological knowledge that informs the knowledge of risk depoliticizes women's resistance through the constitution of psychological abjection and the denial of their actions as endowed with political meaning. When academic research attempts to contest the representation of women as victims, it often reasserts the representation of trafficking as a form of illegal migration. Moreover, such alternative approaches or discourses cannot obliterate the stories of victimhood that exist side by side to stories of migration.

Resisting subjects are simultaneously at a distance from institutional actors and institutionally mediated through the constitution of subjectivity in governmental practices. Particular subjectivities can become reappropriated in the division of subjects that governmentality employs. The particularity of subjectivity and the refusal of dominant forms of subjectivity do not manage to disrupt the legitimate practices of security. As Žižek has indicated in his criticism of Butler, a politics of rupture cannot be thought from the standpoint of particular subjectivities. The complexity of subject positions only makes them disputable in a context of 'indiscernibility of knowledge'.

5
The Politics of Equality

Strategies of unmaking security depend upon the dynamics of practices and representations that redeploy and reappropriate alternative discourses, ethical considerations and subjective resistance within the security *dispositif*. The humanitarian approach insidiously transforms into the governmentality of risk and folds victimhood upon risk factors, bringing trafficked women to their initial status of 'dangerous others'. If suffering is redeployed for the purposes of governmentality, the (imaginary) encounter with the other's suffering body can become part of the management of social problems. Rather than simply related to actors and institutional positions, this reconfiguration of pity can be understood from within the *dispositif* of security that redefines the subjects to be governed.

The previous chapter has shown that documenting the subject's resistance does not necessarily challenge security practices. As traumatized subjects, trafficked women can refuse practices of rehabilitation that discipline and order their behaviour. These refusals are seen as simply symptomatic of a disorder to be 'treated' just like the trauma of trafficking. I have suggested that the institutional mediation of subjectivity is constitutive of the dilemma of resistance that does not disrupt, but functions as a failure that will only spur more governmental interventions to deal with it. Particular forms of subjectivity can always be integrated within forms of governmentality.

I have also suggested that ethical relationality is always translated for the purposes of governmentality and 'infinite responsibility' can be brought under the sway of what is. An analysis of practices unpacks 'what is', the *dispositif* of security that reappropriates forms of resistance and redeploys alternative discourses and strategies. Yet, how can we think politics that can disrupt 'what is', the *dispositif* of security, its interventions and representations constitutive of abjection and its imaginary future?

Ethics propose to transgress the 'state of things', what is, by principles that exceed their governmental incorporation. However, to become politically practicable, these principles need to engage with what is and thus become entangled in the messiness and limitations they tried to avoid. Political strategies and new political possibilities are limited by their anchorage within particular representations of the subject. The imperative to know who trafficked women are precedes politically the possibilities of engagement and leads to the reincorporation of resistance under the banner of governmentality. Resistance risks being re-embedded in the symbolic system, it can be reappropriated in the *dispositif* of security. The impossibility of resistance is due – in Joan Copjec's superb argumentation – to an understanding of the system as positivity. Copjec has reproached Foucault for renouncing the language model in his analysis of power in favour of the battle model. If power functions on the model of war,[1] then there is no negation at work anymore, nothing that transcends the space of social relations. With language, however, there is always the unsaid, the meaning that cannot be captured and risks undermining the whole edifice of what is said. What Foucault shows is always the visible or that which can be made visible within the existing configuration of power.

As the dilemma of numbers made clear, counting trafficked people is one of the strategies of making visible that is never sufficient. More knowledge and more adequate representations are thought to potentially translate into better numbers and more reliable statistics. Copjec suggests a more radical dilemma of counting as making visible: some things cannot be counted, although they are there. They cannot be counted because they negate what is counted and therefore what counts in the situation. Counting is also about the possibility of belonging – to be counted means to be visible, to belong. In this sense, the scandal of the refugee refers to the aporia of counting. Counting should incorporate everybody, but there are always those who cannot be counted because they do not belong and do not count. Visibility needs to be understood as split, as both presentation and representation. In the war model, one exposes these heterogeneous representations and their historical modifications. In the language model, something transcends (and thereby negates) representation. If a governmental analysis focused on the model of war leads to the reproduction of the security *dispositif*, how can the negation of security be theorized beyond representation?

In Foucault, whatever is not visible is so because it is rendered invisible by power. As the invisible exists only in relation to power, when made visible, it can be reintegrated within power relations. The migratory projects of women who become victims of trafficking and their desire to find work are rendered invisible in the encounter with institutional power. Different elements and stories are made visible, stories of abuse, coercion or betrayed trust. Yet, the retrieval of the migration element and of agency, either through interviews or from archival sources, does not challenge the constitution of human trafficking as a criminal law issue or as a migration issue. Trafficked women are either victims or they are illegal migrants; different inscriptions would activate different interventions. We have seen that these interventions can be understood as security practices, as risk management of disorderly conducts.

Foucault's strategy of making heard silenced voices and stories rendered invisible, a strategy shared by feminist and poststructuralist approaches, does not challenge the functioning of the system. Making more explicit the positions and conflicts within the structure of power/knowledge does not say anything about what constitutes the negation of security, what it cannot incorporate except at the risk of radical disruption. Negation has been interpreted either as excess, transgression or the Real. For psychoanalytical theory, negation is the generative principle of a system, the Real that cannot be incorporated in the symbolic and imaginary construction of reality.[2] Deconstruction implies an idea of excess in thinking the ethico-political moment. Yet, it is unclear how these theories translate the relation between the excess and the symbolic system through processes of subjectivation. Although psychoanalysis is analogical in its analysis of societal processes and the formation of subjects, the two remain loosely linked.

I shall reformulate the concept of excess by relating it to subject formation and de-formation. The *dispositif* of security could only be stabilized around the constitution of the subject/abject. Badiou's theorization of the excess as both a subject and a political event, it will be argued, elucidates what is at stake in a disruption which would be heterogeneous to the dominant state of things. The excess allows us to understand how political action surpasses the conditions of possibility of a system, while being linked with processes of becoming subject beyond the forms of subjection inscribed in the system. Next, I explore the implications of his theory for thinking what politics out of security can mean for trafficking in women.

Politics of excess: subjects and events

Badiou offers a conceptualization of politics that is not limited to what is, to exploring power relations. Politics – understood as a disruption of the dominant situation, its representations and modes of interventions – is not of the domain of the possible, it is not linked with the failures of different strategies and the complexity of interventions and representations that cannot entirely constitute subjects. Foucauldians grappling with the concept of resistance have associated the possibility of resistance with the complexity of interventions and representations and the dissonances these entail in the constitution of subjectivity. As the subject is always constituted through complex and sometimes contradictory interventions, the subject experiences a tension and resists (Ransom, 1997). Even if the *dispositif* is an unstable configuration, always redirected by the subject's resistance, resistance can be incorporated under the imperative to govern 'what is'. Badiou's politics, on the other hand, is not a politics of the possible, but of the impossible, of the excess that does not and cannot be part of what is. A politics of the excess, in Žižek's words, is about enacting the impossible, namely what appears as impossible within the coordinates of the existing symbolic system (Žižek and Daly, 2004: 80).

Thinking the excess is not exclusively linked with Badiou's philosophy, but also spans Derrida's deconstructivist philosophy and the psychoanalytical theory indebted to Lacan. It can even be considered the main hypothesis of poststructuralist Marxism: every event that breaks the reproducibility of social structures already presupposes a certain ontological fissure, an inherent lack/excess that prevents the closure (Palti, 2003: 464). For Badiou, politics searches for the most radical consequences of the symptoms and therefore works against the structure (2004a: 84). In this sense, it is opposed to psychoanalysis which tries to reduce symptoms and works towards accommodating the subject to the structure (Badiou, 2004a: 84). While a psychoanalytical approach could illuminate the functioning of security practices in relation to the imaginary of security that sustains them and its role in the constitution of the subject, the overlapping of certain psychoanalytical terms and concepts with the clinical governmental representations of trafficked women has made me wary of a concept of politics that makes use of 'trauma' or of an unbearable encounter with the Real. Derrida's excess is the aporia constitutive of any system; the aporia is not solvable, it can only show the impossibility of closure of a system (Derrida, 1993). This impossibility remains non-negotiable and impracticable politically. The ethics of infinite responsibility was excessive to any instantiation of responsibility and remained trapped in this impossibility, unable to negotiate its own relation to that of an existing order.

In Badiou's theory, the excess also works as negation of how the symbolic order functions. He has argued that situations can never be closed; their definition as sets shows them as infinite, so that they can never be exhaustively represented.[3] The excess of symbolic order is that which is absent and not representable. This excess is a space inhabited by subjects who become political in their connection to an event. For Badiou, the excess is the non-representable in a socio-historical situation. I have shown that governmental interventions depend on the inexhaustible and continuous need for representation of the phenomenon of trafficking and the subjects to be governed. Governing human trafficking requires an understanding of what trafficking is (hence its constitution as a specific field) and a description of subjects. Against governmentality, politics refers to that which cannot be represented, but can only present its own existence (Badiou, 1985). The excess separates the thinking of politics from an analysis of reality as what is, as power relations that shape the social order. Therefore, for Badiou, politics cannot be considered as 'the exercise of power', as with Foucault (Badiou, 1985: 54). Given the immanence of resistance to power in Foucault, politics could be understood as both 'governmental' and 'anti-governmental', concerned both with the functioning and effects of power and with emancipation from particular systems of power (Hindess, 1998: 54). We have seen, however, that 'anti-governmental' politics understood as resistance are not heterogeneous to the situation, but are redeployed as governmental interventions. What Foucault lacks is a theorization of resistance that is not of the order of what is. Furthermore, with both Foucault and Butler resistance is individuated, entangled in the processes that constitute subjects. Badiou argues for a politics of collective subjectification. The subject of politics is no longer the individual, but the collective.

Badiou's politics is different from the Foucault-inspired politics that sheds light on practices of power, analyses configurations of security and risk and makes explicit the existence of gaps or contradictions where the resistance of the subject can gain ground. True political sequences are 'excepted' from the social (Hallward, 2003: 26). Politics is not a question of what is, but of what can be brought to bear upon what is, to disrupt it. Politics does not show the structure of things, politics is that which happens, which interrupts the functioning of the system. Politics cannot be derived from the order of necessity; it is of the order of what happens. Politics is about searching within a situation for 'a possibility *that the dominant state of things does not allow to be seen*' (Badiou, 2004a: 82, emphasis in original).

Unpacking the security *dispositif* that governs human trafficking through risk interventions which make up women as specific categories of risky victims, such a politics remains of the order of what is. It locates existing interventions and representations, but is unable to gauge the transformative potential of any practices. If women refuse to be victims, then they are either illegal migrants to be expediently deported, or traumatized victims who have not come to terms with the violence inflicted upon them. What would disrupt these forms of representation and the interventions they buttress, what would unmake the depoliticization of victims of trafficking and their subjection to practices of security?

An evental politics does away with governmental representations and is harnessed to the excess of symbolic order or, in Badiou's terms, a socio-historical situation. Žižek has succinctly and explicitly formulated the meaning of excess in Badiou's philosophy:

> The 'Excess' ... takes two forms. On the one hand, each state of things involves at least one excessive element which, though clearly belonging to the situation, is not 'counted' by it, properly included in it (e.g., the 'nonintegrated' rabble in a societal situation): this element is presented, but not re-presented. On the other hand, there is an excess of re-presentation over presentation: the agency which brings about the passage from situation to its state (State in society) is always in excess relative to what it structures ... [State power] never simply and transparently re-presents society, but acts as a violent intervention in what it re-presents.
>
> (Žižek, 1998)[4]

The specificity of Badiou's position consists in this doubling of excess, as both the element excessive to the situation and the event that ruptures it. Politics is linked with the localization of excessive subjects in the margin of a situation and of forms of action that would disrupt the situation. Excessive subjects are terms that cannot be organized as part of a situation (Hallward, 2003: 100), while politics is defined as evental excess. Before Badiou, Deleuze had also understood that there is another challenge to power relations that is not framed as subjective resistance. Deleuze is worth quoting at length here as he clarifies the difference between subjectification (in my terminology)[5] and events:

> It definitely makes sense to look at the various ways individuals and groups constitute themselves as subjects through processes of subjectivation: what counts in such processes is the extent to which, as they take shape, they elude both established forms of knowledge and the dominant forms of power. Even if they in turn engender new

forms of power or become assimilated into new forms of knowledge ...
One might equally well speak of new kinds of event, rather than
processes of subjectivation: events that can't be explained by the
situations that give rise to them, or into which they lead.

(Deleuze, 1995: 176)

Unlike Deleuze, Badiou connects processes of subjectification and
events. Subjectification is not simply resistance to relations of power,
but the creation of a collective political subject that suspends classifica-
tions and representations. A political subject emerges through 'fidelity'
to a political event. This subject comes into being through a specific
relationality to the socio-historical situation. Badiou does not want to
replicate an analysis of power/knowledge, as politics is subtraction from
history, that is from any particular regimes of power/knowledge, a particular status quo or a situation (Badiou, 1992: 36). A situation is composed
of the knowledge that circulates in it and assigns a place to different
subsets/categories. 'The state of the situation is the operation which,
within the situation, codifies its parts as sub-sets' (Badiou, 2004b: 154).

The 'state of the situation' can be conceptualized as similar to Foucault's
notion of power/knowledge or governmental practices. Although Badiou
has been criticized for lacking a concept of hegemony à la Gramsci or of
power à la Foucault, Badiou's definition of the 'state of the situation'
can be read as governmental, as practices of counting and representing
categories of subjects. After all, Badiou makes clear that the situation is
structured by virtue of knowledge. If the situation is defined by knowledge
and representation, the event goes beyond power/knowledge. 'Events
are irreducible singularities, the "beyond-the-law" of situations' (Badiou,
2002a: 44). Both excessive subjects and events are non-representable in
the order or structure of the situation. Contrary to Foucault, subjectivation (becoming subjected to power relations and a constituted subject)
is not immanent to subjectification (becoming a subject by resisting
such power relations and refusing the given constitution), as resistance
was immanent to power. Subjectification occurs through the mediation
of a political event and fidelity to it.

Collective subjectification involves excessive subjects that are not
represented in a situation, subjects whose existence can only appear as
non-existence, as negation in a situation. Badiou makes a distinction
between presentation (being in a situation) and representation (the
process of counting the elements of a situation). Representation means
the imposition of consistency upon the inconsistency (disorder) of presentation. Every situation is doubly structured: there is presentation and

representation (Badiou, 1988: 110). The glossary to *L'Être et l'événement* defines the excess as the difference without measure or the power difference between the state of the situation and the situation, or between representation and presentation. Visibility is split between the two; what is visible can be presented, but not necessarily represented with the governmental resources a situation offers. Governing a socio-historical situation is a form of representation that reduces the disorder and multiplicity of presentation. Governing human trafficking can be thought in similar terms, as an attempt to reduce its complexity and politics into a series of categorizations and descriptions whose boundaries should be clearly drawn.

Political events also think the new in a situation. According to Badiou, 'to think the new in situation, we also have to think the situation, and thus we have to think what is repetition, what is the old, what is not new, and after that we have to think the new' (Badiou and Bosteels, 2005: 253). Unlike with Butler, transformation does not emerge out of the iteration of performative acts. The event or the new requires an understanding of the situation, as structured by relations of power/knowledge. What is important is not to fold the event upon the relations of power/knowledge and their tensions or frictions. If power relations produce incoherences and inadequacies that can rupture the subject from her subjection, this would mean equating the event to power/knowledge and bringing forms of collective subjectification back within the gaps of the situation.

Through the event, political subjectification transcends the logic of the situation and suspends its forms of representation and subjection. Hence, subjectification is not a question of inventing other forms of subjectivity, as these would be trapped within the particularity of a situation. Creating different forms of identification for trafficked women does not destabilize existing narratives about who trafficked women and illegal migrants as 'rational entrepreneurs' are. As the previous chapter has argued, women remain risky beings, embodying the danger of 'rational' projects of illegal migration. The particularity of identification brings it under the sway of governmental techniques, makes it representable and countable in the state of the situation.

Excessive subjects cannot be reintegrated within particular representations, as they become political through an event that extricates them from particular governmental forms of representation. An event is attached to the *élément surnuméraire* of a situation or, in Žižek's terms, to the symptomatic element that has no proper place in the situation, although it belongs to it (Žižek, 1999b: 140). The *proletariat* in Badiou's much-favoured example functions as this excessive element of the capitalist system. 'To *think* a situation [*penser une situation*] is always to go toward that which, in it is the least covered or protected by the shelter the general regime of things offers it' (Badiou, 2000: 85).

A political situation of migration, for example, needs to be thought of from the point of view of the *sans-papiers*, the Israeli-Palestinian situation from that of the vulnerable Palestinians. In a situation, the element which is least sheltered is 'like a point of exile where *it is possible* that something, finally, might happen' (Badiou, 2000: 85, emphasis in original). Despite the strict theoretical analysis of the excess, Badiou's political analyses often go back to a rather habitual understanding of vulnerability. While workers were represented in the historical situation of industrial capitalism, the *proletariat* did not exist as a collective subject and could only become so through its identification as excluded and abject other of the capitalism system. Excessive subjects cannot be defined in the terms given by the state of the situation. Disruptions in the situation of trafficking can be linked to the emergence of a subject that is the negation of the situation and that can therefore reconfigure the whole situation. A politics of emancipation does not start with victims of trafficking, but with subjects that would be excessive to this situation. Who are these excessive subjects?

The position of excessive subjects has been cogently articulated by Žižek: '[w]here the logic of excluding a particular group is shown to be part of a wider problem, then you get a kind of distilled version of what is wrong with society as such' (Žižek and Daly, 2004: 142). If not formulated from the position of excessive subjects, but from that of a closed totality, the event becomes a simulacrum; it is reactionary and not progressive politics (Badiou, 2002a). Thus, no change of the situation of migrants from the bias of a societal plenitude (for example what would be better for British people) can qualify as an event. Nazism was also the prototype of the simulacrum as it was an event that formulated fidelity to a social plenitude (the German people). Schmitt's closure of the exception upon the substantive political community of German people would be a simulacrum in this sense.

The event qualifies as *an immanent break*: it proceeds in the situation and it surpasses the situation (Badiou, 2002a: 42). As the event is a disruption, a challenge to the structuring of the situation, it also supersedes the situation and cannot be explainable in the terms of the situation. This disruption is not any formal rupture, its content is what distinguishes an event from its simulacrum. A political event is not only formulated from the position of excessive subjects, but it makes universalizable claims and it enacts equality. It is through its principles, I argue, that political events appear as heterogeneous to practices of security.

If security functions as 'barred universality', practices of security suspend the imaginary of everybody being an equal partaker of security. Challenging practices of security requires a double instantiation of universality. The event addresses everybody equally and is itself a verification of equality as the universal principle of politics. Unlike governmental analyses, an event is not caught within existing representations and their mobilization by power. The enactment of equality requires subjects to dispense with the naming that is ascribed by the situation and changes the descriptions of subjects in a situation. If ethical principles were radically different from the situation, the principles of an event are radically connected with the situation.

The situation of migration, trafficking and excessive women

The first chapter showed that the literature on trafficking tries to subsume the definition of trafficking either under the definitions of migration, prostitution, organized crime or human rights. By ignoring the security framework, humanitarian approaches could not transform the structure within which trafficking is defined and managed. The imbrication of representations of suffering and risk interventions transform trafficked women into 'risky beings', equally subject to pity and compassion, as well as containment and disciplining. To tackle the question of how to unmake security and think politics out of security, I have considered desecuritization, emancipation, ethics and resistance, and analysed their impasses. Now I turn to what politics understood as excess can mean for the situation of trafficking in women. If the phenomenon of trafficking is a socio-historical situation, who are the excessive subjects starting from which an event can lead to the restructuring of the situation and its constitutive practices of security?

As we have seen, every situation is doubly structured as presentation and representation. In Badiou's terms, the situation of trafficking is represented by a specific counting of trafficked women: those who are worthy of pity and those who are not, those who are useful for legal enforcement procedures against traffickers and those who are not. Those who have experienced horrific physical suffering at the hands of their traffickers are to be deemed worthy of pity. The counting of a situation leads to extremely inegalitarian positions. For example, the

Poppy Project in the UK, set up to provide help for all victims of trafficking, is available to women who were brought to the UK and forced to work in prostitution and who have come forward, willing to cooperate with the authorities (Home Office, 2004: 81).[6] Most NGO projects in Europe also work with the distinction between victims of trafficking and migrants. In its manual on developing National Referral Mechanisms (cooperative arrangements at the national level for promoting the human rights of trafficked persons), the OSCE places the process of 'locating and identifying likely victims of trafficking' at the core of anti-trafficking strategies (OSCE, 2004: 16). The identification of victims of trafficking is essential for counting and representing subjects in a situation.

Despite the injunction to achieve adequate victim identification and the detailed procedures specified for this purpose, victim identification appears as a fundamental problem, due to (or rather despite) the recognition that 'those caught up in human trafficking often do not want to reveal their status and experiences to the authorities (OSCE, 2004: 17). Those who do not identify themselves as victims or cannot be identified as such by organizations mandated to engage in the anti-trafficking struggle do not exist in the situation. Similarly, the EU proposal for a short-term residence permit also discriminates among categories of 'worthy' and 'unworthy' trafficked women (European Commission, 2002a). Those who are willing to cooperate with the authorities will receive a temporary residence permit. The granting of permits depends both on the decision of the authorities whether the presence of the victim is useful for the investigation and prosecution of suspects and on their judgement that victims have genuinely severed all links with the traffickers and are really prepared to cooperate. Those who are not useful or are not judged as 'real' victims are unworthy of residence permits. They disappear therefore from the situation as subjects to be counted.

Thinking the situation of trafficking along the lines of an evental politics starts from the excessive subjects of a situation. Locating these elements is by no means equivalent to a contest between victims. What matters here is to see politics out of security in relation to subjectivity. Who are the women that continually fall out of the representational practices undertaken by different authorities? I contend that these excessive elements are illegal migrant sex workers. All other representations of trafficked women are exclusive of this element who-should-not-be-there. 'Real' victims of trafficking are worthy of pity, victims to be rehabilitated and reintegrated in society, or victims traumatized by their experiences of violence. Illegal migrant sex workers do not deny the multiplicity of representations of trafficked women, but constitute the very limit of these representations. They are not supposed to be there, they are illegitimate entrants in the situation of trafficking, excessive migrants who pursue economic interests. At the same time, they are the spectre of the very representation of victims of trafficking from which the latter must be repeatedly dis-identified.

Excessive subjects enter into a different relation with other elements of the situation than the subject/abject discussed so far. Contrary to the dichotomy of subject/abject, Badiou's situation can integrate all these elements and define their interrelations. According to him, there are three modes of appearance in a situation: normality, excrescence (*excroissance*), and singularity (or excess) (Badiou, 1988: 125). A normal element is both presented and represented in the situation. In the situation of trafficking, there is a double construction of normal subjects. On the one hand, there are the legally resident sex workers, the ones who are both presented and represented as endowed with agency. Every element of the category of legally resident sex workers belongs to the situation by virtue of their quality of citizenship. On the other, there are the victims of trafficking, those who are presented and represented as coerced and abused. The normal subjects of a situation do not refer to the governmental meaning of normalization, but to what is taken to be the 'norm' of existence in a situation. Excrescence is represented but not presented in a situation. For example, the state and its institutions are represented but not present as such in the situation of trafficking. The police, immigration officials or even NGOs do not appear as elements of the situation of trafficking in the same way that traffickers or migrants do. Singularity is a term that is present in the situation but not represented in it. Such an element only exists in the situation as a fundamental anomaly (Hallward, 2003: 99), as an excessive subject. By not being represented, these subjects are excessive to the ordering power of the state of the situation.

Badiou's theory of the situation can be used as a cartography of the situation of trafficking. The situation appears now as tripartite, with multiple relations established between the normal and the excrescent elements, the normal and the singular and the excrescent and the singular. This analysis of the situation goes beyond the dual forms of relationality that security studies have dealt with. The self/other or subject/abject relation was mediated through institutions, through the excrescent elements. Badiou's cartography provides us with tools to understand the differentiated relations between normal elements and institutions, between institutions and the anomalous elements and finally between normal elements and the anomalous.

Illegal migrants working as prostitutes are this element which is present in the situation but does not belong to it and is not represented as properly belonging to it. Or rather, it only belongs to the situation by virtue of negation. Illegal prostitutes are those who should not be prostitutes and also those who should not be there. Illegal prostitutes cannot belong either to the category of sex workers or to the category of (regular or legal) migrants. They are an impossible category in the situation of trafficking: illegal migrants cannot be prostitutes – they are suspected victims of trafficking; and vice versa, illegal prostitutes cannot be migrants, as they have been abused and coerced into it. The category of illegal migrant sex workers is consistently dismantled within representations of trafficking. Trafficked women are represented as either unwilling, forced prostitutes or as unwilling, forced migrants. They are thus integrated as a specific subcategory of prostitutes and migrants.

In a different situation, that of society and its moral boundaries, the prostitute herself might be 'excessive'. As Jo Bindman has formulated it, '[s]ex workers, usually referred to as prostitutes, have occupied an anomalous position in societies throughout history ... Outcast status denies them whatever international, national or customary protection from abuse is available to others as citizens, women, or workers' (Bindman, 1997). However, in the situation of trafficking, prostitutes are represented in the trafficking situation by virtue of their citizenship. Prostitution has a more uneasy relationship with workers' and women's rights. The prostitute is the other within the categorical other, 'woman' (Bell, 1994: 2). She is also the other of the 'worker', the one who is not willing to undertake proper work.

In the situation of trafficking, the excessive subject is the illegal migrant sex worker. Even if they can be counted in the situation as an innocent or coerced victims, forced prostitutes or unknowing migrants, this count cannot make sense of women who engage in illegal processes of migration for the purpose of work. Trafficked women overwhelmingly report an intention to migrate to find work (Corso and Trifiro, 2003). The category from which trafficked women are extracted is that of illegal sex workers. Yet, their constitution makes the category of illegal sex workers impossible. The work of trafficked women is not work, they are not willing migrants, they have been coerced, forced, abducted or simply misled; in short, migration for work cannot be part of the situation of trafficking. It only relegates women to the category of migrants who should not be there.[7] This is what is negated by the trafficking situation, although it is upon this very element that the construction of trafficking is built. Women who migrate for work are the symptomal element of the situation inasmuch as they are 'absence embodied' (Hallward, 2003: 90). Victims of trafficking emerge as a category only by the negation of the category of illegal migrant sex workers.

If prostitutes were excessive both to the representation of the worker and the representation of women, illegal sex workers are also excessive to the representation of the nation and state sovereign practices. The Home Office White Paper on migration, 'Secure Borders, Safe Haven' represents illegal sex workers as an excessive presence in a space that is forbidden to them (Home Office, 2002). Berman has shown that the particular combination of the movement, 'race' and gender of migrant East European sex workers turns them into both an external and internal threat by 'disrupt[ing] the ability of the state to adjudicate membership in the political community' (Berman, 2003: 59).

In the situation of trafficking, the prostitute becomes normalized against the representation of illegal sex workers. The prostitute becomes the normal case of the 'free' woman choosing its occupation against the potentially 'forced' foreign and illegal prostitute. Extracting the category of trafficked women from that of illegal sex workers generalizes suspicion to all foreign women who do sex work. The relation between the normal and the excessive elements is presented as one of antagonism. The arrival of large numbers of foreign prostitutes is apparently causing complaints among London prostitutes (The Economist, 2004: 30). The antagonistic representation of the relation between legal prostitutes (citizens or legally resident) and illegal sex workers reiterates security interventions by the state. In this case, division is explained by market logic. As there is competition between prostitutes for clients and prices are going down because of the 'cheaper and more varied offer' of foreign prostitutes, this statist distinction between legality and illegality is served to justify a 'monopoly' position of legal prostitutes. Any possible common fight between the legal and illegal prostitutes seems impossible in this situation. Yet, addressing everybody in the situation of trafficking is at the heart of evental politics.

Principles of an event

Political events do not only start from the excessive element of a situation. According to Badiou, they are not simply formal, but are given content by two principles: universality and equality. Through the mediation of events, subjects achieve forms of political subjectification that are predicated on universality and equality. If excessive subjects engage in the transformation of the situation from outside the *dispositif* of security, universality and equality suspend the possibility of incorporating resistance within governmental interventions and representations.

An evental politics informed by universality and equality is set at the antipode of a politics of formal contestation and agonism and the politics of formal exceptions. Agonism, as put forward by Chantal Mouffe or William Connolly, combines continual tension with respect for the adversary in a mode of 'restrained contestation among friends, lovers and adversaries who exercise reciprocal respect and self-limitation through mutual appreciation of the problematical bases from which they proceed' (Connolly, 1995: 29). Agonism, however, implies that those who would not be restrained have already been displaced, excluded or neutralized. A similar move is to be found in Schmitt, where the sovereign decision on the exception and the definition of politics as the equal relation between friend and enemy obscures Schmitt's treatment of the foe. The definition of politics as friend/enemy delegitimizes the foe or the internal enemy, against whom any measures can be taken. By delegitimizing the foe, Schmitt attempts to delegitimize all forms of collective action that that threaten to disrupt the existing order. He also closes down politics around the state 'as a system of preventive defence against the mass movements that form the basis of civil wars (of classes and of religions) and of revolutions' (Balibar, 1994: 16). If agonistic politics suspends the possibility of collective action, the exception closes down the disruption of existing order.

Evental politics is not just formal, as agonism and exceptionalism are. It is not everything that happens, not any form of resistance. As already argued, an event only emerges in connection to the excess of the situation and it is based on the principles of universality and equality. Badiou opposes all situations of domination by invoking a strictly egalitarian politics inscribed in the event. Equality needs to infuse a strict politics of non-domination that addresses everybody in a situation. The principle of equality sets evental politics at a distance from the politics of exception. The exception is a form of transgression itself, the transgression that is implied in the constitution of normality. The exception is instituted by sovereign decisions that primarily create a relation of inequality. Moreover, the presupposed equality between friend and enemy at the heart of exceptional politics needs to be understood in the context of the delegitimation of the foe. The equality of evental politics is not subject to closure. How are these two principles, universality and equality, to be understood?

Universality is understood only from within the situation and refers to an event that addresses every person present in the situation. This address is not in terms of the particularities of those present, but entails a 'subtraction' from particularity. Badiou agrees that the universal cannot mean the sublation of all particularity and in this sense joins the poststructuralist critiques against the domination of universals which are actually exclusive of particularities. Yet, Badiou's argument goes further in as much as he criticizes respect for particularities (Badiou, 2004b). Respect for particularity still has to construct hierarchies of particularities, to delimit good and bad particularities. The respect for difference or particularity only applies to those differences that are consistent with a tolerant identity (Badiou, 2002a: 24). The much-vaunted liberal concept of toleration is limited in its universal deployment by those who are not tolerant themselves. To translate it in security terms, anybody can claim security, except those who are deemed dangerous.

After the poststructuralist criticism of universality, Badiou's endorsement of the universal might strike us as old-fashioned, but it is a reaction to the problems that particularities have raised for poststructuralist political projects. After all, particularities are always a matter of government, and I have shown that the particular representations of victims of trafficking can be differentially integrated in a *dispositif* of security. Subjects of government are always classified and represented in their particularity. Badiou therefore maintains that 'every universal presents itself not as a regularization of the particular or of differences, but as a singularity that is subtracted from identitarian predicates; although obviously it proceeds via those predicates' (Badiou, 2004b: 145). The universal of the event proceeds through a subtraction from identitarian predicates and particular identifications that integrate subjects in a governmental regime.

In this sense, identity politics is a contradiction in terms (Hallward, 2002). An event disrupts a certain situation by virtue of a principle that needs to hold to all members of a situation. Identitarian predicates cannot hold for the whole of community, they cannot address everybody. Politics can therefore never be linked to a social or economic expressivity (La distance politique, 1991), to interests or positions within the social fabric. Moreover, identitarian predicates cannot break with the dominant forms of representation, as these are caught within governmental representations and interventions. Identities are particular and unequal, while politics is defined by the principles of universality and equality.

However, universality does not mean subordinating the particularity of political sequences to universal moral judgements (Hallward, 2003: 258) anymore than it means the sublation of particularities. Any assertion of the type 'violence is always wrong' or 'suffering is always bad' will blind us to the requirements of the political situation to which we should attend. The universal that Badiou has in mind can only emerge from the particularity of that situation; an event would only use the elements and tools internal to the situation and could not appeal to the universal principles of morality or ethics. As I have shown, there is no infinite responsibility to the other that applies independently of the particulars of a situation. Universality has to remain open, otherwise the event risks becoming a simulacrum. 'If the universal is for everyone' – Badiou implacably asserts – 'this is in the precise sense that to be inscribed within it is not a matter of possessing any particular determination' (Badiou, 2004b: 151). Political movements need to be indifferent to social, national or sexual predicates, and be 'indifferent to differences' (Badiou, 2002a: 27). The indifference to differences consistently defines politics from the emergence of an event to the fidelity to its consequences. Events are subtracted from the regime of governmentality both formally through their linking to the excess and with respect to content through its principles.

The other principle that gives content to politics is equality. Equality is Badiou's chosen 'word for politics', due to its abstraction; equality does not presuppose a closure, does not qualify the terms it refers to and does not prescribe a territory on which to be exercised (Badiou, 1992: 242). One can think of governmental practices that structure and order the social as hierarchical relations and of the event as an egalitarian break. In a lecture on 'Philosophy and politics', Badiou has argued privileged equality against other possible words for politics, namely community and liberty (Badiou, 1992). Rethinking 'community' as more open and less exclusive has been an important way of reconceptualizing politics from liberal political theory to deconstruction and poststructuralism (Agamben, 1993; Nancy, 2001). However, Badiou has argued that the word is incapable of sustaining a politics of emancipation, even if it implies an impossible closure. 'In whichever form', he stresses, 'the word community still contains the supposition of a real being of justice in the form of a collective which is its own truth' (Badiou, 1992: 222). Community would therefore still contain the promise of a future embodiment of real politics. Embodied politics is not politics, as politics is of the order of what happens, of the event.

Similarly, Badiou is wary of freedom as a concept that has been captured by liberalism, by the ideology of commercial and parliamentary freedoms. Freedom can only become of use for politics if it is reconstructed from a different angle, if it is subordinated to another word (Badiou, 1992: 247). He does not attempt, however, to engage with the possibilities of thinking to what words liberty could be subordinated and directly moves on to favour equality. Equality is the word for politics in as much as it does not suppose an achieved totality (*totalité advenue*) (Badiou, 1992: 246). Given the importance that freedom holds in the context of security practices as well as the ontological principle of the modern subject, the next chapter will explore the relation between liberty, equality and security. For the purposes of this chapter, I unpack equality as the content-filling principle of politics.

Equality is de-linked from the social, from the idea of redistribution, solidarity or the state's solicitude towards difference, as any programmatic use would entail a closure of equality upon identity or community. Equality must not be equated with equality of status, of wages, of functions or even less with the supposedly egalitarian dynamics of contracts and reforms (Badiou, 2004a: 71). It cannot be objective and it has nothing to do with the social. Any definitional and programmatic approach to equality transforms it into a dimension of State action (Badiou, 2004a: 73). It is, according to Badiou, a political maxim, a prescription, not 'what we want or what we project, but what we declare in the heat of the event, here and now, as what it is, and not what it should be (Badiou, 2004a)[8]. It is a starting and not an ending point, the objective of political action. As equality cannot be closed and it is indifferent to all particularity and representation, it is universal. The poststructuralist criticism of universality has concerned its 'false' embodiment in a particularity that becomes the stand-in for universality. Through the assertion of equality, universality cannot be closed, but remains open to the contestation of equality. The principle of equality sustains the non-identitarian politics of excess. Is a politics informed by universality and equality possible in the situation of trafficking? I have shown that the situation has as its excessive subjects illegal migrant sex workers. Now I turn to how equality and universality have been formulated in this situation.

Work and equal subjects

Human trafficking has become visible as a form of illegal migration, transnational organized crime and prostitution, a threat to Western states and societies. At the same time, human trafficking has been gradually made visible as a threat to the women who have fallen prey to networks of traffickers. This logic of a double threat (both to states and women) led to an impasse as those who were supposed to be saved (trafficked women) were actually the illegal migrants and potential criminals that states were supposed to neutralize. The 'half-hearted' protection of women (Pearson, 2002: 56) was the logical outcome of prevention that recast women's suffering in the format of risk factors, thus folding back decriptions of victimhood upon risk profiles.

Rather than thinking human trafficking as a complex security issue, the challenge is to think it politically and especially to think an event that would disrupt the structure of the situation in which illegal migration and foreigners are constructed as a threat to Western states. Women's suffering, no matter how intense or life threatening, does not displace the security *dispositif* that governs illegal migration. Following Badiou, the situation of trafficking needs to be thought from the perspective of excessive subjects, of illegal migrant sex workers who are anomalous in the situation of trafficking. Although serving both as a pool for identifying victims of trafficking and as the spectre of the other from which victims must be dis-identified, illegal migrant prostitutes are not coextensive to victims of trafficking.

The shift from victims of trafficking as subjects of pity and suffering to illegal migrant sex workers moves us not only from the normal to the excessive elements but makes possible an understanding of the radical transformation in the trafficking situation. Although they exist in the situation either as 'bogus' victims, the 'happy hookers of Eastern Europe' (*The Spectator*, 25 April 2003: 25), or as illegal migrants, foreign prostitutes are represented in their negativity, as the ones who should not be here or who have got here only by being coerced, forced or deceived.[9] It is only logical that they should be either voluntarily sent 'home' or deported.

Although studies on trafficking have pointed out that anti-trafficking campaigns serve to reinforce stricter migration control and to make migrants even more vulnerable (Deimleiter, 2001; Sharma, 2003), their criticism has hardly had any impact on practices. Similarly, anti-trafficking campaigns have been shown to entail pernicious consequences for prostitutes (Doezema, 2002). Criticism against anti-trafficking measures on grounds of the effects that these entail for specific categories has not challenged the governmentality of trafficking. Such criticism has disallowed any commonality between sex workers and victims of trafficking, creating another form of antagonism besides the antagonism of the market. In this account, the rights of sex workers are threatened by the anti-trafficking campaigns, while the rights of victims of trafficking are threatened by the very existence of prostitution. Divisions create exclusions, thus re-entering the governmental *dispositif* of security.

The division between prostitutes and 'trafficked women' in terms of the effects that anti-trafficking measures have on prostitutes only serves to reinforce the state division between legal and illegal migrants/workers. The antagonism of the market and that of rights is embedded in a construction of migration as the more general context of human trafficking. As the European Commission's proposal for a Council Directive on short-term permit to stay for victims of trafficking has made clear, the permit is to be granted to victims of action to facilitate illegal migration who cooperate with the authorities. According to the proposal, these two actions (trafficking and illegal migration) overlap in practice and measures for the prevention of trafficking have the aim to step up the fight against illegal migration (European Commission, 2002a). Yet, if the problematization of trafficking is vectored by the construction of migration as a security issue, unmaking the security vectoring of trafficking requires the simultaneous unmaking of security practices vectoring trafficking, migration, prostitution, organized crime and human rights.

These divisions and antagonistic relations between sex workers, migrants and victims can be undone exactly from the perspective of illegal migrant sex workers. In the UK, repeated brothel raids have led to the detention of foreign sex workers under the suspicion of having been trafficked. On such an occasion, the *Evening Standard* reported that the women taken into custody were born abroad with most coming from Eastern European countries (quoted in CNN, 2001). In February 2001, the English Collective of Prostitutes tried to stop deportations of women who said they were working independently and earning money to support themselves and their families (International Prostitutes Collective, 2001). What has made possible this form of organization is the egalitarian claim that all prostitutes (be they foreign or not, illegal or not) are workers. This claim is clearly opposed to facts and 'impossible' in the current situation. Laura Agustin has argued that the legalization of prostitution as work does not do anything for the political situation of illegal migrants, as it keeps excluding them from the space of citizenship within which work rights are defined (Agustin, 2005). However, mobilizing the predicate of 'worker' intervenes in the space of citizenship the other way round: it is through work that one can claim rights of residence and citizenship.

As any political event first disrupts that situation, the claim that all prostitutes are workers not only re-names all actors in the situation, but in doing so, it makes differences indifferent. The differences that count for the governing of human trafficking, those between foreigner and native, legality and illegality are suspended. The event also names a wrong that is being done to prostitutes by not considering them as workers and not acknowledging them worker rights as well as for trafficking as a form of exploitation. As workers, foreign prostitutes make visible both the exploitation entailed by the recognition of only certain forms of work as legitimate and the inegalitarian state practices towards foreigners.

My argument that prostitution as work can function as a political event differs from the significant feminist literature which has debated the issue of whether prostitution is or should be work (for example O'Connell Davidson, 1998; Pateman, 1988). According to Maggie O'Neill, feminist analyses have pointed out the social inequalities to which prostitutes are prey and the reproduction of patriarchal hierarchies (1997). From this standpoint, prostitution could be revelatory of all social relations. In one approach, prostitution was thought to be a condition 'true' of all other women. The exploitation that took place in prostitution was just another form of the exploitation of women generally.

> Counting all women's work, including sex work, is a strategy for crossing the divide between sex workers and other women. It strengthens all women's case for compensation, in the form of increased benefits, wages, services and other resources, for the poverty and overwork which have been forced on most of us – the economic power to refuse all forms of prostitution.
>
> (English Collective of Prostitutes, 1997: 100)

When considered from a sociological point of view, such a declaration entails the question whether all other work is similar to prostitution. Much of the feminist debates have focused on the difference between prostitution and other types of work, and the main stances on prostitution are derived from this initial argument. The abolitionist perspective sees 'prostitution as slavery' (Barry, 1995) and degradation of women. The 'work argument' sees prostitution as simply another form of work. Such different approaches to prostitution have been supported by the specific experiences in prostitution; the prostitute body has been contestedly represented as a site of work, a site of abuse, power, sex, addiction and even pleasure (Bell, 1994: 99).

Arguing in favour of prostitution as similar to other types of work or other types of work as similar to prostitution (on the side of the defenders of the sex industry) does not lead politically anywhere, as the debate remains entangled in comparisons and analogies that only show differences and similarities. Prostitution is and is not like other types of work: endless sociological comparisons do not provide any answer to the situation in which trafficked women and prostitutes find themselves nowadays. What counts is not whether prostitution is or is not work, is or is not similar to other forms of work, but whether naming it publicly as 'work' has any political potential. Similarity or dissimilarity to other types of work, analysed with the tools of sociology, does not tell us anything about the political potential of prostitution as work. Hilary Kinnell from the UK Network for Sex Work Project (NSWP) refuses either the equation of all work with prostitution or the acknowledgement that prostitution is a job like any other. She also speaks about 'the total disregard of many anti-trafficking programmes for not only the choices and aspirations of the women and girls targeted, but also for the most basic economic and social realities of their lives' (Kinnell, 2002).

A European Parliament motion for a resolution on the consequences of sex work in the EU shows the impossibility of deciding what prostitution is based on sociological knowledge. There have been no less than seven amendments proposed in the Committee for Women's Rights and Equal Opportunities, all of which are incompatible to one another (European Parliament, 2004). One amendment claims that a clear distinction must be drawn between enforced prostitution, enforced migration and slavery, as the empowerment of individual women – with the aid of state bodies – even vis-à-vis the state, may lead to a self-determined life and career. Another amendment sees the sex industry as having an adverse impact on equality; because it is based on the pursuit of profit by focusing on buyers as a target group (generally men), it constructs an image of unequal relations between men and women (and increasingly frequently also children), in which women are presented as objects for consumption, domination and exploitation; because this industry normalizes sexual violence, it undermines all the efforts which the EU and its Member States have made to give women and men fundamental human rights. The sex industry is deemed to promote and help to create and maintain men's aggression and women's commercialization. Or, in another amendment still, the sex industry can be defined as an undertaking which legally or illegally puts on the market sexual services and/or products for profit making.

We are here in a zone of the indiscernibility of knowledge where political action is needed. Hallward has persuasively formulated this task of political thinking and acting: 'If there is a task specific to politics, it must be to articulate and impose collective principles that break with the infinite complexities, the interminable "negotiations" of culture and psychology' (Hallward, 2001: xx). Prostitution as work breaks with the complexities of knowledge and with the differences that are always to be discovered in analogies between prostitution and other forms of work. Prostitution as work redefines the situation of trafficking from the standpoint of illegal migrants. Yet, this redefinition that brings to the fore those that counted for nothing in the situation of trafficking also reconfigures the relations to other elements in the situation.

Claiming prostitution as work can function as a true rupture in the situation and be emancipatory for women who are otherwise left to the exploitation of traffickers. In this reconfiguration of the trafficking situation, victims of trafficking are not potential harbingers of dangerous irruptions, but equal workers who can claim rights. Forms of abuse and exploitation that had defined victimhood are now assessed from the standpoint of the worker. Rights can be claimed from the perspective of a work and not that of victimhood. The predicate of the 'worker' does not answer the political question of the symbolic and imaginary role of sex work in modern societies. It also does not answer the political problem of capitalism. In the situation of trafficking, it disrupts the security *dispositif* that constitutes others as simultaneously victims and risky beings.

The argument in favour of the political potential of prostitution as work in the situation of trafficking does not mean that issues about the exploitative aspect of prostitution itself are closed. Acting in favour of prostitution as work also means thinking about its effects in a different situation and struggling for more egalitarian forms of work. In a letter to the organizers of the European Conference on Sex Work, the representatives of the English Collective of Prostitutes note that

> [economic] alternatives can only help all of us, whether we want to work in the sex industry or not, to combat violence and discrimination. We do not need to glamorise sex work to get recognition for the rights and skills of the workers who do it. Most other work is not glamorous and workers don't have to claim to love their jobs in order to get recognition as workers. Let's not lower our working class standards.
>
> (Adams and Mitchell, 2005)

Prostitution is reclaimed as a form of labour and this renaming is related to struggles for the 'recognition of women's work, for basic human rights and for decent working conditions' (Kempadoo, 1998: 3). The sex workers' claim that 'we are all workers' – in a form of universal address that refuses to distinguish between native and foreign prostitutes – also points to the gap between rights granted to those who do 'respectable work' and the non-rights of prostitutes. As workers, foreign prostitutes can claim rights by virtue of their work and not their nationality. Kinnell has argued that 'to denigrate women's choices as self-delusional or based on "false consciousness" is not feminism but fascism' (Kinnell, 2002).

Reclaiming prostitution as work has to preserve its element of universality and avoid the closure that partial state recognition of work rights can entail. Work is not a particular identification, it cannot be closed and remains subject to contestation. States, however, attempt to close or exclude the predicate of work as a universal access to citizenship. Even where discussions about prostitution as work are rendered acceptable by the state, such acceptability is limited to regulation within the confines of the nation state and its citizens. Regulation or legalization refers to a system of criminal regulation and government control of prostitutes; some prostitutes are given licenses to work in specific and limited ways. Such laws regulate prostitute businesses and lives, prescribing health checks and registration of health status, telling prostitutes where they may or may not reside, etc. (Prostitutes' Education Network, 2004). Against such system of state control, activists ask for the abolition of laws against prostitution (English Collective of Prostitutes, 2004). In response to the consultation paper on prostitution issued by the Home Office, 'Paying the Price', Cari Mitchell, from the English Collectives of Prostitutes has argued that the licensing of brothels is used by the police to crack down on immigrant women. As they can't get a license, they are forced underground and become easier targets for deportment (Mitchell quoted in BBC, 2004).

The political event of claiming that prostitution is work functions both as the verification of equality (if we are all workers, then worker rights should apply to us too!) and as a form of universal address in the situation of trafficking. By renaming trafficked women, legal and illegal prostitutes as workers, the event disrupts the power relations governing human trafficking. It does so by claiming a new capacity for all sex workers, legal or illegal, foreign or not. The enunciation of prostitution as work challenges state practices against both legal and illegal prostitutes. It shows that an inegalitarian stance leads to increased exploitation of both legally working prostitutes and illegal migrant prostitutes. As the phenomenon of human trafficking takes place in the shadows of the illegality of migrants and the criminalization of prostitution, the equality of the worker disrupts trafficking as a problematization of illegal migration, prostitution, organized crime and risk. Claiming prostitution as work also reconfigures the situation of abuse and coercion in which many trafficked persons have found themselves. Prostitution as work redefines the situation of trafficking from the standpoint of work and therefore tackles the inegalitarian conditions that have been conditions of possibility for abuse and exploitation of victims of trafficking.

Prostitution has been largely unacceptable as a form of labour because it makes explicit the exploitation the market can lead to. On the one hand, prostitution as work points to the hypocrisy of liberal capitalism which accepts certain forms of labour while disregarding others. The idea of the market as the ordering function of society implicitly contains the idea that human beings are marketable beyond their 'labour force'. Rather than a benign force, the market does not distinguish between the demand for beauty products, human organs or sex for that matter. On the other, it shows that state boundaries and the creation of the national labour force is a form of protection against the effects of capitalism. However, the politics of work in the situation of trafficking is discussed in relation to the security *dispositif* and not to capitalism generally. It is nonetheless important to bear in mind that security practices can render capitalist exploitation invisible by legitimating divisions and distinctions within the working force. Exploitation always happens to others, to illegal migrants or trafficked women and is no longer linked with the function that labour plays within capitalism. Alienation and exploitation appear as no longer connected with labour in capitalism – especially when millions of other people would be willing to work under the conditions of Western capitalism.

Having recast prostitution as work within the situation of trafficking does not mean that work does away with any exploitation or that work in general is devoid of any connection with exploitation and oppression. After all, work can also become a mode of governing individuals and populations groups. Nonetheless, a universalizing claim for prostitution as work allows not only for egalitarian claims of illegal migrant women to be enacted but also shifts the description of trafficking towards that of labour exploitation. I do not deny that prostitution can entail forms of more serious exploitation than other types of labour. Prostitute activist networks themselves do not only claim prostitution as work, but attempt to find economic alternatives to it. Several activist groups that work with sex workers and illegal migrants in Europe, independent of the conditions in which they have arrived in the EU, as well as the conditions of their work, have pointed out the need for alternatives that would allow women to move out of prostitution. The English Collective of Prostitutes, in the UK; Cabiria, in France and Comitato per i Diritti Civili delle Prostitute, in Italy do not draw distinctions between the legal and administrative categories of migrant sex workers.[10]

The equality and the universality of work have the potential to radically change the situation of trafficking. Rather than described and divided in categories of legal sex workers, trafficked women and illegal migrants (prostitutes), the situation of trafficking is reconfigured through equality. Trafficked women can no longer be extracted from the category of illegal migrant workers, while work creates a common struggle between sex workers and 'victims of trafficking'. A political event like the claim for prostitution as work renames subjects and radically challenges the security practices governing the situation of trafficking. This does not mean that 'workers' or 'sex workers' cannot become names in other security practices at some other point. Nevertheless, the equality of work and its universal application allow for political actions to take place. As workers, subjects can be political rather than medicalized, psychologized and traumatized victims.

Conclusion

This chapter has argued that the philosophical conceptualization of the excess as that which goes beyond power relations could be used to understand an evental politics that is heterogeneous to dominant practices. Excessive subjects, subjects that are anomalous to a situation and have no place within the representation of the situation, can disrupt the *dispositif* of security, as argued in relation to illegal migrant sex workers. Political events are local formulations of political names, names which are heterogeneous to the state of the situation, followed by fidelity to these formulations. Illegal migrant sex workers, although present in the situation of trafficking, do not belong to its representations or rather only exist through negation. They should not be there – unless having been trafficked – and should not be prostitutes – unless legal residents. 'Work' redefines the situation for illegal migrant workers and turns all these different categories into the sameness of the 'worker'. As all these categories are figures of the worker, all these categories partake of equal rights. Unlike security, equality is a universal formulation without a closure. Following Badiou's concept of politics, equality is enacted by subjects who become political in their fidelity to an event.

What CSS and their equation of emancipation to security have missed is the element of universality that a politics of emancipation entails and security lacks. Security cannot be democratized, it cannot be universally partaken of. Its imaginary is subtended by practices that divide and exclude categories of subjects deemed dangerous or risky. By not looking at the effects of security at the subjective level, desecuritization also misses the element of struggle and emancipation. A politics that would unmake securitization is a politics formulated from the site of the excessive subject, of those who do not belong to the situation. A sociological analysis of the practices of security professionals, as proposed by Bigo, keeps us within the limits of 'what is'. Yet, it is not competing knowledge that can challenge the knowledge of security experts and their practices – rather, as I have argued, subjects that name themselves as equal subjects in politics can radically suspend professional knowledge.

Badiou's conceptualization of a politics of emancipation allows us to think both a more complex situation and the disruption of this situation. The situation is defined as relations between normal, excrescent and excessive elements beyond the dichotomical relation subject/abject. Through the excrescent element of the state and institutions, it has introduced the institutional mediation of practices of subjection. Although normal and excessive elements are differentially governed, Badiou's cartography of the subjects in a situation allows us to understand the specific position of those who should not be there, who represent the negation of the situation. Moreover, the principles of an evental politics are heterogeneous to the governmental practices of security in as much as they destroy the division between the normal and the excessive. They also disrupt the relation of knowledge that excrescent elements have with normal and excessive elements by instating equality. Division becomes equality and exclusion is replaced by universality. Yet, can these political events only exist at a distance from the state? Political events take place at a distance from any state institution, through collective organization. However, illegal migrant prostitutes have emerged as equal political subjects exactly in institutional locations and have made their claims inscribed in law. The next chapter will analyse what these institutional forms of action entail for a politics of emancipation. Can politics be restricted to forms of self-organization by excessive subjects?

6
The Politics of (Ambiguous) Universality

Political events that unmake the security *dispositif* of governing human trafficking are informed by the principles of equality and universality, and connected with the excessive elements of a situation, the anomalous presence of those who should not be there, who are represented as not belonging to the situation. An evental politics harnessed to the excessive subjects of a situation is radically different from the formulation of politics in security studies and IR. Practices of security instantiate and reproduce social order. Analyses of security are harnessed to 'what is', to actors, audiences, representations and interventions. Even Butler's interpretation of speech acts as performatively constitutive of spaces of abjection that could become spaces of resistance does not account for emancipatory politics as radically heterogeneous to practices of security. An evental politics of equality, formulated from the standpoint of excess, suspends differential forms of subjectivity and reconfigures the relationality between excrescent, normal and excessive elements in a situation.

Following Badiou, the collective subjectification of those who are excessive can open the space for a disruption of the security *dispositif*. Illegal migrant sex workers reshape the situation of trafficking from the assignation of risk groups and victimhood to the subjectivity of the worker. Those who were not supposed to be there due to illegality and were not workers due to involvement in prostitution enter the situation of trafficking as equal workers. We have seen that trafficked women are not dangerous as 'victims', as coerced, abused or exploited migrants. They are dangerous inasmuch as they embody the permanent risk of the illegal migrant prostitute, inasmuch as they reactivate the category from which they have been extracted and from which they should dis-identify. Victims of trafficking are other-than-illegal-migrant prostitutes, while simultaneously dangerously close to the latter.

145

Analyses which attempt to think alternative possibilities of subjectification do so by reducing it to private strategies of resistance that can be
incorporated within the *dispositif* of security. Moreover, most attempts
to unmake security practices do not consider how to unmake the exclusionary effects of security. If ethical approaches are acutely aware of the
need for radical principles of politics, the link between radical principles
and existing practices remains unclear.

I have shown that the predicate of 'work' and the collective subjectification of 'worker' – when claimed by prostitutes and trafficked
women – introduces a radical claim of equality within the governmental
practices of security. The claim of equality turns trafficked women from
illegitimate intruders into visible speakers and equal partakers of the
community of workers. Through the body and voice of sex workers, the
migrant other becomes a sharer in the community as a worker. Rather
than radical alterity, the foreign sex worker becomes collectively subjectified, together with all other sex workers. They are the subjects of
their own emancipation, contesting the situation which divides them
into antagonistic categories.

The claim to work introduces an unexpected and, in this sense, evental
claim within the state of the situation. The dangerous or risky trafficked
women are migrants crossing borders and risking their lives in search
of work, who might return even if deported to their countries of origin,
rehabilitated and reintegrated within the normal. Rather than the
predicate of inequality between high-skilled and low-skilled migrants,
legal and illegal, work becomes the signifier of equality, the possibility
of collective subjectivation beyond governmental categorizations into
risk groups.

According to Badiou, this politics is enacted through forms of collective organization at a distance from the state. The distance from the
state is not a form of anti-statism, but politics enacted at a distance from
state institutions. As Badiou has summarized the stakes of the situation
of the *sans-papiers*:

> Considering the fate of the *sans-papiers* in this country, a first orien-
> tation might have been: they should revolt against the state. Today
> we would say that the singular form of their struggle is, rather, to
> create the conditions in which the state is led to change this or that
> thing concerning them, to repeal the laws that should be repealed, to
> take the measures of naturalization (*régularisation*) that should be
> taken, and so on.
>
> (Badiou, 2002b: 98, emphasis in original)

A politics of equality and universality makes prescriptions against the state, without participating in the state and its institutions. Still, a politics that enacts equality and claims the equality of work is not exclusively enacted at a distance from the state institutions through collective subjectification. In his political practice, Badiou has a rather reductionist understanding of the institutional element which is not presented but represented in the situation. Institutions only perform the process of ordering and government. Historicizing the politics of equality and universality yields a different view of the situation and of the role of institutions. Previous forms of collective subjectification and politics might have inscribed their political principles in institutions. In the history of political struggles, equality also exists inscribed in various institutional locales and can be open to verification.

This chapter will explore political struggles that activate institutionally inscribed equality and claim it for categories a priori excluded from its purview. Unpacking the the relationship between institutional politics and the evental politics of excess subjects at a distance from the state yields a more nuanced understanding of how security practices can be undone. As equality and universality already exist as principles inscribed in liberal state institutions, struggles for emancipation start from already existing inscriptions (Balibar, 2004a). Can the excessive elements, that is, illegal migrant sex workers in the situation of trafficking, reclaim these principles from within state institutions?

To answer this question and consider its implications for an evental politics along Badiou's lines, I start by locating the political sites in which equality and universality have informed the political struggles of sex workers and interrogate their relation to an evental politics of collective subjectification. The relation between a politics that unfolds within institutions and a politics that is at a distance from the state will be discussed through the mediation of equality and universality. Finally, I shall consider this double determination of politics for unmaking practices of security.

Equality in history

Badiou's politics of universality and equality is formulated 'at a distance' from the state (Badiou, 2004b: 156). Sex worker activists refuse any involvement with the state on matters of regulating prostitution and claim that anti-trafficking legislation is primarily used to deport sex workers, without any evidences of force or coercion proving the offences (English Collective of Prostitutes, 2004). Their politics could be put in a nutshell as 'those who work here are from here', echoing Badiou's own claim about the *sans-papiers* that 'those who are here are from here [les gens qui sont ici sont d'ici]' (La distance politique, 1996). In a recent action concerning the status of illegal workers in France, *l'Organization politique* has stated that '[p]ayment slips are not fake, even if residence papers are fake. Payments slips are genuine because work is genuine' (Balso, 2005, translation mine). Such a claim evidently enacts an impossibility in the current political situation on the basis of the principles of universality and equality. It also appears articulable only at a distance from state institutions. Yet, an analysis of the situation of human trafficking makes apparent other sites in which an impossibility is enacted.

In the EU, a politics of equality and universality, a politics of the equality of work for migrants who have been rendered illegal has been formulated at other political sites, most notably the European Court of Justice (ECJ). If politics is not just at a distance from the state, but also prescribing against the state, as Badiou argues, then state institutions can become loci for such prescriptions. Just as political events are not exterior to a situation but inherently linked to it through excessive subjects, principles of equality and universality already exist inscribed in the situation, as a logical consequence of other political events and other struggles. Badiou's mathematical ontology makes his theory oblivious of the historicity of the concepts which open avenues for political struggles. As equality is a principle that cannot be subjected to closure, locating it in different situations can allow for its expansion.

Political struggles are often struggles over these inscriptions of equality and universality that exclude certain categories of people as the very possibility of the system functioning. For example, at different points in history, the right to vote excluded different categories of people. Their exclusion from the voting system was part of the functioning of the early-modern capitalist state, which made voting dependent on property. Women's struggle for the right to vote could be read along these lines of challenging the universal inscription in the name of an equality that is denied or suspended. Badiou has been wary of such a politics that he would see as only contributing to an 'oppositional' stance, a position of 'protest from *within* the state-sanctioned structures and rules (parties, elections, trade unions, constitutional amendments ...)' (Badiou quoted in Hallward, 2002, emphasis in original). When such an oppositional stance buttresses or sustains through its principles a politics of emancipation, what role are we to give to this form of politics?

In what follows, I consider how a politics of equality is formulated from within existing institutional inscriptions in the situation of trafficking. An egalitarian statement concerning illegal migrant sex workers has emerged based on an inscription of equality in the Association Agreements signed between the EU and the accession states in the 1990s.[1] These agreements gave the right to nationals from CEECs to 'take up and pursue economic activities as self-employed persons' (European Community, 1991). They extended the right of residence by virtue of work to nationals of other non-EU countries. Work (as self-employment) is extended beyond the realm of the EU and it introduces a claim to equality (as non-discrimination) between CEECs and EU citizens. Although these agreements were set up in the context of an increased liberalization of economic relations between the EU and the accession countries, what interests me here is how these agreements, drafted in completely different circumstances and for a different purpose, are given political purchase in the situation of human trafficking.

The Association Agreements have been at the heart of several cases in front of the ECJ. The right to residence as self-employed workers has been repeatedly invoked by those who had fallen out of the representations of a situation of migration and were present in it only as a negation. They either had their asylum claims rejected or had been in an irregular situation. Although present, they were represented only as anomalous, as excessive and as those who should not be there. In all the cases that have been the subject of judgements by the ECJ – for example, *Gloszczuk* (2001), *Kondova* (2001), and *Barkoci and Malik* (2001) – the right of establishment and residence was formulated from the subjective position of the worker, of the self-employed. The first case concerned two Polish nationals whose applications to stay in the UK as self-employed workers were rejected on the grounds that they had stayed irregularly in the UK. The second case concerned a Bulgarian national who started work as a self-employed cleaner and claimed residence after her asylum application had been rejected. In the third case, two Czech nationals applied for residence as self-employed workers after their asylum claims had been rejected.

In another case, *Jany*, the issue of self-employment and residence became directly connected with that of prostitution. In this case, the ECJ dealt with two Polish and three Czech nationals who wanted to establish themselves as self-employed persons in the Netherlands, but were denied residence permits by the Netherlands Secretary of State for Justice (*Jany*, 2001). The six women were residing in the Netherlands and working in Amsterdam as 'window prostitutes'. In accordance with the Association Agreements between the European Community and

Poland and the Czech Republic, the citizens of the latter states are allowed to 'take up and pursue economic activities as self-employed persons', where *'economic activities* shall in particular include activities of an industrial character, activities of a commercial character, activities of craftsmen and activities of the professions' (*Jany*, 2001, emphasis in original). The women were refused residence permits on grounds that 'prostitution is a prohibited activity or at least not a socially acceptable form of work and cannot be regarded as being either a regular job or a profession' (*Jany*, 2001). The commissioner of the Amsterdam-Amstelland regional police for residence permits rejected the prostitutes' application holding that the expression 'economic activities as self-employed persons' used in the Association Agreements between the EU and Poland and the Czech Republic did not have the same meaning as the same words used in Article 43 of the Treaty of Rome. The six prostitutes asked for a judicial review.

The ECJ had already ruled in *Gloszczuk* (2001) and *Barkoci and Malik* (2001) that the provisions in the Association Agreements represented a 'precise and unconditional principle which is sufficiently operational to be applied by a national court and which is therefore capable of governing the legal position of individuals'. The ECJ also concluded that if a member state accepts prostitution on the part of its own nationals, it could not regard prostitution on the part of Polish and Czech nationals as representing a 'genuine threat to public order' (*Jany*, 2001). The Court decided that the activity of prostitution pursued in a self-employed capacity can be regarded as a service provided for remuneration. The Court also established that such a relation must be carried outside any relationship of subordination concerning the choice of that activity, working conditions and conditions of remuneration; under that person's own responsibility, and in return for remuneration paid to that person directly and in full (*Jany*, 2001).

In all these cases (including *Jany*), the ECJ ruled that the right of establishment has direct effect and CEECs' nationals can invoke it against the member states. Since the *Jany* judgement, several hundred prostitutes have claimed residence as self-employed sex workers (Böcker, 2002: 35). Although not at a distance from the state in Badiou's sense, such a politics still prescribes against the state. Illegal foreign prostitutes, the excessive element of both a situation of migration and trafficking, enact equality and the transformation of prostitution through work from within institutional locales.

Although formally different from the sex worker activist movement, the *Jany* case cannot be considered in isolation from their movement, as it redefines the situation in which sex workers themselves are struggling for the recognition of prostitution as work. The *Jany* case has inscribed prostitution as work in the history of institutions. Institutional struggle over the representation of prostitution and the representation of trafficking will continue. The European Parliament motion and the amendments to it discussed in the previous chapter were a reaction, on the one hand, to the Brussels Declaration on Human Trafficking and ways to fight the phenomenon and to the *Jany* case, on the other. The *Jany* case can consequently only be considered in relation to a struggle of collective subjectification that works in the margins of institutions and challenges, at all times, their authority and their decisions.

The transformation of universality

Badiou's politics of equality and universality is minimally historical. Historicity is reduced to the relation to the situation, to the excessive elements of a situation. The principles which politics itself invokes are not historicized, but are considered as abstract principles which can challenge the state of the situation. If thinking the new entails thinking the old, then thinking politics entails the separation of what can lead to the new and what is a repetition in the situation in relation to equality. Is there a politics of equality that can invoke exactly the history of the principle itself and not amount to a simple repetition of what is? I suggest that the action undertaken in the *Jany* case is a political verification of institutionally inscribed equality, a verification that radically displaces the limits of equality given in the Europe Agreements. Migrant women presented themselves as sex workers and verified the equality of work, thereby bringing prostitution under the remit of work. Equality appears as a maxim of action, a principle that is under verification by subjects who present themselves as equal subjects in politics.

This does not mean that politics should be reduced to institutional politics – we have seen that institutional struggles tend to subvert rather than support the claim of prostitution as work. To understand the role of the *Jany* case and the historicization of equality and universality, evental politics would need to be supplemented by a historical politics of equality and universality. Nevertheless, does this supplementation of evental politics by a historical politics not contradict both the repudiation of historicism and the importance of the excess? The historicization of equality remains linked to the standpoint of excessive subjects, and functions as a verification in a situation where inegalitarian practices and forms of representation are at work. Moreover, the historicization of equality is at odds with analyses of power, which remains within the sphere of what is. If equality can be thought of as the result of struggles whose consequences have been inscribed in institutions, could we not speak about the historicization of a politics of excess?

In a sense, political events exist in history, and the subject's fidelity to an event can lead to the institutional inscription of its consequences. Although a historical element appears as a necessary supplement to Badiou's politics, equality is prescriptive, a maxim and not a consequence of governmental actions. Governmental definitions of equality and calculations of what an optimum would be for the life of the population are not political. The Czech migrant women in the *Jany* case have made use of already existing universal inscriptions. Such inscriptions already exist within the nation-state, or at the level of supra-national institutions.

I have shown that equality can function as radical principle that asserts the equality of political subjects and that it can also be invoked in different institutional locations. Equality has become inscribed in institutions both as a result of struggles or simply contingently, as in the case of Europe Agreements. Political action takes equality out of the economic rationale with which it is linked and moves it to another realm. From the commonsensical understanding of services and of self-employment, equality is transferred rather unexpectedly to the realm of sex industry.

The political verification of equality in different locations can be understood in relation to the ambiguity of universality. The collective subjectification of the worker creates a form of universal address in the situation of trafficking. The worker as an equal subject made those who counted for nothing in the situation, the illegal migrant prostitutes, count for something. Victims of trafficking are transformed from silenced victims of trauma into workers who can process their experience of exploitation and abuse. Work redefines the situation of trafficking and does away with the divisions that security practices had imposed. In the *Jany* case, universality is obviously limited, referring initially to Czech and Polish citizens and subsequently to countries which have Association Agreements with the EU. Moreover, in the newer Association Agreements signed with the Euro-Mediterranean countries, the right of self-employment has been taken out.[2]

How is the unlimited of universality of address linked with the limitations of the scope of equality in the trials before the ECJ? Is work a 'true' universal – does it not entail its own exclusions, that is, those who are unable or unwilling to undertake specific forms of work? Universality has been criticized by poststructuralist and feminist literature both for silencing particular others and for ideologically furthering modern European gendered particularities. Let's take the concept of equality. Feminism has argued that equality stifles difference and attempts to regiment different particularities under 'identity'. Equality erases difference, destroys individuality and suspends freedom. The feminist problematique of equality versus difference derived from the political question of claims to equality, claims which were interpreted as subduing and erasing difference. The equality theorists were thought to accept the basic claims underpinning liberal political theory, that the idea of equality is neutral vis-à-vis gender (Squires, 2000: 118).[3] The difference theorists argued that equality is actually anthropocentric and called for women's specificity to be recognized in feminist struggles rather than effaced in claims for equality. The formal character of liberal equality was seen as 'severely compromised by the character of a (white, bourgeois, male, heterosexual) hegemonic subject' (Brown, 2001: 9).

   In the sense used here, equality is radically separated from identity. Equality is a claim about how to transform social order *by means of equality*. Equality is not about particular characteristics, but about the participation in politics as equal subjects. We could probably say that the universal is a negative universal inasmuch as 'to be inscribed within it is not a matter of possessing any particular determination' (Badiou, 2004b: 151). Rather than linked with a hegemonic subject, equality is actually linked with the 'precarious supplement whose sole strength resides in there being no available predicate capable of subjecting it to knowledge' (Badiou, 2004b: 146). Equality is linked with the excess, with the subjects that are excessive of the hegemonic representation of the elements which are counted in a socio-historical situation. The universality that is linked with excessive subjects is the opposite of hegemony. Work does not create another hegemonic universality, but reformulates the situation of trafficking governed by the security *dispositif*. The function of equality as a non-identitarian and non-hegemonic concept can be better clarified in relation to the ambiguities of universality.

   Balibar has distinguished between three forms of universality: universality as 'reality', universality as 'fiction' and universality as 'symbol' or ideal universality. For our purposes, fictive and ideal universality can clarify the political role of universality. Fictive and ideal universality are political inasmuch they are constructed in confrontation and conflict (Balibar, 2004b). Universality as 'reality' refers to the expansion of institutions and techniques to the entire world, to the interdependency between different parts of the world that analysts of globalization have explored. Despite the existence of a generalized web of economic, political and cultural relations, of an increased interdependency between different areas of the world and of the 'generalisation of minority status', real universality does not mean the extension of universality to humanity, but is actually equivalent to the creation of identities which are 'less isolated *and* more incompatible, less univocal *and* more antagonistic' (Balibar, 1995: 56, emphasis in original). The real universality of economic, political and cultural relations has drawn more boundaries within the humanity and has created more areas of abjection. Although real universality has fostered conflictual relationships, it does not, by itself, hold a political potential. The extension of economic, political and cultural forms to the whole of humanity can be politically challenged in its effects when there are 'fictions' and 'ideals' that purport to address everybody.

Universality as 'fiction' can be understood as synonymous to the concept of hegemony or the dominant discourses that sustain the constitution and reproduction of political order. 'Fictions' refer to the reality constructed by institutions and representations.[4] Historically, fictive universality has taken two forms: religious and national-political (Balibar, 1995, 2002b). Universality as 'fiction' is also ambiguous inasmuch as both nations and religions have spoken to individuals universally, beyond their given forms of subjectification and have served to question relations of inequality and domination. Fictive universality leads dominated groups to struggle for rights in the name of the superior values of the community: the legal and the ethical values of the state itself (Balibar, 2002b: 161). Fictive universality is 'the very point where the two inverse movements of inclusion and exclusion meet and contradict each other' (Balibar, 2004b: 61). The anti-colonial struggle can be seen as a struggle for the universalization of the nation through struggles for self-determination. At the same time, however, religions and nations have been instruments of oppression.

Nevertheless, Balibar argues, fictive universality can achieve hegemony only inasmuch as it has a kernel of true universality. The nation-state, for example, deconstructs subjectivity from its private attachments to reconstruct it as citizenship in the public sphere. By reconstructing the public sphere as the sphere of universal citizenship, fictive universality has made possible struggles against patriarchal domination in the family, for example. Private subjectivity and universal citizenship are opposed in political struggles. These struggles against hegemonic structures denounce the gap or contradiction between official values and practices.

Universality as fiction allows for politics to be formulated in the name of the superior values of the community. These values of the dominated that infuse fictive universality and that are inscribed in institutions create an institutionalized space of struggle that supplements or even buttresses political events at a distance from the state. Such values can be suffrage, justice or freedom and equality.

When universality is dismissed as violent and as the effect of power, then we should ask Balibar's question:

> [H]ow do we account for the fact that, when it attains the universality it requires to fulfil the function that Gramsci will later call 'organic' or 'hegemonic' in a given society, *the dominant ideology must speak the universal and not the particular, enounce the law from the standpoint of the universal or the general interest and not that of privilege*? How do we account for this fact unless we assume that, historically and logically, the dominant ideology comes not from the ideas or values of the dominating group, but *from the dominated themselves*, the bearers of claims to justice, to equality, liberty, emancipation and education, etc.?
>
> (Balibar, 2006: 39, emphasis in original)

No hegemonic form of power can function without some remnant that has come from the language of the dominated. The dominant forces in society, Balibar has argued, 'can speak to the masses in the language of universalistic values (rights, justice, equality, welfare, progress ...) because in this language a kernel remains which came from the masses themselves, and is returned to them' (Balibar, 2002b: 164). The promise of universality functions beyond its historical appropriation within particular power relations.

Universality as 'symbol' or ideal universality introduces the unconditional in politics, the ideal of non-discrimination and non-coercion, of equality and liberty. Universality cannot be reduced to the nation-form or a religious community, but has as an ideal of the subject of politics the common humanity, the individual without particular qualities (Balibar, 2004a: 312). This aspect of universality excludes exclusion as it cannot be subject to closure. Ideal universality refers to the expression of revolt against all discrimination, against inequality, against interdictions and obstacles to freedom of expression or other individual and collective freedoms (Balibar, 1993). The kernel of ideals that infuses fictive universality cannot be limited to the political communities in which universality is expropriated and appropriated by the dominant ideology. Ideals transcend the space of their arbitrary limitations and are excessive to any institutional construction.

The Declaration of Rights that founded the French modern nation-state and the institution of citizenship are based on the 'proposition of equaliberty', which considers all individuals of equal value and is open onto the idea that, at least potentially, all men are citizens (Balibar, 2004b: 59). The existence of forms of universality inscribed in institutions can be understood both as the result of previous struggles for emancipation and as the specificity of how power relations function in modernity. If power is not to be simply repressive or violent (even when its violence means constituting subjects), there is an element of shared universality and values that would bind the governing and the governed. I have shown that practices of security can be bound together by an imaginary of security.

Universality as fictive and symbolic is absent from what I have called the 'barred universal' of security. The tension at the heart of universality that allows for dominant practices to be challenged in the name of equality and even the common humanity of subjects is undermined by the exclusionary move of security practices. Security can only be embodied in forms of life or forms of community to the exclusion of other ones, through a simultaneous imaginary of disorder and insecurity that infuses the imaginary of security and order. Unlike equality or equaliberty, security is subject to closure and boundary drawing. The ambiguity of universality that has led to productive tensions and a politics of emancipatory struggles is barred from security practices. Ideal universality or universality as 'symbol' is the impossible universality in relation to practices of security. Security always appears as a non-event, incapable to address everybody as equal.

Security that could be democratized, extended to every individual refers to real universality. Real universality does not speak politically as fictive and symbolic universality does. Some poststructuralists have interpreted the inter-linking of identities, their fragmentation and destabilization as the conditions of possibility for coming to terms with insecurity and suspending the inflationary practices of security that attempt to govern any form of disorder and instability. Others still have argued against the paranoid security reaction of states to generalized conditions of fragmentation. Real universality is, however, exclusively captured in the terms of what is. It is at the same time increased interconnection and creation of more heterogeneous identities and the exclusion of whole categories of population globally.

Symbolic and fictive universality can also be depoliticized, 'a contradictory combination of an outline of universality and its arbitrary limitation' (Balibar, 1994: 46) suspended, when a different logic is applied, according to which freedom represents a status and equality is a function and right of this status. When human trafficking is governed through risk management, freedoms are bestowed differentially, depending on the degree of riskiness that women show. Equality is defined substantively, only in relation to the allocation in a risk group. Political equality between groups and the equality between all humans as political subjects are suspended. Women are depoliticized by being represented as incapable of being equal subjects: they are traumatized subjects, whose claims and enunciations cannot be fully political.

Challenging the arbitrary limitations that fictive universality can entail is based on an ideal universality, the unconditional principle of the participation of all in politics. According to Balibar, ideal universality is based on the simultaneous enactment of freedom and equality or what he calls *égaliberté* (equaliberty). Equality and liberty became principles of democracy only in the wake of the French Revolution, of specific struggles by the dominated. They have informed political struggles as unconditional principles ever since. The grounding of politics in the principles of the French Revolution could appear as Eurocentric, unaware of the subaltern voices and possibly different modes of thinking and practicing politics. Yet, universality and equality are principles that have been claimed in struggles against Eurocentric hegemonic practices. Security and the state are Eurocentric concepts and practices and it is against their expansion that the same very principles can be mobilized.

Balibar's conceptualization of universality makes apparent both a contradiction and an excess between ideal universality, the universality to which state practices (including dominant practices) must refer and the fictive universality, the universality that appears as split between its particular embodiment and what it excludes. Symbolic or ideal universality is in excess over fictive universality. An analysis of practices lacks a theorization of principles which are in excess over what is and subjects who are excessive or anomalous of what is represented in a situation. Ideal universality makes the arbitrary boundaries of fictive universality contestable through the principle of equal and universal participation in politics. However, universality is both constitutive of the event and excessive to it. Universality is inscribed in institutions as the memory of past political actions for emancipation and simultaneously excessive to the state. This formulation of universality as ambiguity supplements the *prescriptions against the state at a distance from the state* by *prescriptions against the state from within institutions*.

Emancipation and transformation

How can we understand the relation between an evental politics that is
set at a distance from institutions and a politics that supports political
action from within institutions? Can a politics that challenges the arbitrary limitations of universality in the name of unconditional equality
be a supplement to the evental politics that prescribes against the state
from a distance or are these conceptualizations of politics and political
action irreconcilable? Hallward has suggested that Balibar's position is
connected with an oppositional stance from within state-sanctioned
structures and rules (Hallward, 2002). Political events should remain at
a distance from institutions and prescribes against authority. I have
shown, however, that the equivocity of universality leads to different
interpretations of political events. The universality of equality is both
beyond any of its current institutional instantiations and within them.
Balibar's position, which attempts to locate sites where universality
can be opened to intensive contestation, shares with Badiou an understanding of the excess. Badiou sees the excess as linked with the anomalous elements of a situation, while Balibar links it with unconditional
principles that have informed political struggles in history. In a sense,
there is an implicit understanding of equality as excess in Badiou too,
as equality does not pertain to the structuring of the situation but to the
indifferent multiplicity of presentation before and beyond representation.

The tension in the function of universality – both as excessive to the
situation and embedded in institutions – can be seen to define political
action along two axes, which I call following Balibar emancipation
and transformation. Balibar has distinguished among three forms of
politics: emancipation, transformation and civility. He has associated
emancipation with a politics of equality and transformation with a
politics that changes relations of power. These two forms are supplemented by civility, which is a mode of politics that avoids the extremes
of violence and the impossibility of symbolizing social conflicts.

Civility refers to the conditions of possibility of politics itself as transformation and emancipation. Civility is not synonymous to tolerance;
it is a mode of relating to ourselves and of imagining possibilities of
identification and dis-identification that would not take us to the
extremes of violence which are destructive of the space where political
claims can be made. This mode of politics designates the speculative
idea of a politics of politics, or a politics in the second degree, which
aims at creating, recreating and conserving the set of conditions within
which politics as a collective participation in public affairs is possible,

or at least is not made absolutely impossible (Balibar, 2004b: 115). In the situation of trafficking, the politics of civility is kept open through the predicate of work. Work is not only the word that opens the contestation of political equality and universality, but it becomes the predicate of political contestation and enunciation of what Hannah Arendt has called the 'right to have rights' (Arendt, 1986: 296). Politics as civility seems to me to be the necessary form of politics when the 'right to have rights' can no longer be asserted. As entire populations have become superfluous and unnecessary for capitalism, they are reduced to mere existence. The depoliticization and abjectification of life, 'bare life' (Agamben, 1998) can be seen as the consequence of a lack of civility. When conflicts can no longer be symbolized and there is no public space for contesting principles and enunciating equality, politics is replaced either by biolegitimacy and its attendant concern with suffering and pain or by extreme violence. Victims of trafficking are most often represented at these two extremes of the lack of civility: as suffering and impaired bodies whose only legitimacy arises from the biological or as trapped in extremely exploitative and violent relations in the shadows of legality.

Emancipation and transformation create political subjects out of bare life through new predicates of universality and equality. These predicates also inscribe the 'right to have rights', which has been denied or simply inexistent for those who have excessive in a situation. Balibar refers to people whose organs are trafficked and who cannot present themselves as a stand-in for any universal: they are limited to the resources of their bodies for survival. If organ trafficking can create forms of biolegitimacy similar to the worthy victims of trafficking, they do not politicize the situation in terms of emancipation or transformation. While it is impossible to embark upon a discussion of organ trafficking in this book, it is important to point out the difference between the two situations. In the situation of trafficking, the space of politics is kept open through the subjectification of the worker. The situation of trafficking in women is open to a politics of emancipation, in which subjects present themselves as equal participants in politics. By making political claims against the state within institutions such as the ECJ, illegal migrant sex workers transform the power relations that govern the situation. They initiate a process of both self-emancipation and transformation.

According to Balibar, politics as transformation has been given most eloquent theoretical flesh in the works of Marx and Foucault. Despite the nuanced differences between the two thinkers, both were concerned with the possibility of transforming existing power relations. If for Marx such a transformation is led by a world-historical subject, then for Foucault, it is linked with the subject's 'techniques of the self', and their common concern is the transformation of domination. The proletariat emerges as the subject of a future of 'generic equality' and non-domination in Marx, while in Foucault the subject's resistance is always immanent to power relations. Where there is power, there is resistance is one of Foucault's most famous quotes. The problem with their accounts of transformation is that transformation is made of the same fabric as power or domination. The proletariat emerges out of the capitalist relations of domination, while resistance is in a sense coterminous to power. As argued previously, a politics of unmaking security cannot be of the same fabric as security, but needs to radically rupture these practices. As Balibar himself has put it, the problem is that 'the conditions of existence which are to be transformed are woven from the same cloth as the practice of transformation itself' (Balibar, 2002b). The concept of the excess and what is excessive to the fabric of power or a situation structured by domination lead us beyond the entanglement of power and resistance and the impossibility to distinguish between what disrupts and what is simply reappropriated and reincorporated in the symbolic system. If the proletariat has been reinterpreted as an excessive subject, the excess that is absent both in Marx and Foucault is that of ideals which are heterogeneous to the symbolic system. Ideal universality and its principle of equality constitute a break from the *dispositif* of security. With a hint of self-irony, Balibar describes his position:

> Old Marxist, old materialist that I am, I am convinced on this point: the main way of being a materialist, a realist, in politics today is to be 'idealistic' or, more precisely, to raise the question of ideals and choices to be made between ideals. These ideals will necessarily be expressions of very old ideas to which democracy appeals, but of which democracy, in its current manifestations, provides a very sad spectacle ...
>
> (Balibar, 2002b)

The political task of a materialist analysis of power and practices is to see how those depend upon ideals that have emerged out of political struggles. While the *dispositif* of security offers an imaginary of 'barred universality', universality that always already excludes, the universality of equality is only subjected to arbitrary historical exclusions and not to necessary ones. Emancipation and transformation think politics from the standpoint of excessive subjects and ideals. These ideals are not simply ideological or hegemonic, but function in a counter-hegemonic fashion to disrupt the *dispositif* of security and its effects of abjection and domination. Equality and universality are both excessive and historically situated.

In Badiou, the politics of emancipation is triggered by events that are in a sense cut away from history: events happen. However, I have shown that events can only emerge out of a socio-historical situation and its excessive elements. Even if Badiou argues that a politics of radical emancipation cannot originate in a proof of possibility that an analysis of the world could offer (Badiou, 1992),[5] the excess is historically related to the situation. Subjects achieve forms of collective organization in history and excessive principles have themselves a history of their own. Even if events speak of the excess of history itself, of the contingency that cannot be captured by what is, they emerge out a non-historical relation to history. An analysis of the situation can locate the traces that previous events have left in history and this historical awareness of struggles that can support new forms of political action. What is important in naming these two modes of politics is to see that the two axes as not mutually exclusive, but interrelated. The political struggles against the securitizing practices of human trafficking have mobilized both emancipatory and transformative political actions.

Claims about the equal rights of workers rather than about the categories of victims, prostitutes or illegal migrants inscribe a new principle of equality politically. This politics gives new valence to the anomalous and excessive subject of the situation of trafficking, the illegal migrant sex worker. Claims about equal rights of residence by virtue of work that Eastern European sex workers or immigrants have been putting forth activate already existing principles. These claims challenge the restriction of rights to 'decent' and commonsensical forms of self-employment and argue that prostitution is an independent form of work. The challenge to existing migration law on the basis of already inscribed institutional rights relates to the recognition of prostitution as work. Transformative politics is therefore an inscription of equality against its arbitrary limitation and closure. It ties in with emancipatory struggles, the struggles that argue that prostitution is a form of work based on the exchange of labour force against remuneration.

While the event itself ruptures the situation from the standpoint of the excessive elements by means of verifying the principle of equality (excessive to any rationality of domination), the event is linked to a series of struggles that go on in a situation. A political event does not emerge in the interstices of power or from the dissonant complexity of discourses and practices, but from the political struggles that go on in a situation. Illegal migrant prostitutes can claim the equality of work given the existing struggles to rename prostitution as work. Renaming prostitution as work appears as an event in a situation of trafficking inasmuch as it suspends the particular categorization and govern-mentality of security. The ambiguities of a politics of universality have allowed me to show emancipation and transformation as historically and conceptually inseparable. Although mobilizing equality and uni-versality in different situations and by different subjects, emancipation and transformation buttress a politics out of security.

A politics of universality and equality unmakes the inegalitarian and exclusionary security *dispositif*. As previously argued, practices of security are always at the expense of somebody else. Their universal is always a barred one and their imaginary is one of delimiting, categorizing, neutralizing and excluding an-other (where 'other' is to be read as specific categories of population). Unlike the politics of universality and equality, security depends upon the enactment of practices of inequality that divide dangerous and non-dangerous, risk and at-risk, tracing spaces of abjection to be excluded from the space of normal and normalized subjectivity. From the perspective of a politics of equality and universality, practices of security are practices of inequality, particu-larity and closure.

On the contrary, universality and equality remain open and con-testable, despite historical embodiments and arbitrary closures. Fictive universality is historically false, as national and religious communities have simultaneously buttressed practices of security against disorder and practices of normalization against deviants. Yet, it can become political from the standpoint of excess, the excess of ideal universality and of equality. This excess emerges both from within the political community, against the 'normalizing' effects that nations and religions have played and from without, beyond the arbitrary confines that mod-ern political communities have.

A politics of equality and universality begins from a concrete situa-tion that it disrupts and transforms in accordance to egalitarian aspira-tions. Equality and universality as the principles of politics impede its closure. I have called security 'barred universality' inasmuch as closure and the creation of spaces of abjection are intrinsic to its practices. Security cannot remain open; it needs to draw boundaries between those who are to be secure and those who are endangering this security. The horizon of security is, ultimately, fascism, the community that draws impermeable boundaries. The democratization of security, as certain critical security theorists would want, is limited by an arbitrary closure. Yet, if a politics of universality disrupts the *dispositif* of security through collective mobilization and struggle, is this disruption not a form of exceptional politics? Universal prescriptions against the state are still divisive, creating camps in a situation between those who support it and those who do not. The situation of trafficking is divided between those who dismiss the equality of work on the basis on national protection and those who support it. According to Schmitt, universalism can lead to the dehumanization of the enemy and total war. The universalism of liberal principles has created a global matrix of war (Jabri, 2005) where the other is rendered abject. Is the lack of civility not characteristic of the politics of universality and equality too? I maintain that it is not universal principles that Schmitt opposes through his concept of the political, but a politics of rupture that is not formal, but informed by principles of equality.

Schmitt's concept of the political is based on a formal definition. As Žižek has rightly pointed out, 'the decision which bridges a gap [between a normative and actual order] is not a decision for some concrete order, but primarily a decision for the formal principle of order as such' (Žižek, 1999a). The enemy has no form, it is whoever 'calls me into question'. Moreover, the political itself is given no substantive content, it is only defined through 'intensification' (Ojakangas, 2005). Yet, Schmitt limits the formal element of politics and collapses onto a concrete embodiment of the enemy: the enemy cannot be foe. His concept of the political excludes 'internal antagonisms' (Schmitt, 1996: 32). Schmitt effects this closure of politics through the idea of the homogeneous community, whose substance can vary historically from the nation-form to that of the German *Volk*, but whose homogeneity gives content to the state (Müller, 1997).[6] As Carlo Galli has noted, the concept of the political is not just indeterminate, but it is also the principle of collective identity, which is formed in struggle against an external other who is also internal. The exception is not only radical contingency but also the immediacy of identity (Galli, 1996). Schmitt sees liberal universal principles as equivalent to an ideology of pacifism that only leads to more violent and discriminatory forms of war. Still, the politics of ambiguous universality remains open. Closing universality upon forms of political community and collective identity transforms the event into a simulacrum.

Unlike Schmitt's exception, the politics of universality and equality is set at a distance from identity; it is also content-specific inasmuch as it constitutes its own normative basis for criticism and further political action. As the Schmittian exception is formally based upon contingent decisions, it is only power that determines the dominance of one decision over another or the hegemony of a particular form of political community (that is the nation-state). For Schmitt, politics is caught between the necessity of instituting order and the impossibility of firmly or rationally grounding it. The exception speaks to the eternal impossibility of 'giving ground' to order and the necessity to constitute order. A politics of universality and equality disrupts 'what is', not in order to set up another sovereign order, but to institute equality. A politics of universality and equality does not close the contingency of the exception upon the political community or upon a definition of the subject to the exclusion of spaces of abjection.

Conclusion

A politics of (ambiguous) universality has revealed the interdependence rather than mutual exclusion of emancipation and transformation as modes of politics in the situation of trafficking. This chapter has contended that a politics of unmaking the security *dispositif* that governs human trafficking has taken place not only through the collective mobilization of (illegal) sex workers but also within institutions such as the ECJ. Rather than undermining or subverting the collective subjectification of sex workers, Czech and Polish sex workers have helped redefine prostitution as work. Although they have not changed the valence of illegal migrant sex workers within the situation, as they have themselves been dis-identified from illegal migrants through the mediation of the Europe Agreements, they have inscribed the equality of work in an institutional locale. A politics of institutional transformation emerges from the history of political struggles that have inscribed the principle of equality in institutions.

A politics of transformation can be intertwined with a politics of emancipation when the concept of universality is opened up in its ambiguity. The universal ability to address everybody is dependent upon the very definition of what a universal principle is. A universal principle is a principle that exists both in the arbitrary limitation of political institutions and as an unconditional principle of politics, as equality. Emancipation works with an understanding of universality linked to the emergence of excessive subjects as political subjects. It is the subject who is deprived of positivity and representation, and only exists as an anomaly that stands in for universality, sheared of all particular characteristics. To the universality of the subject 'without qualities' in terms of the resources that a situation has to offer, one needs to add the universality of principles such as equality. Fictive universality shows the semblance between universality and the critique of ideology. Universality is embedded, inscribed in institutions, and serves the purposes of domination. Yet, fictive universality is not equivalent to domination, as it is politically contested and subject to reformulations. Its boundaries are challenged both from within the limits of political communities and from outside, through the mediation of ideal universality, a principle of equality that applies to all humanity. Equality is formulated at the jointure of fictive and ideal universality; it cannot be closed or limited, but remains open as a principle to be enacted by political subjects. It is in this impermeability to closure that equality as a principle of politics is qualitatively different from security. Equality is universal in as much as it remains open, while security appears as 'barred universality'. Closure is the constitutive element of security practices.

In discussing ideal universality, Balibar uses an awkward coinage, that of equaliberty. Equaliberty contains the principle of equality, which has been at the heart of the politics out of security explored here and, another contradictory principle of politics, liberty. Equaliberty names the inseparability of equality and liberty. Although the ontological concept of liberty is implied in the very possibility of political subjectification and self-emancipation, liberty has not been thematized in the politics discussed so far. Yet, liberty is the concept we normally associate with attempts to disentangle politics from security. Liberty has been, after all, the concept that has been oppositional to security, the instantiation of contingency against necessity. The next chapter will explore the meaning of liberty for a politics of emancipation and transformation. Is liberty the other universal politics of politics, associated with equality, as Balibar's coinage of equaliberty seems to suggest?

7
The Politics of Freedom

A politics that enunciates the equality and universality of work is both emancipatory and transformative in the situation of trafficking. It is harnessed to the excessive elements of a situation, the illegal migrant sex workers, who are present but represented as not belonging to the situation. By formulating the universal of work from the standpoint of illegal migrant sex workers, a politics of equality addresses everybody in the situation and functions as the self-emancipation of those who did not exist according to the count of the situation. The politics of equality and universality is also transformative, as it challenges the institutional practices and representations of what equality means in the situation of trafficking. The enunciation of equality as an institutionally represented fiction challenges the arbitrary limit that was drawn between categories of EU and non-EU citizens. Through this institutional struggle, the ideal of equality creates the collective subjectification of all those involved in sex work, independent of their citizenship and national belonging. The equality of work does not only challenge the risk management of victims of trafficking, but also the imaginary of security that disposed of the subjects' freedom and equality, depending on national appurtenance, thus disqualifying forms of life from the universal of equality and rendering them abject. The failure of the humanitarian approach can now be seen in the light of the arbitrary limitation of equality and freedom through risk assessment and disavowal of equality for those who fall out of the categories of subjects deemed to be or forced to become responsible, autonomous and prudential. Through risk management, women are supposed to achieve a form of managed freedom. At the same time, the freedom to move, to migrate or to engage in sex work is forbidden to them. What is the relation between managed and regulated freedom and the freedom to resist abjection, to engage in political struggles and self-emancipate? Claims to freedom are absent from any discourse concerning trafficked women.[1] The humanitarian approach is based on their specificity as victims, relegated outside the boundaries of politics where they could make claims to liberty or exercise freedoms. Whatever rights and benefits women can be accorded, it is never in terms of freedom. Temporary shelter, food and (temporary) residence are granted either in exchange for testimonies against the traffickers or on a risk management basis. The humanitarian approach, although claiming a series of rights for trafficked women, has never formulated any criticism in terms of infringement of liberties. Interestingly, the defenders of the rights of victims of trafficking have never made the argument that their liberty (for example, the free movement of persons or freedom to choose a better life) has been trespassed by states that restrict their movement, locate and deport them. States are only cautioned about the dangers of retrafficking that the unnoticed vulnerabilities of victims could cause. As La Strada Moldova has pointed out, echoing largely accepted knowledge among the NGOs, the victims' encounter with the authorities can reinforce the trauma of trafficking, making it more difficult for the victims to get back to 'normal life' and creating the conditions of possibility for retrafficking (La Strada Moldova, 2006: 5).

The assumption at work here is that 'normal life' is defined in terms of managed and regulated freedom, from which freedom of movement is excluded. Hence the spectre of illegal migration or retrafficking parallels all humanitarian measures concerning victims of trafficking. Freedom does not appear as an argument about the women's right to choose whether they want to testify against their traffickers. The assumption of trauma makes any decision by women potentially an unfree decision. Women's freedom is a matter of the needs of the police or of the judiciary. If the investigative and prosecuting authorities decide that women's testimonies are useful for the trial, then they are allowed to stay and testify. If women do not testify, La Strada Moldova reminds us, 'criminals, who made a fortune by selling human slaves, get scot-free and commit new crimes, and more and more people become victims of trafficking in persons' (La Strada Moldova, 2006: 5).

If freedom is denied or limited for the purposes of governing human trafficking, it resurfaces in academic analyses of human trafficking in an ontological sense. Women are ontologically free and therefore resist these practices of abjection. Yet, I have shown that their practices of resistance are reappropriated in a discourse of risk and trauma, thereby having their political implications obscured. A physically and psychologically traumatized subject is also deemed incapable of ontological freedom. Are they also deemed incapable or 'unworthy' of political freedoms? If the depoliticization of subjectivity could be undone through the egalitarian predicate of work, thus opening the space for ontological freedom, I am interested here in the absence of political claims to freedom from the situation of trafficking. In the situation of trafficking, liberty cannot become a direct argument against security. Why is liberty silenced when women and other migrants need it most? Balibar has suggested that equality and liberty are inseparable as the kernel of ideal universality. His 'proposition of equaliberty' can be translated succinctly as 'no equality without liberty, no liberty without equality' (Balibar, 2002b). This equation is especially of interest for a politics out of security as claims to liberty have been used to challenge security practices. For example, civil liberties feature prominently in the activities of those who oppose the practices of the 'war on terror'.

Although liberty is seen as the counter-concept of security, little theoretical work on the political purchase of the concept has been done in critical security studies. The subject that is presupposed by critical security studies is an ontologically free subject.[2] The implicit counterpart to the construction of security as a speech act or to a contingent *dispositif* of discourse and practice is the free subject that can challenge those constructions. Alternative discourses to the constructed discourse of security can be articulated, as long as subjects are supposed to be ontologically free. Even if freedom is institutionally limited, the ontological freedom that is at stake is that of resisting practices of security. Paradoxically, critical approaches cannot accommodate this assumption in an explicit way. The subject's ontological freedom is recognized, but not theorized in relation to security. Ontological freedom provides a resource of agency against security practices, but liberty as a political construct is not theorized. In a way, critical security studies reformulate the debate of security and liberty as the problematique of the modern subject: ontologically free and endowed with agency, yet constituted in relations of power. As long as liberty functions only at the level of ontology, it is unclear how such an ontological premise can play a role politically. Ontological freedom can be denied or reformulated as non-freedom. Is there any role left for the political concept of freedom, a freedom that is enunciated in a claim and enacted as a prescription against the state?

In the first part of this chapter, I explore the role of liberty in the constitution of political communities, in order to understand the impossibility of enunciating the freedoms of victims of trafficking. Through a Foucauldian re-reading of Thomas Hobbes, I show how liberty is reconfigured from an excessive universal into a limited and managed practice. In the second half of the chapter, I unpack liberty as a practice of governmentality and inquire into the conditions of possibility for liberty as a principle for emancipation and transformation. Drawing on Balibar's insight of the inseparability of equality and freedom, I argue that liberty cannot be mobilized against security in the absence of equality. Politics out of security is a politics of inseparable equality and liberty. The enunciation of political freedoms can be formulated only when there is a presumption of equality at work or when equality is axiomatically introduced into a situation.

Governing the excesses of freedom

The political lesson that we associate with Hobbes is that individuals give up freedom for the security they can enjoy in the Leviathan. Yet, freedom does not disappear from the Leviathan, but re-emerges in a different shape, a limited freedom that refutes the dangerous freedoms of the state of nature. Hobbes appears to solve the dilemma of differential freedom by defining freedom in a mechanistic sense, as simply the unimpeded possibility of motion. Despite this understanding of freedom as determined by the laws of motion, the spectre of other freedoms hovers over the Leviathan. The institution of sovereignty is based on the distinction between the two types of freedom: freedom as a prerogative of the individual prior to the social contract (which is shown to be no freedom at all) and freedom within the constraints and limitations of the Leviathan (freedom as necessity). The shift from natural to civil liberty is that from state of nature to the civil state of peace and order.

The shift from the state of nature to the commonwealth is also a change in the status of equality, another concept whose dismissal to the state of nature does not evacuate its political possibility. Equality in the state of nature is depicted as pernicious as it led to the war of all against all. The equality of the state of nature is replaced by the political equality of individual wills that decide to authorize the Leviathan to govern them. There is therefore a moment of political liberty and equality in Hobbes's theory, the constitution of Leviathan by a multiplicity of discrete individual wills. What is more, with Hobbes, nobody is unfit for the task of political community. There are no slaves or people of lesser intellect, who could not join in the constitution of the state and the 'equality of all under one'. Yet, this moment in the constitution of the state contains the very promise of its unmaking. As the Leviathan has been constituted through individual wills, it can also be undone through 'civil war'. The ambiguity of the very constitutive moment of the Leviathan leads Hobbes to set up a mechanism of government that would make the eruption of civil wars impossible.

Richard Ashcraft has suggested that Hobbes's statement that the Leviathan had been 'occasioned by the disorders of the present time' should be read as part of his political theory and not simply as a background note (Ashcraft, 1978: 28). Other Marxist and post-Marxist theorists have seen the problem of revolts and political revolutions as immanent to the constitution of the Leviathan, rather than simply a historical incentive to the theory. Hobbes should be read as a theoretically preventive attempt against the causes and outburst of civil wars. In Balibar's formulation, '[h]is entire organization of the state, including the way in which the distinction between the public and private sphere operates, can be understood as a system of preventive defence against the mass movements that forms the basis of civil wars (of classes and of religions) and of revolutions' (Balibar, 1994: 16). Foucault has also argued that '[i]t is a discourse of struggle and permanent civil war that Hobbes wards off by making all wars and conquests depend upon a contract, and by thus rescuing the theory of the state' (Foucault, 2004b: 99).

This potential reversal of civil peace into civil war is evident from Hobbes's continuous concern with seditions. He dedicated considerable space to seditions in both *De Cive* (1642) and *Leviathan* (1651). *Behemoth* (1682) is entirely devoted to the issue of civil war and seditions; it takes these analytical considerations and applies them historically to the English civil war. Seditions are to be prevented not only through 'forewarning' and 'forearming', as Hobbes suggests in *De cive*, but also through much more subtle and varied tools. The Leviathan does not only provide for the protection of citizens against the state of nature, but also has to ensure the impossibility of its re-emergence and avoid the dissolution of the commonwealth.

The transfer of rights to the state does not do away with the possibility of civil war and excessive freedom. Even when Hobbes attempts to restrict freedom to 'corporeal freedom', or the freedom of moving without impediment, the subject thus constituted seems to be haunted by the spectre of excessive liberty. If individuals give up freedom in search of security, the state is allowed to 'do whatsoever he shall think necessary to be done, both before hand, for the preserving of Peace and Security, by prevention of Discord at home and Hostility from abroad'

(Hobbes, 1985: 233). Although subjects are free to disobey commands that would contradict natural law and free to resist the sovereign when attacked, they cannot challenge the actions of the Leviathan. And yet, the very spectre of sedition and disobedience still haunts the Leviathan.

Who are the subjects of potential seditions, those who threaten the body politic and forebode its dissolution? The very enemies of the Leviathan are its own citizens and the spectre of excessive liberty. Hobbes is adamant against the freedom of man to be the judge of good and evil (1985: 365), as this liberty could be a direct challenge to state action. Citizens cannot be private judges of public affairs and need to submit their judgement to that of the sovereign. This freedom of judgement can only be true of the state of nature, as in the Leviathan the freedom of judgement would undermine the sovereignty of law and would be dangerously close to seditious actions. Hobbes's diatribe against Roman and Greek understandings of liberty, which could buttress claims of individuals against the state (1985: 369), entrenches the boundary between forms of liberty linked to the two forms of life – nature and civilization. In *Behemoth*, he clearly states among the causes of the English civil war the exceeding number of men who had been educated by famous books on ancient Greece and Rome, in which 'popular government was extolled by the glorious name of liberty, and monarchy disgraced by the name of tyranny' (Hobbes, 1990: 3). The liberty that the Leviathan allows can be undermined by the very horizon of excessive liberty.

One could argue that citizens are allowed to enjoy freedom, as long as it does not lead to seditions. The only logically possible freedom is a qualified form of freedom, a freedom with limits enforced by the sovereign state (Walker and Neal, 2003). The rest of the freedoms are defined by the 'silence of the law'; for such silence to be correctly interpreted and not to lead to revolt, ordered and disciplined citizens are required. The preservation of civil peace requires practices of liberty that are consonant with the goals of the state. As David Burchell has put it, civil peace requires both an absolute sovereign and a population trained and educated in the civic virtues of justice, gratitude and complaisance.[3] He persuasively makes the argument that Hobbes's 'education' (*disciplina*, in the Latin original) covered a wide range of 'discipines' by which human beings are made into citizens (1999). Chapter XXX of the *Leviathan* lists the virtues that need to be inculcated into people so as to make rebellion impossible: not to exalt fellow citizens above the sovereign, not to speak evil of the sovereign, to respect their parents, not to deprive fellow subjects of their legitimate possessions, and not to have unjust intentions. The sovereign appears from its inception as governmental, engaged in the normalization of freedom and the prevention of the subject's excessive liberty. The individual is 'the product of the civil society which is to regulate it, and the Hobbesian problem is how to form it so that it will be able and willing to abide by the natural laws and contracts appropriate to civil society' (Connolly, 1988: 27).

Although Foucault has distinguished disciplinary and governmental practices from the prerogatives of the sovereign state, Michel Senellart, the editor of Foucault's lectures on governmentality, has located the *police* function of the sovereign state alongside its military role (Senellart, 1995). Sovereignty needs policing techniques for its own reproduction and perdurability. Peace, security and order can only be achieved through a process of permanent ordering, regulation and normalization of the subject. Ordering entails the normalization and regulation of excessive liberty, a liberty that continues to manifest itself within the Leviathan through excessive practices. Hobbes is wary of the 'multitude', the crowds who shun political unity and resist authority. If the constitution of the Leviathan entails the move from the 'multitude' to the 'people', the multitude reappears in the governing of the state. Yet, it is not the same multitude, but rather the spectre of a multitude endowed with excessive freedom. The multitude of the state of nature was already 'decomposed, reduced in advance (preventively) to the sum of its constituent atoms (people in the state of nature)' (Balibar, 1994: 16), who can enter the social contract only one by one, individually. In the Leviathan, the multitude reappears in a political guise. 'When they rebel against the state, the citizens are the multitude against the people' (Virno, 2002: 10). For Hobbes the multitude appears as a permanent remainder of the state of nature in the middle of the commonwealth.[4] As Virno has noted, the multitude is a negative concept, the very negation of the state of civil peace with its entailing techniques of normalization. In *De Cive*, the problem of the multitude is translated upon the faction, defined as a multitude of subjects united in opposition to the sovereign authority. Factions, Hobbes points out, are unjust, being 'contrary to the peace and safety of the people' (quoted in Ashcraft, 1978: 42).

In rejecting the multitude and other forms of illicit associations such as factions, Hobbes rejects the very possibility of resistance against the Leviathan. He uses the concepts of liberty and equality in a counter-revolutionary move to create a pact, a social contract through which everybody is alienated (Balibar, 2002a). The political equality on which Hobbes bases the constitution of the Leviathan is only a point of departure, distanced both from the equality in the state of nature and the governmental techniques deployed in the functioning of the state for the purposes of its conservation. The moment of political equality is at a distance from the hierarchies of power and honour in the state. Yet, Hobbes's equality is a partial equality, subtended by relations of inequality – hence the continuous concern with disciplining subjects who might revolt against such inequality.

To avoid the peril of its dissolution, the sovereign state reshapes and tames excessive liberty to make it consonant with civil laws. One of these dangerous practices, one of the 'diseases' of the Leviathan, is the practice of excessive words, words improperly used or words without a referent. The body politic is threatened by words and phrases like 'one must listen to the voice of conscience not to the voice of authority' or 'it is right to kill a tyrant' (Rancière, 1992: 43). The greatest fear of the Leviathan is not regicide, or sedition itself, but the naming of regicide as tyrannicide (Rancière, 1992: 369). When the king is called a tyrant, other forms of justification of political action challenge the authority of the Leviathan. Tyrannicide is synonymous to the excessive use of liberty and the enactment of equality against relations of domination. The word 'tyrant' challenges the rightfulness of the sovereign and points to relations of domination and inequality. Claims of tyrannicide also enact the political equality from which Hobbes could make solely a moment of departure of the commonwealth. Political equality is suspended, however, in the functioning of the state, and its reassertion by practices of excessive liberty is what the Leviathan fears most. Political equality cannot last in the functioning of the Leviathan, as the narrative of the constitution of the state is divorced from the insurrectional moment of politics, the moment of collective action against forms of domination and inequality.

Practices of security make possible the separation between the constitution of political communities and the insurrectional moment of equality. Security excludes those internal others deemed dangerous, banishes factions and other associations and drastically limits political equality and liberty. The most troublesome enemies for the state are not those external enemies who threaten its survival in the international 'state of nature' – after all Hobbes is aware of the fact that a state does not die like an individual – but those who threaten to reveal the relations of domination at the heart of the Leviathan. Thus, security is not simply a practice that creates spaces of abjection and exclusion under the guise of a promise for the future. Security practices are also counter-insurrectional practices that attempt to suspend radical claims of emancipation and transformation. If security mobilizes sovereign decisionism and exceptionalism, as Schmitt suggested, it is for the purpose of uprooting another political exception, that of an insurrection against inequality and domination. The limits of liberty and equality are necessary counter-insurrectional limits. Yet, if the spectre of excessive political freedom still haunts the Leviathan, Hobbes undertakes a second move that further obscures that role of insurrection (understood as a politics of emancipation and transformation). Hobbes's lesson is that practices of security are simultaneously a way of suspending forms of excessive liberty against domination and inequality.

Governing through freedom

The separation between the insurrectional and the constitutional moment in the constitution of the state is not a sufficient strategy for preventing the possibility of insurrection. The normalization of liberty in the sovereign imaginary and the distancing of the moment of political equality, in Hobbes, are supplemented by another move that renders the practices of excessive liberty and revolts against injustice and domination unthinkable. Besides the disciplinary taming of excessive liberty, there is another element that appears as part of the state function to prevent seditions. Hobbes's enlarged definition of safety as not just 'bare Preservation, but also all other Contentments of life, which every man by lawful Industry, without danger, or hurt to the Commonwealth, shall acquire to himself' (Hobbes, 1985: 376) spells out another governmental function of the state. Freedoms are produced by the state to ensure the prosperity of the population. They are not only normalized but also fostered, artificially created by the state without any reference to a false/excessive liberty or (non-)freedom. It is no longer the Leviathan that appears as the artificial creation of the social contract, but the individual is being refashioned, artificially recreated.

In *De cive*, following the chapter on seditions, Hobbes prescribes upon the sovereign state the duty to 'ensure that the citizens are abundantly provided with all the good things necessary not just for life but for the enjoyment of life' (Hobbes, 1998: 144). Such an approach deriving from the state function of ensuring prosperity entails a different conceptualization of freedom. This concern with population, its 'multiplication' and prosperity as the other side of disciplinary normalization is encapsulated by biopolitical practices. Foucault had located the emergence of an art of government as early as the 15th and 16th century. Yet, it was only in the 18th century that the art of government found its own rationality by inventing the notion of the population. The population becomes the ultimate end of government itself (Foucault, 1991: 100).

In Hobbes, an account of governmentality *avant la lettre* subordinates the concern for the welfare of the population to the prevention of seditions. The state has, therefore, to take care of the reproduction of the population and of their prosperity, to ensure domestic peace and defence against external enemies. The state does not simply avoid the resurgence of the 'state of nature' through repressive and disciplinary means, but is also supposed to ensure the good living for its subjects, through governmental technologies. The policing function of Leviathan is not simply repressive and dissuasive; it also needs to facilitate the circulation of persons and goods, the provision of goods, use all forces, restrict superfluous spending, etc. The creation of regulated freedoms can prevent resistance to domination. The governmental function of creating prosperity is linked to the prevention of insurrections. In *Behemoth*, the 'admiration [of] the great prosperity of the Low Countries after they had revolted from their monarch' (Hobbes, 1990: 3–4) is again mentioned among the causes of the English civil war. Protected and prosperous, citizens have no reason for discontent with the Leviathan.

What does this 'governmental' function of the state mean for liberty? To ensure the prosperity of the population, the state needs to foster certain liberties, like the liberty of circulation or commerce. Subsequently, the state becomes a producer of freedom; it creates a series of freedoms which can serve to enhance its prosperity and the welfare of the population. It needs freedom and, therefore, it has to produce and organize it. Liberty becomes a *'technical* requirement of governing the natural processes of social life and, particularly, those of self-interested exchange' (Burchell, 1991: 139). These freedoms, however differently interpreted by mercantilism, Keynesianism or (neo-)liberalism, constitute the subject as the artificial *homo economicus*.

Governmentalized freedom as freedom without an outside is no longer defined by its excesses, but immanently, through considerations of proper use. Is the use of liberty aligned to the purposes of the state? The logic of governmentalized freedom is totally different from liberty under conditions of necessity. The creation of artificial freedom eliminates the outside of excessive freedom. Social and economic processes have no outside, but become constitutive of the community, without the mediation of political subjects. Political equality is no longer the basis for the constitution of community; equality as a principle of action is replaced by equality as a goal, by programmatic equality in Badiou's terms. Freedom becomes a governmental creation linked to specific processes that ensure the 'ordered' functioning of the state and its population and also contains the criteria for its own control. The constitution of the subject as self-regulating has become an explicit political stake.

Artificial freedoms are governed according to a different principle of necessity, namely, efficiency. Efficiency is, however, no longer understood as the calculation and adjustment of ends and means which would be part of any political decision.[5] The criteria of efficiency are already given by the knowledge of economic and social processes. Subjects adjust their freedoms to these processes. Governmentality no longer works with a paradigmatic relation between the state and the citizen. With the invention of the population and the use of political economy as a rationality of government, the relation between the state[6] and its citizens or certain spheres to be governed works with the principle of utility. Is the liberty of certain categories of the population or in certain areas desirable for proper government? The answer varies and can only be supported by a detailed knowledge of the population. Only a certain kind of liberty – a certain way of understanding and exercising freedom, of relating to ourselves individually and collectively as subjects of freedom – is compatible with the liberal arts of rule (Rose, 1999).

The differentiation between excess and proper use reframes the double of liberty/security as the triptych of liberty/security/equality.[7] Freedom as excess speaks of the insurrectional moment of politics, the moment in which political equality is allied with freedom in actions against domination. Freedom as proper use suspends the problem of political equality. Equality becomes programmatic and is to be understood as substantive, a goal to be achieved by governmental programmes. Programmatic equality is based on a constitutively inegalitarian society, with subjects labelled as capable or incapable of aligning their actions to the purposes of government. Moreover, this constitutive inequality suspends excessive liberty and the enactment of political equality. The criteria for the proper use of freedom are given by immanent processes which are deciphered by professionals: economists, social scientists, demographers, etc. A proper use of artificially created freedoms – for example, freedom of movement, freedom of commerce – divides populations among categories. Inequality is not only characteristic of social relations, but becomes constitutive of who subjects are. Those who use freedom properly are the self-governing subjects, able to manage themselves and their liberties. The paradigmatic liberal subject is therefore the subject capable of self-control, the subject that harnesses her freedom to the purposes of the state and avoids its excesses. However, such a freedom – Hindess warns us – is not something 'granted to individuals as such and in general: it is granted to certain individuals only and within particular circumscribed domains' (Hindess, 2001: 97). The relation between those who are governed and those who govern is variable, depending on the categorization of the governed. Freedom is to be granted to these self-governing subjects. Those who are not yet capable of self-regulation have their freedoms restricted under the imperative of utility or efficiency.

The liberal state has a long history of people who are deemed not to possess or to display the attributes required for the juridical and political subjects of rights; they are subjected to all sorts of disciplinary, biopolitical and even sovereign interventions (Dean, 1999a). Alongside the minority of self-governing subjects, the rest are constituted as subjects whose freedom is to be severely restricted. The constitution of categories of abjects is made possible through the expert assessment of their use of freedom. Rather than rendered as a denial of freedom, abjection enters a complex relation to the proper use of liberty. I have already shown that security practices constitute categories of subjects and abjects. The governmentalization of freedom introduces a new aspect to the excessive liberties of the multitude. Calling a king a tyrant made visible a wrong and a form of oppression. It was available as a practice to anybody who could hold the state accountable for its practices, it was the insurrectional moment that always haunted the constitution of political communities. Political equality can only appear as superfluous in relation to artificial freedoms that are supposed to ultimately lead to relative equality. The insurrectional moment can no longer be invoked.

As social and economic processes have become naturalized, the state will hold individuals and groups of the population accountable for the proper use of their freedoms, so as not to impinge upon the natural unfolding of these processes. Hobbes has warned against the dangers of commerce in some products. Trading too much can be as dangerous as trading too little. Those who do not conform to the limits and conditions set by the state become dangerous. They are not dangerous to the state itself, but they pose a risk to the good functioning of certain societal and economic processes. Thus, they become dangerous to society and to the rest of the population. The danger posed is not one of direct sedition against the state, but one of indirect disordering of the processes that make up the state. Through governmentalization, freedom is doubly removed from the insurrectional moment of politics. Not only was constitution separated from insurrection, but the constitutive moment is obscured in the temporal rendering of the state as constituted by economic and social processes. If Schmitt's analysis of the role of the state rendered visible the constitutive moment of order, he also joined Hobbes in separating it from insurrection.

Trafficked women are not dangerous only because they have broken the law or because of their difference. They are dangerous given the ways in which illegal migration is understood, as unordered disturbance of the processes of free movement. Women pose a threat to freedom of movement – a governmental process devised by the EU as a method of effective government. Breaking the parameters set by the state for what freedom of movement should be turns women into risky others. As the risk they pose is one of renewed migratory projects, it must be understood as a risk to a process, not to the state. Similar to migration, organized crime also refers to the non-sanctioned improper use of the freedom of commerce. Organized crime functions in the shadow of law, by ignoring the definitions of proper and improper use of freedom of trade authorized by the state.

What is at stake in the construction of risk and danger around the (im)proper use of freedom appears more clearly when one considers the French so-called 'seuil de tolérance' [threshold of tolerance] regarding migration. Migrants can be tolerated as long as they as they play a role in the functioning of social and economic processes, as long as they do not migrate in higher numbers and do not raise any claims politically. Interestingly, as Balibar has pointed out, the question of the 'seuil de tolérance' has not been raised in relation to labour, but in relation to housing, welfare, education, everything that serves for the reproduction of labour force (Balibar, 1992). Migrants become a problem when they try to have access to social housing, welfare benefits, when they manage to bring their families, when their children go to schools, when they are no longer reduced to raw labour force. Migrants become dangerous when they do not simply enact qualified freedoms granted to them in certain areas, but attempt to enact political equality, claim equal treatment or equal rights.

Victims of trafficking are also represented as dangerous when their use of freedom is improperly made to function as part of migratory processes. Their riskiness becomes most evident when they refuse institutionalization, deportation and therapy. When they become associated with sex workers and claim political equality, they become the dangerous migrant other. In light of the reformulation of the relation between liberty, equality and security, one can say that migrants become dangerous when they attempt to reactivate the insurrectional moment of politics. The threat of trafficking and the risk that victims of trafficking pose is embedded in the threat that illegal migrant (sex) workers – the category from which victims of trafficking are extracted – can pose. Illegal migrant (sex) workers can activate an insurrectional politics that challenges the inegalitarian premises of the constitution of states and the exclusionary effects of their governmental practices.

The two forms of freedom that appear in Hobbes, liberty and its excesses, on the one hand, and artificial freedoms and their proper use, on the other, point to a differential relation between liberty, equality and security. Although Hobbes thought that equality (or the lack of enough difference) between men led to the war of all against all, political equality was the point of departure in the constitution of the Leviathan. If this equality was suspended through preventive disciplinary practices of excessive liberty, it always harboured the risk of being reactivated by 'factions' and 'multitudes of citizens' as a form of insurrectional politics challenging state practices. The artificial freedoms that the state creates suspend equality by dividing the population into categories depending on their capacity for self-governance and proper use of freedom. Without an outside or a fiction of excess, artificial freedoms naturalize the inequality of political subjects. Equality as the form of action, as the principle that informs insurrections and revolts is replaced by programmatic equality, a form of substantive equality that attempts to progressively reduce existing inequalities. Those who resist state practices are categorized as unable to behave properly, or as unequal in some other way, by virtue of some particularity (class, race, nationality, mental or intellectual condition, etc.). The specification and categorization of subjects gives rise to a limited concept of freedom, a managed and regulated freedom aligned with the purposes of the state.

The freedom of trafficked women is therefore doubly unthinkable: both as excessive liberty and as properly used freedom. Freedom of movement cannot be practiced by subjects who are not useful to the social and economic processes sanctioned by the state. Also, trafficked women cannot enact excessive freedoms as they are not participants in the constitution of the political community where they attempt to claim rights. Hobbes's lesson is that the freedom of women who cross borders in search for work – making themselves vulnerable to abuse and exploitation – is unthinkable inasmuch as the insurrectional moment of politics has become unthinkable.

Inseparable equality and liberty

My reading of Hobbes has attempted to retrieve an understanding of excessive liberty linked with equality in forms of insurrectional poli-tics that have been suspended by the constitution and functioning of the Leviathan. Political theory has often gone along with this suspension of an insurrectional understanding of liberty and equality and has seen equality as substantive and liberty as a status, both being derived from a subject's particularity and her belonging to a specific political community. Consequently, equality and freedom could be thought only as separable and incompatible rather than intrinsically related. Liberalism, for example, is characterized by the paradox of liberty and equality. 'Premising itself on the natural equality of human beings', Wendy Brown has argued, 'liberalism makes a political promise of universal individual freedom in order to arrive at social equality, or achieve a civilized retrieval of the equality postulated in the state of nature' (Brown, 1995: 67). With liberalism, equality is deferred, turned into a goal to be achieved, while liberty is seen as primary. Consequently, while making a promise of potential equality, liberalism also legitimizes existing inequalities.

In coining the rather awkward-sounding concept of equaliberty, Balibar has argued that equality and liberty are inseparable, that privileging either equality or liberty is equivalent to denying both. The concept of equaliberty posits the inseparability of equality and liberty as a historical realization:

> ... the reasoning that underlies the proposition of equaliberty ($E = F$) is not essentialist. [I]t is based on is the historical discovery, which can legitimately be called experimental, that their *extensions* are necessarily identical. To put it plainly, the situations in which both are either present or absent are necessarily the same.
>
> (Balibar, 1994: 48, emphasis in original)

Equality and liberty can only be verified in particular situations, none is given substantively. Equaliberty is to be verified by political actors in concrete situations. The proposition of equaliberty can be translated as the historical inseparability of equality and liberty or that equality is identical to freedom. In practice, '*neither* can true liberty go without equality *nor* can true equality go without liberty' (Balibar, 1994: xiii, emphasis in original). As the equation of liberty and equality has emerged out of historical practice, there is no proof of this truth but a negative one: equality and liberty are always contradicted together (Balibar, 1994: 48). Equality and liberty are contradicted in the same situations, there can be no situations which suppress or repress freedom and do not also suppress or diminish equality. In the situation of trafficking, the inequality of illegal migrants is also a form of unfreedom, be it freedom of movement or even freedom of choice.

The opposite of the proposition of equaliberty is therefore the proof of its truth: situations of constraints on freedom also mean social inequality. Unfreedom is identical to inequality as freedom is identical to equality. The deferral of equality through the creation of the Leviathan would make the liberty granted to citizens a form of unfreedom. The creation of artificial freedoms is in itself a strategy of division and inequality of categories of the population. The body politic is constituted through a double deferral of equality: first, citizens can enjoy only formal liberty and, second, the majority of the population is subjected to practices of unfreedom. Balibar has emphasized three aspects of equaliberty that contradict the Hobbesian constitution of the body politic. The first is that politics is founded on the recognition that neither freedom nor equality can exist without each other, that the suppression or even the limitation of one necessarily leads to the suppression or limitation of the other. Secondly, equaliberty implies universality. Democracy is a historical process of the extension of rights to all humanity. In the third place, equaliberty implies ... 'a universal right to *politics*, the right of every man and every woman to become the 'subject' or agent of politics' (Balibar, 1994: 49, emphasis in original).

The imperative of security constitutes political communities through practices of inequality and unfreedom. Those who make use of excessive liberty to resist tyranny or to resist oppressive practices challenge the inequality of domination. The multitude challenges the right of the sovereign to judge on good and evil and manifests itself as an equal judge. Governmental freedoms depend upon an inegalitarian premise; through the distinction that is traced among categories of the population, freedoms become unfreedoms. Equaliberty refers to the freedom of every subject to resist oppression and domination; such freedom can only be enacted or claimed through equality. Equality challenges the very logic of population division (as the logic of security) and therefore opens a space for liberty. Equaliberty is universal in that nobody can be excluded from politics by virtue of particular characteristics or predicates; it functions in the tension between fictive and ideal universality, between the arbitrary limitation of politics and its universal promise.

The equality that informs emancipation and transformation needs to be set at a distance from the concept of difference. As Badiou has separated the politics of emancipation from any cultural predicates, equality needs to be separated from the very popular concept of difference. In a recent article on Balibar's concept of equaliberty, Alan Johnson has argued that it has an affinity with the feminist 'equality-versus-difference' debate (Johnson, 2003). Despite apparent similarities, I contend that political equality needs indifference to difference.

The feminist problematique of equality-versus-difference derived from the political question of claims to equality, claims which were interpreted as subduing and erasing difference. Therefore, the question that has beset feminist struggles and political theory is: how can women claim equality with men, while at the same time needing claims based on difference? The equality theorists were thought to accept the basic claims underpinning liberal political theory, that the idea of equality is neutral vis-à-vis gender (Squires, 2000: 118). The difference theorists argued that equality is actually anthropocentric and called for women's specificity to be recognized in feminist struggles rather than effaced in claims for equality. The formal character of liberal equality was seen as 'severely compromised by the character of a (white, bourgeois, male, heterosexual) hegemonic subject' (Brown, 2001: 9).

One of the ways out of the quandary of equality-versus-difference has been to refuse the terms of the question altogether, to refuse the dichotomous mould in which the question of equality-versus-difference has been formulated. The deconstruction or displacement of the dichotomy has challenged the connection of equality with sameness and of difference with dichotomous sexual difference. Sexual difference could be deconstructed in a criticism of dichotomous thinking (see Lloyd, 1984; Prokhovnik, 2002) and its simplification of the world. On the side of equality, a similar strategy of displacement has consisted in the deconstruction of the equality–sameness equation. The definition of equality as sameness, 'a condition in which humans share the same nature, the same rights, and the same terms of regard by state institutions' is intrinsic to liberalism (Brown, 1995: 153). The conceptual force of equality rests on the assumption of difference, which should be in some respect valued equally (Squires, 2000: 129).

Joan Scott has proposed to 'relax' the concept of equality by redefining it as 'deliberate indifference to specified differences' (Scott, 1994: 294). Equality no longer presupposes sameness, but a deliberate ignorance of some differences. Yet, relaxing the concept of equality was at the antipode of theoretical debates that were defining theoretical feminism. Rather than indifference to specified differences, equality was thought to silence the claims of women by the equality of Woman (defined as white, middle-class, and straight). Thus, the equality-versus-difference debate shifted onto the side of difference, of differences-within-difference, the different voices of oppressed and dominated women under the category of Women. Feminism had to preoccupy itself with how to give voice to these different categories rather than engage with the meaning of political equality.

Yet, my contention has been that a continual emphasis on 'differences that differ' can lead to a political impasse. Victims of trafficking are already different; one can create other differences, be indifferent to certain differences, while pointing out others. What counts politically is not a list of differences, but how one gets out of listing differences that can be subjected to more and more detailed governmental representations and interventions. It is an important insight of the intersection of feminism and poststructuralism that subjects are different from their constitution through history and practices of power, that representation does not exhaust presentation. However, this awareness is not enough for political struggles. Why should one difference be supported as opposed to another? The answer has variedly concerned the history of injustice or the hierarchization and polarization of differences. Contrary to these positions, I have argued that emancipation cannot be linked with cultural predicates, with that which is represented and given as partial. The struggle of sex workers addresses everybody in the situation of trafficking under the predicate of work.

Struggles for the emancipation of women have been best of the question of equality-versus-difference. Scott has brilliantly shown how 'difference' and 'sameness' have both been present – although in tension – in the struggle of women, as early as the French Revolution. Feminism is the paradoxical expression of that contradiction in its effort both to have 'sexual difference' acknowledged and to have it rendered irrelevant (Scott, 1996: 168). In her own words,

> Feminism was a protest against women's political exclusion; its goal was to eliminate 'sexual difference' in politics, but it had to make its claims on behalf of 'women' (who were discursively produced through 'sexual difference'). To the extent that it acted for 'women', feminism produced the sexual difference that it sought to eliminate. This paradox [...] was the constitutive condition of feminism as a political movement throughout its long history.
>
> (Scott, 1996: 3–4)

The use of sexual difference or equality arguments is therefore contextual. Yet, Scott's comments reveal that equality is reinterpreted in identity terms, as sameness. In the sense employed here, equality is not about identity. Equality is a claim, an enunciation or a practice. Rather than unifying, it is a practice of dis-unity, de-classification and de-categorization.

Geneviève Fraisse has objected to the subsumption of equality to identity in feminist theory. She has asked why a philosophical, onto-logical concept such as difference – whose correspondent is obviously identity – has been connected with a political principle such as equality – whose correspondent is liberty (Fraisse, 2001: 251–3). Feminist literature has brought together the ontological discussion of identity/difference and the political one of equality/liberty through a combination of equal-ity and difference.[8] The rationale for such a move takes equality through the ontological prism of identity and assumes that equality is destructive of difference. Yet, difference itself is hierarchical and leads to inequality. Fraisse has suggested that the 'difference of the sexes' should not impede the formulation of a politics of equality and liberty. Instead of opposing identity and difference, one should play upon their possible conjunction: women are different from and similar to men. Here, para-doxically, she has joined Scott in the intimation that claims to identity/difference can be formulated depending on the context.

Drawing inspiration from the critique that Fraisse formulates, my contention is rather that the question of equality/liberty is incompatible to that of identity/difference. An emphasis on particularity, on difference undermines equality as it undergirds the *dispositif* of security. The equality–difference debate in feminism obscures the importance of equality as a principle for politics, by reducing it to an identitarian concern. While it is true that inequalities are also gendered and feminist research has brought to light the gendered deployment of power, it is important that one should not lose the political potential of equality by subsuming it under identity. Badiou is worth quoting at length here, as his comments are an interesting alternative to the feminist debates around identity/difference:

> The progressive formulation of a cause that engages cultural or communal predicates, linked to incontestable situations of oppres-sion and humiliation, presumes that we propose these predicates, these particularities, these singularities, these communal qualities, in such a way that they become situated in another space and become heterogeneous to their ordinary oppressive operations ... But in the end, between this particularity present in the practical, con-crete support of any political process, and the statements in the name of which the political process unfolds, I think there is *only* a relation of support, but not a relation of transitivity. You can't go from one to the other, even if one seems to be 'carried' by the other.
>
> (Badiou, 1998: 118–19)

'Difference' arguments can be mobilized contextually in support of a politics of equality, but they are not transitive to a politics of equality. The struggle of dominated groups is never simply formulated in terms of 'being black', 'being women', 'being gay', etc. but is a struggle against inequality and abjection in which subjects emerge as other-than-represented.

Equality is not identity, as this would mean a denial of freedom. Such is the problem that feminism encounters once more when it attempts to think politics for the woman-other. I have suggested that a transformative and emancipatory politics for trafficked women has to be divorced from identity/difference concerns, even if sexual difference and the naturalization of women (or a certain category of women) have been instrumental in the imaginary of prostitution. The situation of prostitution can be approached politically by means of questions of inequality and unfreedom rather than difference.

This insight bears a lot of weight for my previous discussion of the divisibility of freedom exactly through the construction of difference. If difference is the primary instrument of political struggles, it can become consonant with governmental strategies of population categorization and division. As the defining principle of politics, equality suspends the possibility of such categorization. The separation of equality and freedom allows for the deployment of practices of security. Politics out of security, politics of transformation and emancipation is based on the insurrectional enactment of equality and liberty as indeterminate principles whose extensions are to be verified in particular situations.

Although Balibar does not consider inequality as preceding unfreedom, my analysis of governmentality and security has made clear that hierarchy and division precede unfreedom. Governmental freedoms operate through the division and categorization of populations. The case of trafficking in women is one of those historical instantiations of the absence of both equality and freedom. The unthinkability and absence of freedom or liberty is linked with the absence of equality. Freedom can only become thinkable from the standpoint of a form of equality, the equality of work. Balibar's proposition of equaliberty offers an important insight as claims to freedom are impossible in the absence of equality. Trafficked women are categorized by the state as a specific population group, whose risk is to be ascertained and upon whom a variety of sovereign, disciplinary and governmental technologies are to be deployed. It is the difference of the trafficked women that makes them unequal and risky. Politics starts with a subjectification that is universalizing and not differential. The predicate of work suspends the specifications of difference in the situation of trafficking.

If (in)equality precedes (un)freedom, transformative and emancipatory struggles enact the principle of equality in order to politicize liberty. Liberty can become thematized, politicized, contested or enacted only from the standpoint of equality. Otherwise liberty remains presupposed as the 'unlimited power of the negative' (Badiou, 2003: 74), the ontological freedom of the modern subject to resist oppression and domination. Equality disrupts the dividing practices of security and allows the dangerous and risky to enter the stage of politics, to invent egalitarian names for themselves and derive political freedoms from these names.

The relation between equality and freedom understood as the political practice of emancipation and transformation reconfigures situations defined by inequality and unfreedom. Rather than substantively defined, equality and freedom can only be understood in relation to practices of inequality and unfreedom. In this sense, equality and freedom are maxims for action, principles that are not linked to any form of particularity or difference, but which intervene in any situation in which difference is formulated as domination or discrimination. Contrary to Balibar, I understand equality as the condition of liberty. Without the prerequisite of non-discrimination, of equality, interventions against domination cannot be formulated. It is the unconditional equality of all subjects as political subjects and participants that supports the enactment of liberty in situations of domination. Liberty is a word for politics inasmuch as a politics of transformation and emancipation is a politics of excessive liberty, of forms of insurrection that take rights and freedoms beyond the boundaries assigned to them and challenge situations of domination.

The emancipatory and transformative politics in the situation of trafficking suspends what I called in the first chapter the 'vectoring' of security by suspending its structuring of the situation as a situation of domination and discrimination. The situation of trafficking can be reconfigured through the enunciation of equality that starts from those who would count for nothing and that transforms, through political action, into a struggle for liberty and equality.

Conclusion

This chapter has questioned another absence in the struggles that unmake practices of security in the situation of trafficking, namely that of claims to freedom. I have started by questioning the absence of freedom in the situation of trafficking in women and have offered an account of the conditions of (im)possibility of political freedom. To this purpose, I have revisited the conceptualization of freedom and its relation to equality and security in Hobbes's political theory. Through a re-reading of Hobbes, I have shown that what makes claims to liberty unthinkable in relation to the situation of trafficking is not security, but the absence of equality. Hobbes's definition of liberty entails several moves away from equality as a political principle of insurrectional politics. Firstly, the state curtails the possibility of excessive liberties and minimizes citizenship through disciplinary and repressive practices that attempt to prevent and make impossible insurrections against situations of domination and discrimination. Secondly, the state also creates freedoms to be enjoyed as part of the immanent social and economic processes of the population. These freedoms are to be differentially enjoyed, depending on the capacity for self-government in accordance to state goals. The move from liberty to freedom can be read as an intensified attempt at suspending equality and insurrectional politics. The governmentalization of freedom undermines equality even more as it classifies individuals in different categories depending on their capacity for governing their freedom. Political equality remains only a moment of departure in the Leviathan, a moment from which the Leviathan departs in its functioning.

The risky and the dangerous are not simply abject others to be subjected to normalizing and disciplinary interventions, but those subjects who could reactivate the spectre of the insurrection beyond the constitution of the state through the social contract or its reproduction through the governance of social and economic processes. Security practices do not only create divisions and categorizations within the 'normal' subjects, but simultaneously target the excessive or excrescent subjects in a situation. Those who could enact a politics of equality and liberty against situations of domination and discrimination are to be incapacitated through practices of security. Trafficked women become dangerous through the excessive and disallowed use of freedom of movement. As non-nationals, non-citizens, migrants are a priori excluded from freedom of movement. Other differences such as risk profiles reconstruct victims of trafficking as a category continually prompted to endanger processes of migration and freedom of movement defined by the EU and its member states. Trafficked women are already outside the equality of citizenship and its national content. Their past biographies add to this social inequality, the inequality of 'nature': they are unable to govern their freedom and permanently incapacitated from the use of freedom.

Yet, beyond this constitution of danger there is the spectre of the more dangerous illegal migrant (sex) workers, the category from which the victims of trafficking are extracted. Illegal migrant (sex) workers embody the danger of reactivating insurrectional politics by making claims against inequality and unfreedom and exposing what is wrong with society as such. If forms of insurrection can suspend the vectoring of security in the situation of trafficking, if a politics of emancipation and transformation happens, it is because an instantiation of equality has been made possible. Equality disrupts situations of discrimination and suspends the division of freedom depending upon categories of subjects. Enunciations of equality make possible claims to freedom against the *dispositif* of security that governs human trafficking.

Conclusion: Politics Happens

On 18 October 2005, the European Commission issued a communication on 'Fighting trafficking in human beings – an integrated approach and proposals for an action plan'. After naming 'human rights' as the fundamental concern in tackling human trafficking, the document immediately emphasizes its dimensions of organized crime and illegal migration. 'High profits from labour and sexual exploitation', the Commission points out, 'are often subject to money laundering and may enable traffickers to engage in other criminal activities and to achieve economic, social or even political power' (European Commission, 2005a: 4). In January 2006, the UK government also issued a consultation paper on trafficking, which features a neologism, 'organized immigration crime', to refer to trafficking and other intersections between organized crime and illegal immigration (Home Office, 2006). The problematization of human trafficking, a phenomenon which, in the words of the Home Office, 'causes great harm to the individuals involved and to our society as a whole' (Home Office, 2006: 3), is paralleled by another important development. At the same time that the European Commission was preparing its action plans, Brussels was the location of another event: sex workers organized an international meeting that would lead to a Declaration of the Rights of Sex Workers in Europe (The International Committee on the Rights of Sex Workers in Europe, 2005). The Declaration reiterates international rights that should apply to all citizens – including sex workers. In the section on 'Freedom from Slavery and Forced Labour', the Declaration states the following:

> Measures should be taken to ensure that sex workers enjoy full labour rights, are informed of them and have access to the full range of measures and standards to end exploitative working conditions.

Measures should be taken to provide appropriate assistance and protection to victims of trafficking, forced labour & slavery like practices with full respect for the protection of their human rights. Provision of residency permits should be provided to ensure effective access to justice and legal remedies, including compensation, irrespective of their willingness to collaborate with law enforcement. Trafficked persons must not be returned to situations in countries that will lead to their re-trafficking or result in other harms.

(The International Committee on the Rights of
Sex Workers in Europe, 2005: 10)

The Declaration also points out that the non-recognition of prostitution as work has 'adverse consequences on the working conditions of sex workers'. These two quasi-simultaneous declarations, the EU's and the sex workers', display two modalities of action and engagement with social problems. On the one hand, there is the security problematization and governmentality of human trafficking and, on the other, a politics that verifies equality and enacts liberty. The Declaration of the Rights of Sex Workers in Europe verifies the equality of rights as stated in various EU and international documents. The Commission communication reiterates the politics of security in perfect consonance with a politics of human rights and concern for the particular other.

The Commission communication and the sex workers' Declaration of rights speak of the two modes of politics that this book has explored. A politics of security, of closure and of particularity, versus a politics of universality, of equality and of freedom. I started by exploring what security means and what it does in the context of human trafficking. Although security was not theorized and largely absent from political and scholarly interventions in the context of human trafficking, the presence of security entailed effects upon what could be said and done about human trafficking. As a nexus of representation and intervention, security creates spaces of abjection, spaces of exclusion and particularity. Security also depoliticizes the actions of equal subjects by mobilizing clinical knowledges to understand and describe those who are dangerous as well as those who are to be protected. The management of trafficking as a security issue relied on the management of migration, organized crime and prostitution. The practices that were deployed for governing human trafficking in all these aspects turned victims of trafficking into risky beings, victims of earlier childhood traumas likely to undertake high-risk actions such as illegal migration. The reading of trauma and psychological disorder into women's actions suspends critical considerations of their situation, their relation to the 'rehabilitation and reintegration' programmes or to the prospects for the future that such programmes define. The actions of victims of trafficking fall either under the heading of illegal migration or under that of clinical reactions to traumatic experiences.

Politics out of security starts from a shedding away of particularity, from a suspension of classification and representation. The concept of excess, of excessive subjects to a situation can inform a politics that transcends particularity and suspends the governmental vectoring of security. Excessive subjects are not seen as part of the situation, they are not representable, but only exist as an anomaly, as those who should not be there. Illegal migrant sex workers are those who do not belong to the situation of trafficking; they are anomalous inasmuch as they should not be there. A situation that is reconfigured from the standpoint of those-who-should not-be-there starts with the predicate of work. Work reframes the situation of trafficking without excluding either illegal migrants or victims of trafficking. As victims of trafficking are caught in the representations mobilized for the purposes of prevention, new names and identifications that are heterogeneous to governmentality need to be invented to reconfigure their situation. The figure of the worker disrupts the representations and interventions that mobilize clinical and psychological knowledge for the purposes of risk management.

The figure of work formulates exploitation as a 'wrong' of equality rather than as the result of psychological vulnerability leading to victimhood. It does not erase stories of abuse and violence and does not deny the unwillingness of foreign migrant women to be prostitutes. The figure of work redefines the situation in which illegal sex workers did not exist and exploited workers could only exist as victims to be voluntarily returned and rehabilitated. Work also addresses everybody in the situation and radically challenges the valence of the element which did not exist as positively individuated in a situation. From nothing, illegal migrant prostitutes can become something. Work can open a new form of collective action and redefine the boundaries of the political community. Those who work become part of the situation and could even claim residence and a 'path' to citizenship rights. A politics of emancipation and transformation radically changes the way people are counted and count in a situation.

The institutional claim by illegal migrant sex workers that they are self-employed workers and hence should be given residence rights is different from the forms of institutional struggles that a Bourdieuean analysis of fields would conceptualize. The Commission communication was supposed to be a response to a document written up by the European Experts Group on Human Trafficking, a consultative group formed of NGO representatives, academics and activists. Notwithstanding the recommendations of the 2004 Report they presented to the Commission, the present communication reiterates the EU policies regarding trafficking. Even recommendations to make residence independent of the victim's testimony or to ensure that victims of trafficking are not deported (Experts Group on Trafficking in Human Beings, 2004) have been ignored, despite the knowledge and the expertise mobilized by NGOs. Institutional struggles reproduce existing interests, unless considered from the standpoint of those who are excessive, who do not count in the situation.

Excessive subjects formulate egalitarian prescriptions against the state. They challenge situations of inequality and unfreedom by calling into question the particular mode of counting and representation in a situation. A politics of unmaking security functions as a political event by disrupting the abjectifying effects of security, on the basis of a claim to equality and universality. The profoundly inegalitarian claim of security which separates those who are dangerous or risky from those who are not is therefore challenged on the basis of a political claim to equality. This axiomatic claim to equality implies a dimension of universality – equality remains by definition open, addressing everybody.

The inscriptions of equality support liberty and inform insurrectional actions against relations of domination. Yet, the tradition that has opposed liberty to security in political theory has failed to analyse the practices of inequality that allow for the normalization or regulation of freedom. The reading of Hobbes that I have proposed has drawn on a Marxist concern with an insurrectional politics against situations of inequality and unfreedom. Even when it makes room for qualified liberty or creates artificial freedoms, security disavows and attempts to prevent forms of insurrectional politics that are based on the enactment of equality and liberty. Rendering the other dangerous has appeared as a process of rendering them first unequal, taking away forms of insurrectional actions and reducing them to a shadowy existence. Liberty and equality are therefore inseparable, both in their negation and in their enactment. Just as restrictions on liberty or unfreedoms can only function through an a priori denial of equality, a politics of equality is also a politics of liberty. Equality and liberty are not goals to be achieved, programmes to be implemented, but principles of action, maxims that are manifest in struggle.

Through the local verifications of equality and liberty a transformative-emancipatory politics challenges the governmentality of security. Under the imaginary of a universal promise, security deploys symbolic practices that transform the social into situations of inequality and unfreedom. A politics of universality, equality and liberty un-vectors the practices of security. How are we therefore to think the relation between politics and security? Security has appeared as coextensive to practices of government, the ultimate horizon of politics understood as the analytics of power relations. In a Schmittian reading, security is the very condition of possibility of order. In this dual aspect as both the condition and regulation of order, security depends on the specification of particularized subjectivities that create forms of inequality and suspend the excessive use of freedom.

The analysis of security in the Leviathan has linked this governmental analysis with a larger concern about insurrectional politics. A transformative-emancipatory politics is a form of insurrectional politics, the politics that practices of security have always tried to suspend. In Butler's terms, practices of security do not only create spaces of abjection, but they also prevent excessive subjects from making excessive claims of equality and liberty. In the separation from insurrectional politics, the constitution and functioning of the Leviathan have entrenched inequality and domination. Equality is only a point of departure in the constitution of the state; the inequality to the sovereign becomes the dominant relation in the functioning of the state. Liberty is disciplined or unequally fostered in particular categories of citizens. Without considerations of what political struggles cut across the fabric of the social, we would be caught within a governmental *dispositif* that creates 'legitimate' forms of exclusion in the name of order, survival, economic processes, welfare, etc.

If security is coextensive to the governmentality of populations, politics unmakes its dividing and exclusionary effects through the enunciation of universality and the inseparability of equality and liberty. Rather than the horizon of society, security is the negation of a politics of equality and liberty against any situation of domination and discrimination. A problematization of the problematization of security would steep security back into the political struggles and antagonisms which it tries to silence. Politics explores ongoing struggles in local situations and retrieves their enactment of equality, liberty and universality that practices of security attempt to neutralize.

Yet, is work and especially sex work the predicate of universality, equality and freedom as suggested here? As Marx has argued in the case of the proletariat, workers are free, but as they do not possess anything, they can only sell their labour force. Work is not just the form of an egalitarian collective subjectification, but also the key that opens the door of capitalism. For example, a claim like 'We are all workers' implies – besides an equalitarian subjectification – the freedom to sell one's labour force. Illegal migrants and trafficked women can break free from conditions of more serious, more violent exploitation by selling their labour force in the regulated framework of the market. One has to, however, concede to a Marxist critique the fact that the position of the worker entails other forms of exploitation, not necessarily of a much subtler nature than the exploitation of trafficked women in the shadows of illegality. While this form of emancipation remains partial, it represents an emancipatory move from the securitizing practices that categorize women as risky others. Unlike security, equality does not qualify the terms it refers to and it does not presuppose a territory for its exercise (Badiou, 1992). Equality is also its own measure that can be assessed by anybody in the here and now, rather than in an indeterminate future.

A politics of universality, equality and freedom is not devoid of conflict and division; it also creates divisions between adherents and opponents. However, it is not the division that delegitimizes politics, but the closure. The division of prescriptive principles is a division without closure, while the divisions of governmentality are reified and closed in their particularity. Security is one of the modalities in which inequality and unfreedom are entrenched, legitimated and reproduced. 'Politics out of security' has addressed this modality of structuring and counting situations and people and its un-vectoring, without making claims about domination more generally. Politics out of security un-vectors the security problematization of human trafficking and draws attention to the deployment of a particular *dispositif* that attempts to close off collective struggles against the closure of political communities.

Notes

Introduction: On the Contradictions of Trafficking in Women

1. The story was reported in all the major print and Internet media (for example, Britten, 1 October 2005; Gillan and Bindel, 5 October 2005; Smith, 3 October 2005).
2. This book focuses on trafficking in women, as it is the dominant construction at the European level. Therefore, it will use 'trafficking in women', 'human trafficking', and 'trafficking' interchangeably. Although trafficking in children, trafficking for domestic work and trafficking in organs are gaining increasing prominence, this thesis does not explicitly engage with them. Questions of subjectivity and the construction of political agency would need to be thought in these concrete contexts.
3. The Poppy Project (2006), which has published a report on the asylum claims of victims of trafficking in the UK, explains it by the lack of specific legislative measures that would ensure that trafficked women are not returned to their countries of origin once any police proceedings against their traffickers are at the end.
4. Foucault defines truth as these ordered procedures that govern statements.
5. I paraphrase here a question formulated by Slavoj Žižek contra Michel Foucault's analysis of micro-practices. While Žižek would agree with analyses of micro-practices, of the local functioning of power relations, he would ask, 'what holds together this plurality?' (Žižek, 1995: 198).
6. Some of these methodological clarifications have been inspired by Mariana Valverde (2003).
7. The critique of Foucault's positivity of the social, undertaken in Chapter 5, does not refute the importance of 'surfaces', but indicates the need to conceptualize negativity and excess as present, but not represented within a situation.
8. The abject has been defined by Judith Butler as the domain of those who are not yet subjects, but who form the constitutive outside of the domain of the subject (Butler, 1993).

1 Problematizing Trafficking in Women: In the Absence of Security

1. On this largely accepted understanding of representation see Shapiro (1988).
2. Both the UN and Council of Europe definitions of trafficking in persons include deception and force (Council of Europe, 2005; UN, 2000).

3. Legal archive for case R/1418/05, at the Galati Court of Justice, consulted in January 2006.
4. See also Chapter 4 in this book and Aradau (2004a).
5. For how these criticisms are played out in Carl Schmitt, for example, see Rasch (2003).

2 Problematizating Securitiy: The Presence of an Absence

1. This is not however, the only element that makes human trafficking a security issue. Bush adds the humanitarian element, the global concern with the plight of trafficked people.
2. The literature on organised crime and security has flourished since the 1990s, typical widening analyses being present in the journal *Transnational Organised Crime*. Similar approaches have been given by P. Williams (1994).
3. 'Schools' are arbitrary delimitations of how security is analysed. Yet, Waever's 'school' terminology has stuck, as it captures some of the main disagreements in security studies (*c.a.s.e. collective*, 2006; Waever, 2004). Nevertheless, not all the approaches discussed here can be labelled as schools.
4. I do not consider the question of the 'audience' here, as in the securitization framework, the audience is thought as a separate, already given entity. Analysing the problematization of security emphasizes the constitutive effects that representations and interventions have in constituting subjects and abjects. In the latter sense, we are all part of security practices rather than simply acquiescing them from a distance.
5. For a compelling discussion of the case of Rosa Parks and of the differences in Butler's and Bourdieu's accounts of agency, see Lovell (2003).
6. There is an ambiguous use of 'police' in Bigo's work, one directly connected with the analysis of police work and a more comprehensive one derived from Foucault. In the latter sense, 'police ... is the ensemble of mechanisms through which order is ensured' (Foucault, 2001: 17, translation mine).
7. M. C. Williams (1997) and Ceyhan (1998) make similar arguments.
8. In this form of argumentation, ontological insecurity has fared better in security studies. If at the heart of the modern subject is insecurity, one needs to come to terms with this insecurity.
9. A more detailed critique of Beck's concept of risk and its appropriation in security studies is undertaken in Aradau and van Munster (2007).
10. Both Campbell and Dillon have also offered influential analyses of security practices inspired by Foucault's work (Campbell, 1992; Dillon, 1995b).
11. Critical Security Studies, with capital 'C', has also been named the Welsh School, given the location of Ken Booth and Wyn Jones at the University of Aberystwyth (Smith, 2000).
12. For the purposes of this chapter, I do not engage with the debates about the concept of human security, but simply rely on a contradiction that the concept cannot capture.
13. Cynthia Weber sets out a feminist interpretation of performative identity in IR (Weber, 1998).

3 Unmaking Security: Desecuritization, Emancipation, Ethics

1. Ethical approaches are not singular in defining the exclusionary relation to the other as security. However, they are considered predominantly for the alternative to security that they present.
2. On the exceptionalism of security according to a Schmittian logic, see especially Huysmans (1998a; 2004), Williams (2003), and *c.a.s.e. collective* (2006).
3. Personal communication with Ole Waever, Paris, June 2005.
4. For a theoretical discussion of how the exceptionalism of security practices becomes entangled with the practices of normal politics, see Aradau and van Munster (2008).
5. Similar definitions of democracy have been formulated by Alain Badiou, Jacques Rancière, Miguel Vatter or Slavoj Žižek. In Chapter 7, I offer a redefinition of security that is consistent with this reformulation of politics and democracy.
6. See my reply to Andreas Behnke (Aradau, 2006; Aradau 2004b).
7. On biopolitics and security, see Dillon and Lobo-Guerrero (2008, forthcoming).
8. See, for example, Stern (2006) for a critical engagement with the effects of security practices.
9. For a Foucault-inspired approach to ethics as 'aesthetics of the self', see Jabri (1998). Although ethics of the self and ethics of the other cannot be totally separated, Foucault has been rightly faulted for not making more room for the other in his consideration of ethics (Butler, 2005: 23). The constitution of the individual as a moral subject is inseparable not just from the existence of the other, but also from the intersubjective dimension of norms that govern this relationality.
10. Kearney's answer to the question of indetermination takes him beyond Levinas and into hermeneutics (2002: 10).
11. Campbell has undertaken such a work of translation in the case of Bosnia (1998b).

4 Subjects, Knowledge, Resistance

1. Even in Italy, where the law gives victims of trafficking the right to a residence permit if they enter a programme of rehabilitation, the general rule is one of deportation.
2. On a similar engagement with 'governmentality', but which reads security through the prism of criminalization, see Ericson (2007).
3. Despite the peril of exoticism, Foucault's coinage '*dispositif*' has been preserved as such in English contexts, due to the perceived inadequacy of translations such as mechanism, apparatus or assemblage. Neither equivalent could account for the heterogeneity that *dispositifs* imply. A *dispositif* is characterized by instability rather than smooth functioning that mechanism or apparatus would imply. An assemblage also loses the connotations of 'disposition', the ways in which objects are disposed of and dispositions are fostered in subjects.

4. Most of the NGOs in Western Europe have integrated anti-trafficking work in their work with sex workers. I have encountered this 'history' with NGOs from Italy (On the Road, TAMPEP, Commitato per le Diritti Civili delle Prostitute), France (Cabiria), Germany, the Netherlands Foundation against Trafficking in Women (STV).

5. I was involved in working on a report that considered the role and pitfalls of cooperation between different institutions regarding the problem of trafficking (Danish Red Cross, 2005).

6. Oficiul National de Prevenire a Traficului de Persoane si Monitorizare a Protectiei Victimelor Traficului (National Office for the Prevention of Human Trafficking and Monitoring of Victims of Trafficking), http://www.politiaromana.ro/Prevenire/trafic_persoane.htm, accessed 26 March 2005.

7. In January 2004, I conducted interviews with representatives of the IOM Bucharest, Ad Pare Bucharest, Reaching Out Piteşti and Save the Children Romania. Psychological counselling and therapy was foremost on their agenda, all victims of trafficking having to go through a therapy programme. However, they were all aware of the importance of the economic and social context. The task of helping women find jobs or get out from poverty proved daunting for most of them, Reaching Out being the only NGO that makes sure women have a job before they leave the shelter.

8. La Strada is one of the first NGOs funded by the EU to prevent trafficking in women in Central and Eastern Europe.

9. The conditions for obtaining temporary residence permits imply either the cooperation of women in the prosecution of the trafficker or exceptional cases of threat or abuse. Most women are either 'voluntarily returned' or deported.

10. The EU STOP programme has financed NGOs to tackle trafficking in women, while DAPHNE has provided funding to NGOs fighting violence against children, young people and women (European Commission, 2002b).

11. Based on archival research of testimonies in trafficking trials at the Galati Court of Justice, Romania, in January 2004 and January 2006. Information is based on the following files: 2922/P/2003 in 2004 and files 494/2005, 956/P/2002 and 16/P/2005 in 2006 and the testimonies of women included in these legal files.

12. Testimonies in case 956/P/2002, Galati Court of Justice.

13. Personal communication, 13 January 2006.

14. Author's interview with IOM spokesperson, Bucharest Romania, January 2004.

15. See the section on 'Reaching Out', a Romanian NGO in Danish Red Cross (2005).

16. Author's interview, Bucharest, January 2004.

17. The Stockholm syndrome as a manifestation of the victim's trauma has been promoted by the NGOs working with trafficking women.

18. Research carried out in January 2004 and January 2006 in the archives of the Galati Court of Justice, Romania.

19. Andrijasevic has shown how the IOM public anti-trafficking campaigns are based on the idea that women should stay home, in their countries. Danger becomes directly connected with border crossing (Andrijasevic, 2004, Chapter 5).

5 The Politics of Equality

1. Foucault (2004b) details the model of war and its use for the analytics of power.
2. The Real is understood here differently from my interpretation of 'really' in Chapter 2. Psychoanalysis uses both the concept of the Real and of reality to convey this distinction. The Lacanian Real is – unlike our concept of 'real' objective/collective experience – that which resists representation and resists its symbolization. The Real is therefore the lack in the Symbolic Order, that which always threatens the coherence and wholeness of the symbolic. Unlike the Real, reality is the subjective representation of symbolic and imaginary articulations (Ewans, 1996).
3. Given that he understands situations as indifferent multiplicities, Badiou relies on mathematics for the understanding of ontology. Mathematics appears as a modality of thinking multiplicity without any predicates. The mathematical side of Badiou's philosophy is less important for my purposes, as I rely on his understanding of situations. I accept the basic premise that situations cannot be closed, although the state of the situation attempts to close the multiplicity of presentation.
4. Žižek is wrong to equate Badiou's 'state of the situation' with the State. Badiou plays on the difference between 'état' (state) and 'État' (State, although the noun is not capitalized in English), and makes the State equivalent to the state of the situation, to the ordering of people and things in a situation.
5. I use the distinction subjectivation (from the verb 'to subject') and subjectification (from the verb 'to subjectify') to refer to the process of becoming subjected to power and of becoming a subject by resisting power, respectively. Although the two are closely intertwined in Foucault, this distinction is at the heart of the concept of politics proposed here.
6. The rationale for such discrimination is again one of risk management and containment. The Consultation Paper goes on to state that '[i]t is hoped that co-operation with the authorities will allow information to be gathered on the traffickers and so lead to the disruption of trafficking networks' (Home Office 2004: 81).
7. When the exploitation of other illegal migrants is revealed, this does not lead to a reconsideration of labour laws or labour relations but to debates about migration policies and the role of border controls.
8. Translation mine. Feltham and Clemens translate it as 'under fire of the event' (Badiou, 2004a).
9. The European Council Framework Decision on combating trafficking in human beings defines trafficked women as victims of coercion, force or threats, including abduction, deceit or fraud, abuse of authority or vulnerability (European Council, 2002).
10. For Cabiria, see http://www.cabiria.asso.fr/ (accessed 20 April 2006), for the English Collective of Prostitutes, http://www.allwomencount.net/EWC%20Sex%20Workers/SexWorkIndex.htm (accessed 20 April 2006) and for Comitato per i Diritti Civili delle Prostitute, http://www.lucciole.org/ (accessed 20 April 2006).

6   The Politics of (Ambiguous) Universality

1. The Europe Agreements (or Association Agreements) were part of the pre-accession strategy and concerned Bulgaria, the Czech Republic, Cyprus, Estonia, Hungary, Latvia, Lithuania, Malta, Poland, Romania, Slovakia, Slovenia and Turkey. At present, all these countries have become EU members, with the exception of Turkey.
2. For example, the difference between the agreement signed with Morocco in 1996 and the one signed with Egypt in 2001. In the latter, there is no longer any mention of the right of establishment.
3. I return to the problem of equality and difference in the next chapter.
4. Balibar uses 'fictions' for what I have called 'symbolic practices'. Universality as 'symbol' or 'ideal' is linked with what my tripartite distinction between real, symbolic and imaginary reserved for the imaginary.
5. '... une politique d'émancipation radicale ne s'origine pas dans une preuve de possibilité que l'examen du monde fournirait' (translation mine).
6. See also my reply to Andreas Behnke, (Aradau, 2006 and *c.a.s.e. collective*, 2007).

7   The Politics of Freedom

1. Freedom and liberty will be used interchangeably here. For a discussion of the subtle difference between liberty and freedom in Arendt, see Pitkin (1988).
2. The concept of 'ontological security', recently introduced in security studies can be considered as the counterpart of ontological freedom. The constituted subject is ontologically insecure, not ontologically primarily free. Ontological security raises important political questions not just in relation to the constitution of the social, but about the modern subject more generally. What happens to politics when its subjects are no longer constituted by freedom, but by insecurity?
3. 'Man is made fit for society, not by nature, but by education' (Hobbes quoted in Burchell, 1999).
4. Malcolm Bull has suggested that it is a 'faction' as a simulacrum of the people and not the multitude that Hobbes opposes (Bull, 2005). Yet, factions are a 'multitude of citizens', in many ways similar to other illicit organisations that Hobbes finds dangerous.
5. I am grateful for this point to Lene Hansen.
6. The state is understood here in its Foucauldian sense, including practices of 'government at a distance'. For a discussion of state practices and government at a distance, see Rose and Miller (1992).
7. Huysmans has analysed border control and surveillance as different types of technologies to tackle the excesses of freedom. In the context of the EU, he defines security policy 'those political and administrative practices that address excesses (e.g. a sudden inflow of very large numbers of immigrants) *endangering* the orderly conduct of freedom' (Huysmans, 2004a: 305).
8. Ontological equality (understood as identity/difference) can be linked with the previously discussed concepts of ontological freedom and security. However, what interests me here is the politicization of concepts rather than their ontologization.

References

Adams, Niki (2003) Anti-trafficking Legislation: protection or deportation? *Feminist Review* 73: 135–8.

Adams, Niki and Cari Mitchell (2005) *Letter to the Conference Organisers. European Conference on Sex Work, Human Rights, Labour and Migration. 10 October 2005.* English Collective of Prostitutes. Accessed 20 April 2006. Available from http://www.allwomencount.net/EWC%20Sex%20Workers/LetterEuroConference.htm.

Agamben, Giorgio (1993) *The Coming Community.* Translated by Michael Hardt. Theory out of Bounds. Minnesota: University of Minnesota Press.

—— (1998) *Homo Sacer: Sovereign Power and Bare Life.* Translated by Daniel Heller-Roazen. Stanford: Stanford University Press.

Agustin, Laura (2005) Migrants in the Mistress's House: Other Voices in the 'Trafficking' Debate. *Social Politics: International Studies in Gender, State and Society* 12, no. 1: 96–117.

—— (2007) *Sex at the Margins: Migration, Labour Markets and the Rescue Industry.* London: Zed Books.

Alternative sociale (2005a) *Metodogie de lucru in centrele de asistenta si protectie a victimelor traficului de persoane.* Accessed 19 September 2005. Available from http://www.antitrafic.ro/_media/Program_A4_Nicoleta.pdf.

—— (2005b) *Traficul de fiinte umane. Infractor, victima, infractiune.* Iasi: Alternative sociale.

Amnesty International (2004) *'So does it mean that we have rights?' Protecting the human rights of women and girls trafficked for forced prostitution in Kosovo.* Accessed 5 August 2006. Available from http://web.amnesty.org/library/index/ENGEUR/700102004.

Amnesty International and Anti-Slavery International (2005) *Safety Fears for Women Rescued in UK Brothel Raid.* Accessed 29 December 2005. Available from http://www.antislavery.org/archive/press/pressrelease2005UKrescue.htm.

Anderson, Bridget and Julia O'Connell Davidson (2003) *Is Trafficking in Human Beings Demand Driven? A Multi-Country Pilot Study.* Geneva: IOM Migration Research Series, 15.

Andrijasevic, Rutvica (2003) The Difference Borders Make: (Il)legality, Migration and Trafficking in Italy among Eastern European Women in Prostitution. In *Uprootings/Regroundings: Questions of Home and Migration,* eds Sarah Ahmed, Claudia Castaneda, A. Fortier and M. Sheller: 251–72. Oxford: Berg.

—— (2004) *Trafficking in Women and the Politics of Mobility in Europe.* University of Utrecht. Ph.D. Thesis.

—— (2007) Beautiful Dead Bodies: Gender, Migration and Representation in Anti-Trafficking Campaigns. *Feminist Review* 86: 45–66.

Anti-Slavery International (2002) *Human Trafficking, Human Rights. Redefining Victim Protection.* London.

Apap, Joanna, Peter Cullen and Felicia Medved (2002) *Countering Human Trafficking: Protecting the Victims of Trafficking* EU/IOM STOP European Conference on Preventing and Combating Trafficking in Human Beings.

Accessed 30 May 2006. Available from http://www.belgium.iom.int/ StopConference/Confdocs/Confpapers/index.htm.

Aradau, Claudia (2004a) The Perverse Politics of Four-Letter Words: Risk and Pity in the Securitization of Human Trafficking. *Millennium: Journal of International Studies* 33, no. 2: 251–77.

—— (2004b) Security and the Democratic Scene: desecuritization and emancipation. *Journal of International Relations and Development* 7, no. 4: 388–413.

—— (2006) Limits of Security, Limits of Politics? A Response. *Journal of International Relations and Development* 9, no. 1: 81–90.

—— (2007) Law Transformed: Guantanamo and the 'Other' Exception. *Third World Quarterly* 28, no. 3: 489–502.

Aradau, Claudia and Rens van Munster (2007) Governing Terrorism through Risk: Taking Precautions, (Un)Knowing the Future. *European Journal of International Relations* 13, no. 1: 89–115.

—— (2008 forthcoming) Taming the Future: The Dispositif of Risk in the 'War on Terror'. In *Risk and the War on Terror*, eds Louise Amoore and Marieke de Goede. London: Routledge.

Arendt, Hannah (1986) *The Origins of Totalitarianism*. New York: Meridian Books.

Ashcraft, Richard (1978) Ideology and Class in Hobbes' Political Theory. *Political Theory* 6, no. 1: 27–62.

Austin, J. L. (1975 [1962]) *How To Do Things with Words*. Oxford: Oxford University Press. 2nd edition.

Badiou, Alain (1985) *Peut-on penser la politique?* Paris: Editions du Seuil.

—— (1988) *L'Être et l'événement*. Paris: Editions du Seuil.

—— (1992) *Conditions*. Paris: Editions du Seuil.

—— (1998) Politics and Philosophy. Interview with Peter Hallward. *Angelaki* 3, no. 3: 113–33.

—— (1999) *Manifesto for Philosophy*. Translated by Norman Madarasz. New York: SUNY Press.

—— (2000) *Deleuze: The Clamor of Being*. Translated by Louise Burchill. Minnesota: Minnesota University Press.

—— (2002a) *Ethics: An Essay on the Understanding of Evil*. London: Verso.

—— (2002b) Politics and Philosophy: An Interview with Alain Badiou. In *Ethics: An Essay on the Understanding of Evil*, ed. Peter Hallward: 95–144. London: Verso.

—— (2003) Seven Variations on the Century. *Parallax* 9, no. 2: 72–80.

—— (2004a) *Infinite Thought: Truth and the Return of Philosophy*. Translated by Oliver Feltham and Justin Clemens. London: Continuum.

—— (2004b) *Theoretical Writings*. Translated by Ray Brassier and Alberto Toscano. London: Continuum.

Badiou, Alain and Bruno Bosteels (2005) Can Change Be Thought? A Dialogue with Alain Badiou. In *Alain Badiou: Philosophy and Its Conditions*, ed. Gabriel Riera: 244–60. New York: State University of New York.

Baker, Tom (2000) Insuring Morality. *Economy and Society* 29, no. 4: 559–77.

Balibar, Étienne (1992) *Les frontières de la démocratie*. Paris: La Découverte.

—— (1993) *Quel universalisme aujourd'hui?* Accessed 2 February 2006. Available from http://www.cerclegramsci.org/archives/balibar.htm.

—— (1994) *Masses, Classes, and Ideas: Studies on Politics and Philosophy Before and After Marx*. London: Routledge.

—— (1995) Ambiguous Universality. *Differences: A Journal of Feminist Cultural Studies* 7, no. 1: 48–74.

—— (2002a) Le Hobbes de Schmitt, le Schmitt de Hobbes. Préface. In *Le Léviathan dans la doctrine de l'Etat de Thomas Hobbes*, ed. Carl Schmitt: 7–65. Paris: Editions du Seuil.

—— (2002b) *Politics and the Other Scene*. London: Verso.

—— (2004a) Is a Philosophy of Human Civic Rights Possible? Reflections on Equaliberty. *The South Atlantic Quarterly* 103, no. 2/3: 311–22.

—— (2004b) *We, the People of Europe? Reflections on Transnational Citizenship*. Princeton: Princeton University Press.

—— (2006) Constructions and Reconstructions of the Universal. *Critical Horizons* 7: 21–43.

Balso, Louise-Judith (2005) Ouvriers sans papiers in France: loi d'exception et mensonge d'Etat. *Le Journal politique*, no. 1. Accessed 26 February 2006. Available from http://orgapoli.net/article.php3?id_article=64.

Barbir Mladinovic, Ankica (15 June 2006) *Croatia: A Human Trafficking Victim Speak with RFE/RL*. Accessed 5 August 2006. Available from http://www.thewarproject.org/node/10086.

Barry, Kathleen (1995) *The Prostitution of Sexuality: The Global Exploitation of Women* New York: New York University Press.

Bauman, Zygmunt (1991) *Modernity and Ambivalence*. London: Polity Press.

—— (2001) *Community: Seeking Safety in an Insecure World*. London: Polity.

BBC (2004) *Prostitution Laws Facing Overhaul*. Accessed 20 October 2004. Available from http://news.bbc.co.uk/1/hi/uk/38980009.stm.

BBC Radio 4 (2005) Home Office Minister Tony McNulty answers questions raised by a *Today Programme* report into people trafficking. In *Today Programme*. London: BBC.

Beck, Ulrich (1999) *World Risk Society*. Cambridge: Polity Press.

—— (2002) The Terrorist Threat: World Risk Society Revisted. *Theory, Culture and Society* 19, no. 4: 39–55.

Behnke, Andreas (1999) Postmodernising Security. *ECPR Joint Sessions* 1999 Mannheim.

—— (2000) The Message or the Messenger? Reflections on the Role of Security Experts and the Securitization of Political Issues. *Cooperation and Conflict* 35, no. 1: 89–105.

Bell, Shannon (1994) *Reading, Writing and Rewriting the Prostitute Body*. Bloomington: Indiana University Press.

Berman, Jacqueline (2003) (Un)Popular Strangers and Crisis (Un)Bounded: Discourses of Sex Trafficking, the European Political Community and the Panicked State of the Modern State. *European Journal of International Relations* 9, no. 1: 37–86.

Bertone, Andrea Marie (2000) Sexual Trafficking in Women: International Political Economy and the Politics of Sex. *Gender Issues* 18, no. 1: 4–22.

Bigo, Didier (1996) *Polices en Réseaux. L'expérience européenne*. Paris: Presses de Sciences Po.

—— (2000) Liaison officers in Europe: New Officers in the European Security Field. In *Issues in Transnational Policing*, ed. J. W. E. Sheptycki: 67–99. London: Routledge.

—— (2001a) Migration and Security. In *Controlling a New Migration World*, eds Virginie Guiraudon and Christian Joppke: 121–49. London: Routledge.

—— (2001b) The Möbius Ribbon of Internal and External Security(ies). In *Identities, Borders, Orders. Rethinking International Relations Theory*, eds Mathias

Albert, David Jacobson and Josef Lapid: 91–116. Minneapolis: University of Minnesota Press.
—— (2002) Security and Immigration: Toward a Critique of the Governmentality of Unease. *Alternatives* 27, Special Issue: 63–92.
—— (2006) Globalized (In)Security: The Field and the Ban-opticon. In *Illiberal Practices of Liberal Regimes: The (In)Security Games*, ed. Collection Cultures & Conflits: 5–50. Paris: L'Harmattan.
Bindman, Jo (1997) *Redefining Prostitution as Sex Work on the International Agenda*. Network of Sex Work Projects. Accessed 19 April 2006. Available from http://www.walnet.org/csis/papers/redefining.html.
Böcker, Anita (2002) *The Establishment Provisions of the Europe Agreements: Implementation and Mobilisation in Germany and the Netherlands*. Zentrum fuer europaeische rechtspolitik Bremen. Accessed 30 January 2006. Available from http://www.zerp.uni-bremen.de/english/pdf/dp1_2002.pdf.
Boltanski, Luc (1999) *Distant Suffering: Morality, Media, and Politics*. Translated by David Burchell. Cambridge: Cambridge University Press.
Bolton, Sally (2005) *Mini-series Explores the Inhumanity of Human Trafficking*. UN Chronicle. Accessed 11 June 2007. Available from http://www.un.org/Pubs/chronicle/2005/webArticles/110905_Trafficking.html.
Booth, Ken (1991) Security and Emancipation. *Review of International Relations* 17, no. 4: 313–26.
—— (1995) Human Wrongs and International Relations. *International Affairs* 71, no. 1: 103–26.
—— (1997) Security and Self: Reflections of a Fallen Realist. In *Critical Security Studies*, eds Keith Krause and Michael C. Williams: 83–120. London: UCL Press.
—— (2004) Realities of Security: Editor's Introduction. *International Relations* 18, no. 1: 5–8.
Booth, Ken and Peter Vale (1997) Critical Security Studies and Regional Insecurity: The Case of Southern Africa. In *Critical Security Studies*, eds Keith Krause and Michael C. Williams: 329–58. London: UCL Press.
Bourdieu, Pierre (1990) *In Other Words: Essays towards a Reflexive Sociology*. Translated by Matthew Adamson. London: Polity Press. Choses dites, Editions de Minuit, 1987.
—— (1991) *Language and Symbolic Power*. Cambridge: Cambridge University Press.
Boutellier, Hans (2000) *Crime and Morality: The Significance of Criminal Justice in Post-Modern Culture*. London: Kluwer Academic Publishers.
Britten, Nick (1 October 2005) Sex Slaves Freed as Police Smash Human Trafficking Operation: Campaigners Seek Greater Protection for Victims of 'Brutal Industry'. *Daily Telegraph*, 12.
Brown, Wendy (1995) *States of Injury: Power and Freedom in Late Modernity*. Princeton: Princeton University Press.
—— (2001) *Politics out of History*. Princeton: Princeton University Press.
Brownlie, Julie (2001) The 'Being-Risky' Child: Governing Childhood and Sexual Risk. *Sociology* 35: 517–37.
Bruggeman, Willy (2002) *Illegal Immigration and Trafficking in Human Beings Seen As A Security Problem for Europe. Speech at the IOM-EU Conference on Combating Human Trafficking, 19 September 2002*. Accessed 26 October 2004. Available from http://www.belgium.iom.int/STOPConference%20Papers/20%20Bruggeman%20Brussels%20IOM.19.09.02.pdf.

Bull, Malcolm (2005) The Limits of Multitude. *New Left Review* 35: 19–39.

Burchell, David (1999) The Disciplined Citizen: Thomas Hobbes, Neostoicism and the Critique of Classical Citizenship. *Australian Journal of Politics and History* 45, no. 4: 506–24.

Burchell, Graham (1991) Peculiar Interests: Civil Society and Governing 'The System of Natural Liberty'. In *The Foucault Effect: Studies in Governmentality*, eds Graham Burchell, Colin Gordon and Peter Miller: 119–50. Chicago: University of Chicago Press.

—— (1993) Liberal Government and Techniques of the Self. *Economy and Society* 22, no. 3: 267–82.

Bush, George (2003) *President Bush Addresses United Nations General Assembly.* Accessed 31 January 2006. Available from http://www.whitehouse.gov/news/releases/2003/09/20030923-4.html.

Butler, Judith (1993) *Bodies that Matter: On the Discursive Limits of 'Sex'.* London: Routledge.

—— (1997a) *Excitable Speech: A Politics of the Performative.* London: Routledge.

—— (1997b) *The Psychic Life of Power: Theories of Subjection.* Stanford: Stanford University Press.

—— (2005) *Giving an Account of Oneself.* New York: Fordham University Press.

Buzan, Barry (1991) *People, States and Fear: An Agenda for Security Studies in the Post-Cold War Era.* London: Harvester Wheatsheaf.

—— (1997) Rethinking Security after the Cold War. *Cooperation and Conflict* 32, no. 1: 5–28.

Buzan, Barry, Ole Waever and Jaap de Wilde (1998) *Security: A New Framework for Analysis.* Boulder: Lynne Rienner.

c.a.s.e. collective (2006) Critical Approaches to Security in Europe: A Networked Manifesto. *Security Dialogue* 37, no. 4: 443–87.

—— (2007) Europe, Knowledge, Politics – Engaging with the limits. The c.a.s.e. Collective Responds. *Security Dialogue* 38, no. 4: 559–76.

Campbell, David (1992) *Writing Security: United States Foreign Policy and the Politics of Identity.* Manchester: Manchester University Press.

—— (1998a) Epilogue: The Diciplinarizing Politics of Theorizing Identity, Writing Security, revised edition. In *Writing Security: United States Foreign Policy and the Politics of Identity*, ed. David Campbell: 207–27. Manchester: Manchester University Press.

—— (1998b) *National Deconstruction: Violence, Identity and Justice in Bosnia.* Minneapolis: University of Minnesota Press.

—— (1999) The Deterritorialization of Responsibility: Levinas, Derrida, and Ethics after the End of Philosophy. In *Moral Spaces. Rethinking Ethics and World Politics*, eds David Campbell and Michael Shapiro: 29–56. Minneapolis: University of Minnesota Press.

Campbell, David and Michael Dillon (1993) *The Political Subject of Violence.* Manchester: Manchester University Press.

Campbell, David and Michael J. Shapiro (1999) Introduction: From Ethical Theory to the Ethical Relation. In *Moral Spaces: Rethinking Ethics and World Politics*, eds David Campbell and Michael Shapiro: VII–XX. Minneapolis: University of Minnesota Press.

Caputo, John D. (1997) *The Tears and Fears of Jacques Derrida: Religion without Religion.* Bloomington, IN: Indiana University Press.

Castel, Robert (1981) *La gestion des risques: De l'anti-psychiatrie à l'après-psychanalyse*. Paris: Les Editions du Minuit.
—— (1991) From Dangerousness to Risk. In *The Foucault Effect: Studies in Governmentality*, eds Graham Burchell, Colin Gordon and Peter Miles: 281–98. Chicago: University of Chicago Press.
Castel, Robert, Françoise Castel and Anne Lovell (1982) *The Psychiatric Society*. Translated by Arthur Goldhammer. New York: Columbia University Press.
Centrul pentru prevenirea traficului de femei (2002) *Traficul de femei in Moldova. Realitate sau mit [Trafficking in Women in Moldova: Reality or Myth]*. Accessed 31 October 2004. Available from http://www.antitraffic.md/materials/reports/cptf_2002_05/.
Ceyhan, Ayse (1998) Analyser la sécurité: Dillon, Waever, Williams et les autres. *Cultures et conflits* 31–2. Accessed 30 April 2006. Available from http://www.conflits.org/document541.html.
CNN (2001) *London Brothel Raids Net 31*. Accessed 20 October 2004. Available from http://edition.cnn.com/2001/WORLD/europe/UK/02/16/britain.vice/.
Connolly, William (1988) *Political Theory and Modernity*. Oxford: Basil Blackwell.
—— (1991) *Identity/Difference: Negotiations of a Political Paradox*. Ithaca: Cornell University Press.
—— (1995) *The Ethos of Pluralization*. Minneapolis: University of Minnesota Press.
—— (1999a) Suffering, Justice and the Politics of Becoming. In *Moral Spaces: Rethinking Ethics and World Politics*, eds David Campbell and Michael Shapiro: 125–53. Minneapolis: University of Minnesota Press.
—— (1999b) *Why I Am Not a Secularist*. Minneapolis: University of Minnesota Press.
Corso, Carla and Ada Trifiro (2003) *E siamo partite! Migrazione, tratta e prostituzione straniera in Italia* Firenze: Giunti.
Council of Europe (2005) *Convention on Action Against Trafficking in Human Beings*. Accessed 20 June 2007. Available from http://www.coe.int/T/E/human_rights/trafficking/PDF_Conv_197_Trafficking_E.pdf.
Council of the European Union (2002) *Framework Decision on Combating Trafficking in Human Beings. 2002/629/JHA*. Accessed 31 October 2004. Available from http://europa.eu.int/eur-lex/pri/en/oj/dat/2002/l_203/l_20320020801en00010004.pdf.
—— (2004) *The Hague Programme: Strengthening, Freedom,Security and Justice in the European Union*. Accessed 16 January 2006. Available from http://www.eu.int/comm/justice_home/doc_centre/doc/hague_programme_en.pdf.
Counter-Trafficking Regional Clearing Point (2003) *First Annual Report on Victims of Trafficking in South Eastern Europe*. Accessed 31 October 2004. Available from http://www.iom.int//DOCUMENTS/PUBLICATION/EN/RCP_trafficking_south eastern_europe.pdf.
Coward, Ros (26 March 2003) Slaves in Soho. *The Guardian*. Accessed 24 May 2006. Available from http://www.guardian.co.uk/comment/story/0,,921977,00.html.
Critchley, Simon (2004) Five Problems in Levinas's View of Politics and the Sketch of a Solution to Them. *Political Theory* 32, no. 2: 172–85.
Danish Red Cross (2005) *Good Practices in Response to Trafficking in Human Beings. Cooperation between Civil Society and Law Enforcement in Europe*. Copenhagen.
David, Alain (2002) Unlimited Inc. *Parallax* 8, no. 3: 78–89.
Dean, Mitchell (1999a) *Governmentality: Power and Rule in Modern Society*. London: Sage.

—— (1999b) Risk, Calculable and Incalculable. In *Risk and Sociocultural Theory: New Directions and Perspectives*, ed. Deborah Lupton: 67–84. Cambridge: Cambridge University Press.

—— (2002) Liberal Government and Authoritarianism. *Economy and Society* 31, no. 1: 37–61.

Dean, Mitchell and Barry Hindess, eds (1998) *Governing Australia: Studies in Contemporary Rationalities of Government*. Cambridge: Cambridge University Press.

Deimleiter, Nora V. (2001) The Law at Crossroads: The Construction of Migrant Women Trafficked into Prostitution. In *Global Human Smuggling: Comparative Perspectives*, eds David Kyle and Rey Koslowski: 257–93. Baltimore: The Johns Hopkins University Press.

Deleuze, Gilles (1990) *Pourparlers*. Paris: Editions de Minuit.

—— (1995) *Negotiations*. Translated by Martin Joughin. New York: Columbia University Press.

den Boer, Monica (1998) Crime et immigration dans l'Union européenne. *Cultures & Conflits*, no. 31/32. Accessed 30 April 2006. Available from http://www.conflits.org/document551.html.

Der Derian, James (1992) *Antidiplomacy: Spies, Terror, Speed and War*. London: Blackwell Publishers.

Derrida, Jacques (1993) *Aporias: Dying – Awaiting (One Another at) the 'Limits of Truth'*. Stanford: Stanford University Press.

—— (1994) The Deconstruction of Actuality: An interview with Jacques Derrida. *Radical Philosophy* 68: 28–41.

Diamantopoulos, Anna (2001) *EU to Protect Sex Slaves, 8 March 2001*. Accessed 29 March 2002. Available from http://news.bbc.co.uk/hiworld/europe/newsid_1208000/1208454.stm.

Dillon, Michael (1995a) Security, Philosophy and Politics. In *Global Modernities*, eds Mike Featherstone, Scott Lash and Roland Robertson: 155–77. London: Sage Publications.

—— (1995b) Sovereignty and Governmentality: From the Problematics of the New World Order to the Ethical Problematic of the World Order. *Alternatives* 20: 323–68.

—— (1996) *The Politics of Security: Towards a Political Philosophy of Continental Thought*. London: Routledge.

—— (2004) The Security of Governance. In *Global Governmentality: Governing International Spaces*, eds Wendy Larner and William Walters: 76–94. London: Routledge.

—— (2005) Cared to Death: The Biopoliticised Time of Your Life. *Foucault Studies* 2: 37–46.

Dillon, Michael and Luis Lobo-Guerrero (2008 forthcoming) The Biopolitics of Security. *Review of International Relations*.

Dillon, Michael and Julian Reid (2001) Global Liberal Governance: Biopolitics, Security and War. *Millenium: Journal of International Studies* 30, no. 1: 41–66.

Doezema, Jo (1998) Forced to Choose: Beyond the Voluntary v. Forced Prostitution Dichotomy. In *Global Sex Workers: Rights, Resistance, and Redefinition*, eds Kamala Kempadoo and Jo Doezema: 34–50. London: Routledge.

—— (2000) Loose Women or Lost Women? The Re-Emergence of the Myth of White Slavery in Contemporary Discourses of Trafficking in Women. *Gender Issues* 18, no. 1: 23–50.

—— (2002) Who Gets to Choose? Coercion, Consent and the UN Trafficking Protocol. *Gender and Development* 10, no. 1: 20–7.

Donzelot, Jacques (1984) *L'invention du social. Essai sur le déclin des passions politiques.* Paris: Fayard.

Dunne, Tim and Nicholas J. Wheeler (2004) 'We the Peoples': Contending Discourses of Security in Human Rights Theory and Practice. *International Relations* 18, no. 1: 9–23.

Edkins, Jenny (2000) *Whose Hunger? Concepts of Famine, Practices of Aid* Minneapolis: University of Minnesota Press.

—— (2002) After the Subject of International Security. In *Politics and Post-Structuralism: An introduction*, eds Alan Finlayson and Jeremy Valentine: 66–82. Edinburgh: Edinburgh University Press.

Edwards, Adam and Pete Gill (2002) The Politics of Transnational Organized Crime: Discourse, Reflexivity and the Narration of Threat. *British Journal of Politics and International Relations* 4, no. 2: 245–70.

El-Cherkeh, Tanja, Elena Stirbu, Sebastian Lazaroiu and Dragos Radu (2004) *EU-Enlargement, Migration and Trafficking in Women: The Case of South Eastern Europe.* Hamburg: Hamburg Institute of International Economics, 247.

Elbe, Stefan (2005) AIDS, Security, Biopolitics. *International Relations* 19, no. 4: 403–19.

English Collective of Prostitutes (1997) Campaigning for Legal Change. In *Rethinking Prostitution: Purchasing Sex in the 1990s*, eds Graham Scambler and Annette Scambler: 83–104. London: Routledge.

—— (2004) *Why We Are Campaigning to Abolish the Prostitution Laws.* Accessed 30 June 2007. Available from http://www.allwomencount.net/EWC%20Sex%20Workers/Abolish.htm.

Enloe, Cynthia (1989) *Bananas, Beaches & Bases: Making Feminist Sense of International Politics.* London: Pandora Press.

—— (1993) *The Morning After: Sexual Politics at the End of the Cold War.* Berkeley: University of California Press.

Ericson, Richard V. (2007) *Crime in an Insecure World.* London: Polity Press.

Ericson, Richard V. and Kevin D. Haggerty (1997) *Policing the Risk Society.* Oxford: Clarendon Press.

European Commission (2001) *Joint Report from Commission Services and Europol. 'Towards a European Strategy to Prevent Organised Crime'.* Brussels: SEC (2001) 433.

—— (2002a) *Proposal for a Council Directive on the short-term residence permit issued to victims of action to facilitate illegal immigration or trafficking in human beings who cooperate with the competent authorities.* Accessed 30 June 2007. Available from http://europa.eu.int/eur-lex/en/com/pdf/2002/en_502PC0071.pdf.

—— (2002b) *'Trafficking in Women: The Misery behind the Fantasy; From Poverty to Sex Slavery; A Comprehensive European Strategy'.* Directorate General Justice and Home Affairs. Accessed 12 November 2004. Available from http://europa. eu.int/comm/justice_home/news/8mars_en.htm#b1.

—— (2005a) *Communication from the Commission to the European Parliament and Council. Fighting Trafficking in Human Beings – An Integrated Approach and Proposals for an Action Plan.* Accessed 30 June 2007. Available from http://europa. eu.int/eur-lex/lex/LexUriServ/site/en/com/2005/com2005_0514en01.pdf.

—— (2005b) *EU Action against Trafficking in Human Beings and the Sexual Exploitation of Children.* Accessed 30 June 2007. Available from http://

europa.eu.int/comm/justice_home/fsj/crime/trafficking/fsj_crime_human_traf
ficking_en.htm#.

European Community (1991) *Europe Agreement with Poland*. Accessed 1 May 2006.
Available from http://mba.tuck.darmouth.edu/cib/trade_agreements_db/
archive/EC-Poland.pdf.

European Council (1999) *Tampere European Council: Presidency Conclusions*.
Accessed 30 June 2007. Available from http://europa.eu.int/council/off/
conclu/oct99/oct99_en.htm.

—— (2002) *Council Framework Decision on Trafficking in Human Beings*. Accessed
30 June 2007. Available from http://europa.eu.int/eur-lex/pri/en/oj/dat/2002/
l_203/l_20320020801en00010004.pdf.

European Parliament (2001) *Report on the Proposal for a Council Framework
Decision on Combating Trafficking in Human Beings. A5-0183/2001*. Rapporteur
Eva Klamt. Accessed 4 May 2006. Available from http://www.europarl.
eu.int/omk/sipade3?PUBREF=-//EP//NONSGML+REPORT+A5-2001-
0183+0+DOC+PDF+V0//EN&L=EN&LEVEL=2&NAV=S&LSTDOC=Y.

—— (2004) *Amendments to a Motion for Resolution on the Consequences of Sex
Industry in the European Union*. Committee on Women's Rights and Equal
Opportunities. Accessed 31 January 2006. Available from http://www.
europarl.eu.int/meetdocs/committees/femm/20040406/522602en.pdf.

Europol (2003) *Crime Assessment: Trafficking in Human Beings in the European
Union*. Accessed 20 October 2004. Available from http://www.europol.eu.int/
index/asp?page=publcrimeassessmentTHB.

—— (2004) *Trafficking in Human Beings – A Europol Perspective*. Accessed 20 March
2006. Available from http://www.europol.eu.int/publications/SeriousCrime
Overviews/2004/OverviewTHB2004.pdf.

Ewald, François (1986) *L'Etat providence*. Paris: Editions Grasset.

—— (1991) Insurance and risk. In *The Foucault Effect: Studies in Governmentality*,
eds G. Burchell, C. Gordon and P. Miller: 197–210. Chicago: University of
Chicago Press.

Ewans, Dylan (1996) *An Introductory Dictionary of Lacanian Psychoanalysis*.
London: Routledge.

Experts Group on Trafficking in Human Beings (2004) *Report of the Experts Group
on Trafficking in Human Beings*. Brussels: European Commission/DG Justice,
Freedom and Security.

Fassin, Didier (2001) The Biopolitics of Otherness: Undocumented foreigners
and racial discrimination in French public debate. *Anthropology Today* 17,
no. 1: 3–7.

—— (2004) Le corps exposé. Essai d'économie morale de l'illégitimité. In *Le
gouvernement des corps*, ed. Didier Fassin: 237–66. Paris: Éditions de l'École des
hautes études en sciences sociales.

Fink-Eitel, Hinrich (1992) *Foucault: An Introduction*. Translated by Edward Dixon.
Philadelphia: Pennbridge Books.

Finkenauer, James O. (2001) Russian Transnational Organized Crime and
Human Trafficking. In *Global Human Smuggling: Comparative Perspectives*, eds
David Kyle and Rey Koslowski: 166–86. Baltimore: The Johns Hopkins
University Press.

Fondazione Rosselli (1999) *Organised Criminality: Security in Europe*. Turin:
European Commission Forward Studies Unit.

Foucault, Michel (1980) Truth and Power. In *Power/Knowledge: Selected Interviews and Other Writings 1972–1977*, ed. Colin Gordon: 109–33. New York: Pantheon Books.

—— (1982) The Subject and Power. In *Michel Foucault: Beyond Structuralism and Hermeneutics*, eds Hubert Dreyfus and Paul Rabinow: 208–26. Chicago: University of Chicago Press.

—— (1991) Governmentality. In *The Foucault Effect: Studies in Governmentality*, eds Graham Burchell, Colin Gordon and Peter Miller: 87–104. Chicago: University of Chicago Press.

—— (1997) What is Critique? In *The Politics of Truth*, ed. Sylvere Lotringer: 23–82. Cambridge, MA: The MIT Press.

—— (2000a) About the Concept of 'Dangerous Individual' in Nineteenth Century Legal Psychiatry. In *Power: Essential Works of Foucault 1954–1984*, ed. James D. Faubion: 176–200. London: Penguin Books.

—— (2000b) Omnes et Singulatim: Toward a Critique of 'Political Reason'. In *Power: Essential Works of Foucault 1954–1984*, ed. James D. Faubion: 298–325. London: Penguin Books.

—— (2000c) The Subject and Power. In *Power: Essential Works of Foucault 1954–1984*, ed. James D. Faubion, 3: 326–48. London: Penguin Books.

—— (2001) La politique de santé au XVIIIe siècle. In *Dits et écrits II, 1976–1988*, eds Daniel Defert and Francois Ewald: 13–27. Paris: Gallimard.

—— (2002) *The Archaeology of Knowledge*. Translated by A. M. Sheridan Smith. London: Routledge.

—— (2004a) *Abnormal: Lectures at the College de France, 1974–1975*. Translated by Graham Burchell. Basingstoke: Palgrave Macmillan.

—— (2004b) *Society Must Be Defended*. Translated by David Macey. London: Penguin Books.

Fraisse, Geneviève (2001) *La controverse des sexes*. Paris: Presses Universitaires de France.

Frederick, John (2005) The Myth of Nepal-to-India Sex Trafficking: Its Creation, Its Maintenance, and Its Influence on Anti-Trafficking Interventions. In *Trafficking and Prostitution*, eds Kamala Kempadoo and Jyoti Sanghera: 127–48. London: Paradigm Publishers.

Galli, Carlo (1996) *Genealogia delal politica. Carl Schmitt e la crisi del pensiero politico moderno*. Bologna: il Mulino.

Giddens, Anthony (1991) *Modernity and Self-Identity: Self and Society in the Late Modern Age*. Stanford: Stanford University Press.

Gillan, Audrey and Julie Bindel (5 October 2005) Home Office Defers Expulsion of Women Held in Brothel Raid. *The Guardian*. Accessed 5 October 2005. Available from http://www.guardian.co.uk/immigration/story/o,15729,1585087,00.html.

Gilpin, Robert G. (1981) *War and Change in World Politics*. Cambridge: Cambridge University Press.

Girard, René (1986) *The Scapegoat*. Translated by Yvonne Freccero. Baltimore: The Johns Hopkins University Press.

Hacking, Ian (1983) *Representing and Intervening*. Cambridge: Cambridge University Press.

—— (1995) *Rewriting the Soul: Multiple Personality and the Sciences of Memory*. Princeton: Princeton University Press.

—— (1998) *Mad Travelers: Reflections on the Reality of Transient Mental Illnesses*. Charlottesville: University Press of Virginia.

—— (2002) The Archaeology of Michel Foucault. In *Historical Ontology*, ed. Ian Hacking: 73–86. Cambridge, Massachusetts: Harvard University Press.

Hallward, Peter (2001) *Absolutely Postcolonial: Writing Between the Singular and the Specific*. Manchester: Manchester University Press.

—— (2002). Badiou's Politics: Equality and Justice. *Culture Machine* 4. Accessed 30 June 2007. Available from http://culturemachine.tees.ac.uk/Cmach/Backissues/j004/Articles/hallward.htm.

—— (2003) *Alain Badiou: Subject to Truth*. Minnesota: Minnesota University Press.

Hansen, Lene (1997) A Case for Seduction? Evaluating the Poststructuralist Conceptualization of Security. *Cooperation and Conflict* 32, no. 4: 369–97.

—— (2000) The Little Mermaid's Silent Security Dilemma and the Absence of Gender from the Copenhagen School. *Millenium* 29, no. 2: 285–306.

Harrington, Carol (2005) The Politics of Rescue: Peacekeeping and Anti-Trafficking Programmes in Bosnia-Herzegovina and Kosovo. *International Feminist Journal of Politics* 7, no. 2: 175–206.

Herman, Judith Lewis (1997) *Trauma and Recovery: From Domestic Abuse to Political Terror*. London: Pandora. 2nd edition.

Hindess, Barry (1998) Politics and Liberation. In *The Later Foucault: Politics and Philosophy*, ed. Jeremy Moss: 50–63. London: Sage.

—— (2001) The Liberal Government of Unfreedom. *Alternatives: Global, Local, Political* 26, no. 2: 93–112.

Hobbes, Thomas (1985) *Leviathan*. London: Penguin.

—— (1990) *Behemoth or the Long Parliament*. Chicago: University of Chicago Press.

—— (1998) *On the Citizen*, eds Richard Tuck and Michael Siverthorne. Cambridge Texts in the History of Political Thought. Cambridge: Cambridge University Press.

Home Office (2002) *Secure Borders, Safe Haven: Integration with Diversity in Modern Britain*. Accessed 20 October 2004. Available from http://www.official-documents.co.uk/document/cm53/5387/cm.5387.pdf.

—— (2004) *Paying the Price: Consultation Paper on Prostitution*. Accessed 30 March 2005. Available from http://www.homeoffice.gov.uk/documents/paying_the_price.pdf.

—— (2006) *Tackling Human Trafficking – Consultation on Proposals for a UK Action Plan*. Accessed 30 June 2007. Available from http://www.homeoffice.gov.uk/documents/TacklingTrafficking.pdf.

Hornby, A. S. (2000) *Oxford English Dictionary*. Oxford: Oxford University Press.

House of Commons (2006) *Human Trafficking: Twenty-sixth Report of Session 2005–2006*. Joint Committee on Human Rights. Accessed 30 June 2007. Available from http://www.publications.parliament.uk/pa/jt200506/jtselect/jtrights/245/24502.htm.

Hughes, Donna (2000) The Natasha Trade: The Transnational Shadow Market of Trafficking in Women. *Journal of International Affairs* 53, no. 2: 625–51.

Hunt, Alan and Gary Wickhham (1994) *Foucault and Law: Towards a Sociology of Law as Governance*. London: Pluto Press.

Huysmans, Jef (1998a) The Question of the Limit: Desecuritisation and the Aesthetics of Horror in Political Realism. *Millennium* 27, no. 3: 569–89.

—— (1998b) Revisiting Copenhagen: Or, On the Creative Development of a Security Studies Agenda in Europe. *European Journal of International Relations* 4, no. 4: 479–505.

—— (1998c) Security! What Do You Mean? From Concept to Thick Signifier. *European Journal of International Relations* 4, no. 2: 226–55.

—— (2004a) A Foucaultian View on Spill-Over: Freedom and Security in the EU. *Journal of International Relations and Development* 7, no. 3: 294–318.

—— (2004b) Minding Exceptions: Politics of Insecurity and Liberal Democracy. *Contemporary Political Theory* 3, no. 3: 321–41.

—— (2006) *The Politics of Insecurity: Fear, Migration and Asylum in the EU*. London: Routledge.

ICMPD (2002) *Regional Standard for Anti-Trafficking Police Training in SEE*. Vienna, Austria: International Centre for Migration Policy Development.

—— (2004) *Regional Standard for Anti-Trafficking Training for Judges and Prosecutors in SEE*. Accessed 22 June 2007. Available from http://www.icmpd.org/829.html.

International Prostitutes Collective (2001) *Opposing Trafficking Laws Being Used to Deport Women*. Accessed 19 April 2006. Available from http://www. allwomencount.net/EWC%20Sex%20Workers/IPCpage.htm#Opposing% 20trafficking%20being%20used%20to%20deport%20women.

International Research & Exchange Board (2003) *Building Civil Society Women's Empowerment Programs: Anti-Trafficking, Crisis Counselling, NGO Strenghtening, Domestic Violence Prevention*. Accessed 30 May 2006. Available from http:// www.irex.org/women/about.asp.

IOM (1999) *Trafficking in Migrants: IOM Policy and Responses*. Geneva: IOM.

—— (2000) Poster created for the 'Prevention of Trafficking in Women in the Baltic States' information campaign. IOM Lithuania. Available from http:// iom.fi/content/view/138/8.

—— (2001) *Vulnerability to Trafficking in Human Beings of Young Female Population of Romania. Main findings of sociological research on risk factors and geographical distribution, The Center for Urban and Regional Sociology (CURS), the Institute for Life Quality Research (ILQR) and Mercury Research and Marketing Consultants 2001*. Bucharest: IOM Office in Romania.

—— (2002) *Brussels Declaration on Preventing and Combating Trafficking in Human Beings: Draft Recommendations, Standards and Best Practices*. STOP Conference. Accessed 30 October 2004. Available from http://www.belgium.iom.int/ STOPConference/Conference%20Papers/brudeclaration.pdf.

—— (2003) *Who Is the Next Victim? Vulnerability of Young Romanian Women to Trafficking in Human Beings*. Accessed 30 June 2007. Available from http:// www.iom.hu/regpublications.html.

IOM Ukraine (2007) *Combating Trafficking in Human Beings in Ukraine. Statistics updated on 31 March 2007*. IOM Accessed 20 June 2007. Available from http://www.iom.org.ua/docs/Eng%20Stat%20mar_07_1%20doc.pdf.

Irwin, Mary Ann (1996) *White Slavery as Metaphor: Anatomy of a Moral Panic, Ex Post Facto; The History Journal V*. Accessed 30 June 2007. Available from http://www.walnet.org/csis/papers/irwin-wslavery.html.

Jabri, Vivienne (1998) Restyling the Subject of Responsibility in International Relations. *Millenium: Journal of International Studies* 27, no. 3: 591–611.

—— (2005) Critical Thought and Political Agency in Time of War. *International Relations* 19, no. 1: 70–89.

Johnson, Alain (2003) Equalibertarian Marxism and the Politics of Social Movements. *Historical Marxism* 11, no. 4: 237–66.

Jordan, Ann D. (2002) Human Rights or Wrongs? The Struggle for a Rights-Based response to Trafficking in Human Beings. *Gender and Development* 10, no. 1: 28–37.

Kearney, Richard (2002) *Strangers, Gods and Monsters: Interpreting Otherness.* London: Routledge.

Kelly, Liz and Linda Regan (2000) *Stopping Traffic: Exploring the Extent of, and Responses to, Trafficking in Women for Sexual Exploitation in the UK.* Accessed 15 October 2007. Available from http://www.homeoffice.gov.uk/rds/prgpdfs/frs/25.pdf.

Kempadoo, Kamala (1998) Introduction: Globalizing Sex Workers' Rights. In *Global Sex Workers: Rights, Resistance and Redefinition,* eds Kamala Kempadoo and Jo Doezema. London: Routledge.

Kinnell, Hilary (2002) *Why Feminists Should Rethink on Sex Workers' Rights.* Accessed 30 June 2007. Available from http://www.nswp.org/pdf/KINNELL-FEMINISTS.PDF.

Koser, Khalid (1998) Out of the Frying Pan and into the Fire: A Case Study of Illegality amongst Asylum-Seekers. In *The New Migration in Europe. Social Constructions and Social Realities,* eds Khalid Koser and Helma Lutz: 185–98. London: Macmillan Press.

Krause, Keith (1998) Critical Theory and Security Studies: The Research Programme of Critical Security Studies. *Cooperation and Conflict* 33, no. 3: 3–10.

Krause, Keith and Michael C. Williams (1997) From Strategy to Security: Foundations of Critical Security Studies. In *Critical Security Studies: Concepts and Cases,* eds Keith Krause and Michael C. Williams: 33–60. London: UCL Press.

Kvinnoforum (1999) *Crossing Borders Against Trafficking in Women and Girls in the Baltic Sea Region.* Accessed 25 February 2006. Available from http://www.qweb.kvinnoforum.se/misc/tiw-ResourceBookBody-Nov99.rtf.

Kyle, David and Rey Koslowski (2001) Introduction. In *Global Human Smuggling: Comparative Perspectives,* eds David Kyle and Rey Koslowski. Baltimore: The Johns Hopkins University Press.

La distance politique (1991) *Le mode historique de la politique.* 1. Accessed 23 November 2006. Available from http://membres.lycos.fr/orgapoli/.

—— (1996) *Entre sans-papiers et lois Debre.* 19/20. Organisation Politique. Accessed 23 November 2006. Available from http://membres.lycos.fr/orgapoli/.

La Strada (2007) *Who are the Victims of Trafficking?* Accessed 30 June 2007. Available from http://www.strada.org.pl/index_en.html.

La Strada Moldova (2006) Identification of Trafficked Persons. *La Strada Express* 2: 1–50.

Laclau, Ernesto (1996) *Emancipation(s).* London: Verso.

Laclau, Ernesto and Chantal Mouffe (2001) *Hegemony and Socialist Strategy: Towards a Radical Democratic Politics.* London: Verso. 2nd edition.

Laczkó, Frank and David Thompson, eds (2000) *Migrant Trafficking and Human Smuggling in Europe: A Review of the Evidence with Case Studies from Hungary, Poland and Ukraine.* Geneva: IOM.

Lautsen, Carsten Bagge and Ole Waever (2000) In Defence of Religion: Sacred Referent Objects for Securitisation. *Millenium* 29, no. 3: 705–39.

Levinas, Emmanuel (1998) *Entre Nous: On Thinking-of-the-Other.* New York: Columbia University Press.

Limanowska, Barbara (2002) *Trafficking in Human Beings in South-Eastern Europe: Joint UN, OSCE and Unicef Report.* Accessed 30 June 2007. Available from http://www.osce.org/publications/odihr/2005/04/13771_211_en.pdf.

Lippert, Randy (1999) Governing Refugees: The Relevance of Governmentality to Understanding the International Refugee Regime. *Alternatives* 24: 295–328.

Lloyd, Genevieve (1984) *The Man of Reason: 'Male' and 'Female' in Western Philosophy.* London: Methuen.

Lobo-Guerrero, Luis (2006) Kidnap and Ransom Insurance: Micro-Practices of Security through Risk Embracing. Paper presented at the *47th Annual Convention of the International Studies Association.* San Diego.

Lovell, Terry (2003) Resisting with Authority: Historical Specificity, Agency and the Performative Self. *Theory, Culture and Society* 20, no. 1: 1–17.

Lupsha, Peter (1996) Transnational Organised Crime versus the Nation-State. *Transnational Organised Crime* 2, no. 1: 21–48.

Lupton, Deborah (1999) Risk and the Ontology of Pregnant Embodiment. In *Risk and Sociocultural Theory: New Directions and Perspectives,* ed. Deborah Lupton: 59–85. Cambridge: Cambridge University Press.

Meijer, Irene Costera and Baukje Prins (1998) How Bodies Come to Matter: An Interview with Judith Butler. *Signs* 23, no. 2: 275–86.

Miller, Peter and Nikolas Rose (1990) Governing Economic Life. *Economy and Society* 19, no. 1: 1–31.

Minnesota Advocates for Human Rights (2005) *Health Consequences of Trafficking.* Stop Violence Against Women. Accessed 1 April 2006. Available from http://www.stopvaw.org/Health_Consequences_of_Trafficking.html.

Moon, Katherine (1997) *Sex among Allies: Military Prostitution in U.S. – Korea Relations.* New York: Columbia University Press.

Müller, Jan (1997) Carl Schmitt – An Occasional Nationalist? *History of European Ideas* 23, no. 1: 19–34.

Murray, Alison (1998) Debt-Bondage and Trafficking: Don't Believe the Hype. In *Global Sex Workers: Rights, Resistance, and Redefinition,* eds Kamala Kempadoo and Jo Doezema: 51–68. London: Routledge.

Nancy, Jean-Luc (2001) *The Inoperative Community.* Theory and History of Literature. Minnesota: Minnesota University Press.

NSWP (1999) *Commentary on the Draft Protocol to Combat International Trafficking in Women and Children Supplementary to the Draft Convention on Transnational Organised Crime.* Accessed 3 February 2003. Available from http://www.nswp.org/mobility.

O'Connell Davidson, Julia (1998) *Prostitution, Power, and Freedom.* Ann Arbour: University of Michigan Press.

O'Neill, Maggie (1997) Prostitute Women Now. In *Rethinking Prostitution: Purchasing Sex in the 1990s,* eds Graham Scambler and Annette Scambler: 3–28. London: Routledge.

Ojakangas, Mika (2005) Philosophies of 'Concrete Life': From Carl Schmitt to Jean-Luc Nancy. *Telos* 132: 25–45.

OSCE (1999) *Trafficking in Human Beings: Implications for the OSCE; Background Paper Published for the OSCE Review Conference, September 1999.* Vienna: OSCE.

—— (2004) *National Referral Mechanisms: Joining Efforts to Protect the Rights of Trafficked Women; A Practical Handbook.* OSCE/ODIHR. Accessed 30 June 2005. Available from http://www.osce.org/publications/odihr/2004/05/12351_131_en.pdf.

Palti, Elias (2003) Poststructuralist Marxism and the Experience of Disaster. On Alain Badiou's Theory of the (Non-)Subject. *The European Legacy* 8, no. 4: 459–80.

Pateman, Carol (1988) *The Sexual Contract.* Cambridge: Polity Press.

Pearson, Elaine (2002) Half-Hearted Protection: What Does Victim Protection Really Mean for Victims of Trafficking in Europe? *Gender and Development* 10, no. 1: 56–9.

Pettman, Jan Jindy (1996) *Worlding Women: A Feminist International Politics.* London: Routledge.

Pitkin, Hanna Fenichel (1988) Are Freedom and Liberty Twins? *Political Theory* 16, no. 4: 523–52.

Poku, N.K. and David Graham, eds (2000) *Migration, Globalisation and Human Security.* London: Routledge.

Pomodoro, Livia (2001) Trafficking and the Sexual Exploitation of Women and Children. In *Combating Transnational Organised Crime: Concepts, Activities and Responses,* eds Phil Williams and Dimitri Vlassis: 237–42. London: Frank Cass.

Poppy Project (2004) Image for the Poppy Project Campaign, March 2004. Available from http://www.eaves4women.co.uk/POPPY_Project/About_Us.php.

—— (2006) *Hope Betrayed: An Analysis of Women Victims of Trafficking and Their Claims for Asylum.* London. Accessed 15 October 2007. Available from http://eaves4women.co.uk/POPPY-Project/Documents/Recent-Reports/Hope%Betrayed.pdf.

Prodi, Romano (2002) *Priorities for Seville: Better Regulation and Immigration: Speech by Romano Prodi, President of the European Commission.* 12 June 2002. Accessed 28 April 2006. Available from http://europa.eu.int/rapid/pressReleasesAction.do?reference=SPEECH/02/278&format=HTML&aged=1&language=EN&guiLanguage=en.

Prokhovnik, Raia (2002) *Rational Woman: A Feminist Critique of Dichotomy.* Manchester: Manchester University Press. 2nd edition.

Prostitutes' Education Network (2004) *Prostitution Law Reform: Defining Terms.* Bayswan. Accessed 20 April 2006. Available from http://www.bayswan.org/defining.html.

Pupavac, Vanessa (2004) International Therapeutic Peace and Justice in Bosnia. *Social & Legal Studies* 13, no. 3: 377–401.

Rabinow, Paul (2003) *Anthropos Today: Reflections on Modern Equipment.* Princeton: Princeton University Press.

Rancière, Jacques (1992) *Les noms de l'histoire. Essai de poétique du savoir.* Paris: Seuil.

—— (2003) *The Philosopher and His Poor.* Translated by John Drury, Corrinne Oster and Andrew Parker. Durham: Duke University Press.

Ransom, John S. (1997) *Foucault's Discipline.* Durham: Duke University Press.

Rasch, William (2003) Human Rights as Geopolitics. Carl Schmitt and the Legal Form of American Supremacy. *Cultural Critique* 54, no. 120–147.

Rees, Wyn (1999) *Organized Crime, Security and the European Union.* ECPR Workshop, Grenoble. Accessed 2 February 2006. Available from http://www.essex.ac.uk/ECPR/events/jointsessions/paperarchive/grenoble/ws8/rees.pdf.

Romano, Elisa and Rayleen De Luca (1997) Exploring the Relationship between Childhood Sexual Abuse and Adult Sexual Perpetration. *Journal of Family Violence* 12, no. 1: 85–98.

Rose, Nikolas (1989) *Governing the Soul: The Shaping of the Private Self.* London: Routledge.

—— (1998) *Inventing Our Selves: Psychology, Power, and Personhood.* Cambridge: Cambridge University Press.

—— (1999) *Power of Freedom: Reframing Political Thought.* Cambridge: Cambridge University Press.

—— (2001) The Politics of Life Itself. *Theory, Culture and Society* 28, no. 6: 1–30.

Rose, Nikolas and Peter Miller (1992) Political Power beyond the State: Problematics of Government. *British Journal of Sociology* 43, no. 2: 172–205.

Salt, John (2000) Trafficking and Human Smuggling: A European Perspective. *International Migration* 38, no. 3: 31–56.

Salt, John and Jeremy Stein (1997) Migration as a Business: The Case of Trafficking. *International Migration* 35, no. 4: 467–94.

Saward, Michael (2003) Enacting Democracy. *Political Studies* 51, no. 1: 161–79.

Scarry, Elaine (1985) *The Body in Pain: The Making and Unmaking of the World.* Oxford: Oxford University Press.

Schaaf, Kristin and Thomas McCanne (1998) Relationship of Childhood Sexual, Physical, and Combined Sexual and Physical Abuse to Adult Victimization and Posttraumatic Stress Disorder. *Child Abuse and Neglect – International Journal* 22, no. 11: 1119–33.

Schmitt, Carl (1996) *The Concept of the Political.* Translated by Tracy B. Strong. Chicago: University of Chicago Press.

Scott, Joan Wallach (1994) Deconstructing Equality-versus-Difference: Or, the uses of poststructuralist theory for feminism. In *The Postmodern Turn: New perspectives on Social Theory*, ed. Steve Seidman: 282–98. Cambridge: Cambridge University Press.

—— (1996) *Only Paradoxes to Offer: French Feminists and the Rights of Man.* Cambridge, Massachusetts: Harvard University Press.

Senellart, Michel (1995) *Les arts de gouverner. Du regimen médiéval au concept de gouvernement.* Des Travaux. Paris: Seuil.

Shannon, Sarah (1999) Prostitution and the Mafia: The Involvement of Organized Crime in the Global Sex Trade. In *Illegal Immigration and Commercial Sex: The New Slave Trade*, ed. Phil Williams: 119–44. London: Frank Cass.

Shapiro, Michael (1988) *The Politics of Representation: Writing Practices in Biography, Photography and Policy Analysis.* Madison, Wisconsin: University of Wisconsin Press.

Sharma, Nandita (2003) Travel Agency: A Critique of Anti-Trafficking Campaigns. *Refuge: Canada's Periodical on Refugees* 21, no. 3: 53–65.

—— (2005) Anti-Trafficking Rhetoric and the Making of Global Apartheid. *NSWA Journal* 17, no. 3: 88–111.

Sipaviciene, Audra (2002) 'You Will Be Sold like a Doll!' In *NIKK Magazine*, 1: 10–15.

Smith, Joan (3 October 2005) The Ugly Truth about 'Cuddles'. *Independent on Sunday*, 23.

Smith, Steve (2000) The Increasing Insecurity of Security Studies: Conceptualizing Security in the Last 20 Years. In *Critical Reflections on Security and Change*, eds Stuart Croft and Terry Terriff: 72–101. London: Frank Cass.

Squires, Judith (2000) *Gender in Political Theory*. London: Polity Press.

Stateva, Milena and Nadya Kozhouharova (2004) Trafficking in Women in Bulgaria: A New Stage. *Feminist Review* 76, no. 1: 110–16.

Stern, Maria (2006) 'We' the Subject: The Power and Failure of (In)Security. *Security Dialogue* 37, no. 2: 187–205.

Sylvester, Christine (1994) *Feminist Theory and International Relations in a Postmodern Era*. Cambridge: Cambridge University Press.

—— (1996) The Contributions of Feminist Theory to International Relations. In *International Theory: Positivism & Beyond*, eds Steve Smith, Ken Booth and Marysia Zalewski: 254–78. Cambridge: Cambridge University Press.

Taylor, Ian and Ruth Jamieson (1999) Sex Trafficking and the Mainstream of Market Culture. *Crime, Law and Social Change* 32, no. 3: 257–78.

The Economist (4–10 September 2004) It's a Foreigners' Game. 29–30.

The Evening Standard (10 October 2002) Saved from the Sex Slave Gangs, 16.

The International Committee on the Rights of Sex Workers in Europe (2005) *Declaration of the Rights of Sex Workers in Europe*. Accessed 17 January 2006. Available from http://www.sexworkeurope.org/DeclRightsBrussels05.pdf.

The Spectator (25 April 2003) Happy Hookers of Eastern Europe, 5.

Tickner, Ann (1992) *Gender in International Relations: Feminist Perspectives on Achieving Global Security*. New York: Columbia University Press.

—— (2001) *Gendering World Politics: Issues and Approaches in the Post-Cold War Era*. New York: Columbia University Press.

Tudorache, Diana (2004) General Considerations on the Psychological Aspect of the Trafficking Phenomenon. In *Psychosocial Support to Groups of Victims of Trafficking in Transit Situations: Psychosocial Notebooks*, ed. Guglielmo Schinina. Geneva: IOM.

UK Government (2005) *UK Presidency of the European Union: UK Priorities*. Accessed 15 October 2005. Available from http://www.eu2005.gov.uk.

UN (1949) *Convention for the Suppression of Traffic in Persons and the Exploitatio of the Prostitution of Others*. Accessed 31 May 2006. Available from http://www. ohchr.org/english/law/trafficpersons.htm.

—— (2000) *Protocol to Prevent, Suppress and Punish Trafficking in Persons, especially Women and Children, Supplementing the United Nations Convention against Transnational Organized Crime*. United Nations. Accessed 20 August 2003. Available from http://www.uncjin.org/Documents/Conventions/dcatoc/final_documents_2/convention_%20traff_eng.pdf.

UNODC (26 March 2007) *UNODC Launches Global Initiative to Fight Human Trafficking*. Accessed 30 May 2007. Available from http://www.unodc.org/unodc/press_release_2007_03_26.html.

Urban Justice Center (2007) *Statement on Trafficking in Persons for the 51st Session of the Commission for the Status of Women on the 'Elimination of All Forms of Discrimination and Violence against the Girl Child'*. Accessed 23 June 2007. Available from http://www.urbanjustice.org/ujc/publications/sex. html.

US State Department (2002) *Romania Human Rights Report*. Accessed 26 January 2006. Available from http://www.ncbuy.com/reference/country/humanrights. html?code=ro&sec=6f.

Valverde, Mariana (1996) 'Despotism' and Ethical Liberal Governance. *Economy and Society* 25, no. 3: 357–72.

——— (2003) *Law's Dream of a Common Knowledge*, ed. Austin Sarat. The Cultural Lives of Law. Princeton: Princeton University Press.

Van Impe, Kristof (2000) People for Sale: The Need for a Multidisciplinary Approach towards Human Trafficking. *International Migration Special Issue* 1.

Veyne, Paul (1997) The Final Foucault and His Ethics. In *Foucault and His Interlocutors*, ed. A. I. Davidson. Chicago: University of Chicago Press.

Virno, Paolo (2002) *Grammaire de la multitude. Pour une analyse des formes de vie contemporaines.* Translated by Veronique Dassas. Paris: Editions de l'Eclat & Conjonctures.

Vocks, Judith and Jan Nijboer (2000) The Promised Land: A Study of Trafficking in Women from Central and Eastern Europe to the Netherlands. *European Journal on Criminal Policy and Research* 8: 379–88.

von Struensee, Vanessa (2000) Sex Trafficking: A Plea for Action. *European Law Journal* 6, no. 4: 379–407.

Waever, Ole (1995) Securitization and Desecuritization. In *On Security*, ed. Ronnie Lipschutz: 46–86. New York: Columbia University Press.

——— (2000) The EU as a Security Actor: Reflections from a Pessimistic Constructivist on Post-Sovereign Security Orders in International Relations. In *International Relations Theory and the Politics of European Integration*, eds Morten Kelstrup and Michael C. Williams: 250–94. London: Routledge.

——— (2004) Aberystwyth, Paris, Copenhagen: New 'Schools' in Security Theory and Their Origins between Core and Periphery. Paper presented at the *45th Annual Convention of the International Studies Association*. Montreal.

Walker, R. B. J. (1997) The Subject of Security. In *Critical Security Studies. Concepts and Cases*, eds Keith Krause and Michael Williams: 61–81. London: UCL Press.

Walker, R. B. J. and Andrew Neal (2003) Notes on European Liberty and Security: Problems, Principles, and Contradictions. ELISE.

Walkowitz, Judith R. (1980) *Prostitution and Victorian Society: Women, Class, and the State*. Cambridge: Cambridge University Press.

Walt, Stephen (1991) The Renaissance of Security Studies. *International Studies Quarterly* 35, no. 2: 211–39.

Walters, William and Wendy Larner (2002) The Political Rationality of the 'New Regionalism': Toward a Genealogy of the Region. *Theory and Society* 31: 391–432.

Weber, Cynthia (1998) Performative States. *Millenium: Journal of International Studies* 27, no. 1: 77–95.

Weiner, Myron (1992/1993) Security, Stability and International Migration. *International Security* 17, no. 3: 91–126.

Weir, Lorna (1996) Recent Developments in the Government of Pregnancy. *Economy and Society* 25, no. 3: 373–92.

Wijers, Marjan and Lap-Chew, Lin (1999) *Trafficking in Women: Forced Labour and Slavery-like Practices*. Utrecht: STV/GAATW, 2.

Wijers, Marjan and van Doorninck, Marieke (2002) Only Rights can Stop Wrongs: A Critical Assessment of Anti-Trafficking Strategies. Paper presented at *EU/IOM STOP European Conference on Preventing and Combating Trafficking in Human Beings*. Brussels.

Williams, Michael C. (1997) The Institutions of Security: Elements of a Theory of Security Organizations. *Cooperation and Conflict* 32, no. 3: 287–307.

—— (2003) Words, Images, Enemies: Securitization and International Politics. *International Studies Quarterly* 47: 511–31.
Williams, Phil (1994) Transnational Criminal Organisations and International Security. *Survival* 36, no. 1: 96–113.
—— (1999) Human Commodity Trafficking: An Overview. In *Illegal Immigration and Commercial Sex: The New Slave Trade*, ed. Phil Williams: 1–10. London: Frank Cass.
Wyn Jones, Richard (1999) *Security, Strategy, and Critical Theory*. London: Lynne Rienner.
Zimmerman, Cathy (2003) *The Health Risks and Consequences of Trafficking in Women and Adolescents: Findings from a European Study*. Accessed 24 February 2004. Available from http://www.lshtm.ac.uk/hpu/docs/traffickingfinal.pdf.
Zimmerman, Warren (1995) Migrants and Refugees: A Threat to Security? In *Threatened People, Threatened Borders: World Migration and U.S. Policy*, eds Michael S. Teitelbaum and Myron Weer. New York: The American Assembly, Columbia University.
Žižek, Slavoj (1995) *The Metastases of Enjoyment*. London: Verso. 2nd edition.
—— (1998) Psychoanalysis and Post-Marxism: The Case of Alain Badiou. *South Atlantic Quaterly Spring* 97: 235–61.
—— (1999a) Carl Schmitt in the Age of Post-Politics. In *The Challenge of Carl Schmitt*, ed. Chantal Mouffe: 18–37. London: Verso.
—— (1999b) *The Ticklish Subject: The Absent Centre of Political Ontology*. London: Verso.
—— (2004) *Organs without Bodies: On Deleuze and Consequences*. London: Routledge.
Žižek, Slavoj and Glyn Daly (2004) *Conversations with Žižek*. Oxford: Polity Press.

ECJ Cases

Barkoci and Malik (27 September 2001) European Court of Justice, Case C-257/99.
Gloszczuk (27 September 2001) European Court of Justice, Case C-63/99.
Jany (20 September 2001) European Court of Justice, Case C-268/99.
Kondova (27 September 2001) European Court of Justice, Case C-235/99.

Index